Our McGinty Family in America

Gerald Kirk McGinty Sr.

2018

Seventh Avenue Productions
Minneapolis

Seventh Avenue Productions
© 2011 2013 2018
Gerald K. McGinty, Sr.

ISBN-13: 978-0-9838854-1-2
LCCN: 2011916023
Printed in the United States of America.

Cover design by Lupi

All photographs either in the public domain, part of the author's personal collection or have been used with permission. Inquiries should be addressed to Gerald K. McGinty Sr. at mcgintyboy@aol.com.

Back cover photos L to R: Elisabeth Smith McGinty, Mollie Redd and Wiley Patterson McGinty, and Wiley Patterson McGinty Jr.

ACKNOWLEDGEMENTS

I would like to thank my brother and fellow researcher, Phil McGinty for his major contributions to this book. The family mysteries that we have solved together are many.

I would also like to thank family members and other McGinty researchers for their valuable contributions over the years. This is truly a team effort.

I am also grateful to my son and author, Mark McGinty, who assisted me in editing and publishing this book.

CONTENTS

FOREWORD

The history of our McGinty family has always been of great interest to me. We must not only appreciate and enjoy our history today, but also pass it on to future generations. In the 1950's, my grandfather, Wiley P. McGinty Sr., and his wife, Tinnie Mae Hunt, who lived in rural McGinty, AL, researched our family and created *Our McGinty Book*. This book was a collection of genealogical charts on some of the McGinty relatives that they were aware of at the time. They primarily used the U.S. mail to correspond with the various limited sources of information that were known to them. This was before computers and the Internet. Their research on our McGintys inspired me to expand on the project and it was a valuable resource to begin tracking down our other ancestors.

As I began this project, I quickly learned that there are many resources available today and my use of the Internet has resulted in the discovery of a network of researchers and historians who are also interested in the McGinty family. Many of them were newly found relatives. From these many sources, new material has surfaced on a regular basis. Genealogy as a hobby has become very popular. Various libraries, historical societies, state and federal archives and other professional organizations are open and eager to assist researchers in their quest for information. All of this has resulted in more comprehensive and accurate information regarding our family.

I have made every attempt to only present information that has been documented and to correct the errors in earlier research, of which there were many, because assumptions were made without documentation. I have not footnoted every source, but my rather extensive files do contain documentation for the vast majority of information presented here. At some point in the future, I hope to donate my research to an institution for safekeeping and use by future researchers. For now, questions are welcome by me.

Since those early days in Pennsylvania, when the first McGintys arrived in America over 250 years ago, I have documented these nine successive generations in my immediate family tree:

John McGinty I – Gr. Gr. Gr. Gr. Grandfather
Robert McGinty – Gr. Gr. Gr. Grandfather
George Washington McGinty – Gr. Gr. Grandfather
William Pitts McGinty – Gr. Grandfather
Wiley Patterson McGinty Sr. – Grandfather
Wiley Patterson McGinty Jr. – Father
Gerald K. McGinty Sr. – Me
Gerald K. McGinty Jr. – My Son
Macon Henry McGinty – My Grandson

Because of the proliferation of the McGintys, due to many large families, my intent in this document was to concentrate mainly on my direct lineage. However, I have also included some of the descendants of each generation. This will provide a base of information for other researchers. I have also posted an extensive family tree on Ancestry.com along with various articles on state archive sites. My Ancestry.com family tree is expanded to include any known McGinty connections. There are now over 4000 names there.

This search has been and continues to be extremely enlightening and gratifying to me, and I hope that current and future generations of McGintys will find it useful in helping them to know more about their heritage and gain inspiration and strength from the accomplishments of their fathers. Their record is one of patriotism, civic pride, and strong religious beliefs. Our ancestors defended this country in virtually every war since arriving in America. Many of them gave their lives for the country that we enjoy today. The first McGintys were true pioneers. Let us hope that future generations will improve on what our family has accomplished so far during its long history.

Although many of the people reviewed here have passed on, this continues to be a living document. Interested researchers and other McGinty historians are discovering new information about our relatives, and this is being shared like never before.

There are now web sites containing information on the McGinty family, and who knows what the future might hold? Researchers in the past did not have the sources of information that we have today. Many assumptions were made in earlier research that has since proven to be in error. I can only see improvements in the amount and quality of documented information as we move ahead into future generations.

Our McGinty Family in America

The Old Country: Before 1750

The explanation of why our McGinty family - whose surname contains the Scottish prefix "Mc" or "Mac" meaning "son of"- came to America from Ireland, instead of Scotland, is found in the history of the Scottish Presbyterians who were referred to as Ulster Scots or Scotch-Irish, as opposed to plain "Irish" which were Catholics. The Ulster area of Ireland contains several counties, including the county of Donegal.

COUNTY MAP OF IRELAND
Courtesy of
Irish Genealogical Society, Int'l
P. O. Box 16585
St. Paul, Minnesota 55116

The Scotland from which the McGintys came was one of the poorest and most backward of European countries. Poverty-stricken, generally lawless, still lingering in the Middle Ages in the seventeenth century, with agricultural methods hardly better than primitive, there was every reason why an ambitious Scot should look elsewhere for improvement in his condition. They voluntarily relocated to the Ulster area in the seventeenth century as part of a plan by Elizabeth I of England (ruled from 1558-1603), and implemented by her successor, James I of England (prior to this he was James IV of Scotland), of planting colonies of Protestants in Ireland in an attempt to domesticate those "wild Irish" who were in constant rebellion against England.

The scheme involved driving the Irish from their lands and granting these acres to English lords and gentry who would agree to bring in enough settlers to establish the "Plantation". The scheme did not work smoothly because the Irish would return from the bogs and hills where they had been driven, and raid, burn and harass the new settlers. However, the toll from starvation and defeat finally became so severe that in 1603 the Irish submitted to the English pressure and the "Plantation of Ulster" began in 1610. As a result, vast amounts of Irish Catholic-owned land in Northern Ireland was seized and given to the "planted" Protestants. By the late 1600's eighty-five percent of Ireland had been overtaken by English landlords.

Of the six counties of the Plantation, County Donegal and County Tyrone were given almost wholly to the Scots. Scot lowland tenant farmers from the territory south of the narrow waist of Scotland between Glasgow and Edinburg, and the coastal strip north of Edinburg, relocated to this land. As tenant farmers, they owed their "lairds" specific rents, and various services, such as work on the lord's estate (especially at harvest), cutting and carrying peat, or thatching his buildings; and if the lord had a mill, the tenant must have his grain ground there for a fee. The tenant also owed military service to the nobleman, who was one step above the lord. They were humble folk with ambition and qualities of character that made them good pioneers.

There were problems that developed in Ulster. The Ulster Scot Presbyterians were ordered to worship in the Church of England, which they would strongly resist. In 1660 Charles II forbade these Presbyterians to hold family worship if anyone that was not of the immediate family was in the house. This act was one of the incentives for many Scots to leave for the Western Hemisphere.

The Ulstermen developed, in rapid succession, two new industries in Northern Ireland. Both woolen and linen manufacturing flourished, bringing remarkable prosperity to the area. However, the competition of this Irish cloth aroused uneasiness among the English manufacturers and in 1698 they petitioned the king for protection. The Woolens Act of 1699 prohibited the exportation of Irish cloth to any places except England and Wales. This left all of the other markets wholly to the English. It was a crippling blow to the industry of Ulster. We know that there were McGinty families involved in the growing of flax which is the fiber used to make linen, but have not yet been able to directly link them to our family in America. The linen industry was organized on a piecework basis and was distributed widely among the women who made items in their homes. We know that later, in Kentucky, the noted Anne McGinty brought the first spinning wheel to the area and weaved cloth from nettle and buffalo hair (see James McGinty in Kentucky).

Another reason for mass immigration to America was caused by rack-renting. The Ulstermen typically leased their land from the plantation landlord for a period of thirty-one years. They improved their holdings by building homes and developing the land. When some of these landlords decided to increase the rent substantially with the renewal of a lease, the Scotch-Irish farmers refused to accept this departure from the traditional practice. This issue drove many Presbyterian Ulstermen to America. It was so serious, that whole villages in Ireland lost their farmers to America.

The pull of America was powerful. By 1717 English colonials had already been in the New World for a century. Some of the colonies were flourishing and others were optimistic. Reports from William Penn's settlements were enthusiastic as to the quality of the land and the treatment of colonists. Conditions in Ireland were not good. Disease and crop failures added to their problems. Because of all this and the lure of the American colonies, thousands of people left Ireland between 1717 and 1775 and sailed to America where they became pioneers.

There were two drawbacks. One was the peril of crossing the ocean. The voyage was on a small, overcrowded sailing vessel and took three months. As many as 250 passengers might be on a ship.

Passengers were subject to epidemics such as smallpox. The other was the cost of the trip which was typically five British Pounds for each adult and under one Pound for children. They usually brought their own food and supplies. The ship furnished water, which was usually inadequate and became foul during the voyage. One Pound of currency represented a month's wages for a laborer. The captain often offered free passage to anyone agreeing to sell himself (become bonded labor or an indentured servant) which contract, in turn, was sold to a landlord upon arrival in America. The term of indenture was one to five years. In Pennsylvania, where our McGintys lived, the regulations were such that a freed servant, after his indenture was complete, was entitled to fifty acres of land. Thus he was then able to start out as a free man under excellent conditions.

Based strictly on family lore, it is thought that our McGintys in America came from County Donegal during this period in history. However, there is no official record confirming this. Based on other research, specifically that of the Jackson families, our McGintys could have come from a different area of Ireland. There is still a large concentration of McGintys in the Donegal area of Ireland. County Donegal had been formed in 1606 at the beginning of the plantation movement. There was a full-page map of old Ireland with an article that was published in the *Chicago Tribune,* on St. Patrick's Day, March 17, 1952. The title of the article was "First Families of Old Ireland." It shows the names and locations of the major families that lived in the various Irish counties hundreds of years ago. The "MacGinty" family is shown only in County Donegal. Our name is not shown in any other area of Ireland.

I visited County Donegal and Donegal Town in August 2003. There, I met several McGintys. This is truly McGinty country. On one street, there were seven houses, all McGinty, and they were not all related. I visited the St. Agatha Catholic Church cemetery in Clar, which is near Donegal Town, and found at least twenty-five McGinty graves. The oldest ones were from the mid 1800's. Our McGintys have been thought to be Presbyterians in Ireland; however, they could have been Quakers. Again, there is no record confirming their religion there.

The Tenement Act of 1842 provided for a uniform valuation of all property in Ireland. Richard Griffith was appointed Commissioner of Valuation and conducted this survey. *Griffith's Valuations* were published between 1848 and 1864. This survey shows 114 McGinty households in County Donegal. The county is divided into parishes and Donegal parish shows fifty-two McGinty households, Kilteevoge parish has twenty-six and Stranorlar parish shows nine. All of these parishes are in the area around Donegal Town. More research is needed in Ireland.

Our McGinty family decided to make the long voyage and build a new life in America. Since people from Ireland were already British citizens, no documentation was required for their passage, making it difficult to trace the exact timing of their movement. There is documentation showing that our McGintys were present in Pennsylvania before 1753. The total number of Scotch-Irish who came to America during these years is estimated at over 200,000 and included our McGinty family.

The surname McGinty is Scottish and derives from an ancient Celtic family. According to *Surnames in Ireland,* by Sir Robert E. Matheson, McGinty is a derivative of the name McGinity. Other variations of this name were Maginnetty, M'Entee, M'Ginety, M'Ginnety and McGinnitty. The name originates from the Celtic word, Mag Fhinneachta, which means "Son of Fair Snow." Two separate authorities, Patrick Woulfe and Edward MacLysaght who are noted publishers of Scotch/Irish research have confirmed this as the meaning of our name.

It is interesting to note that nine of the early Presidents of the United States were of Scotch-Irish decent, and as some research shows, we are possibly related to President Andrew Jackson.

Our McGinty Family

The following male generations are the ancestors and direct descendants of the author Gerald K. "Jerry" McGinty Sr. They are listed with the most recent generation first.

Most Recent Generation

Macon Henry McGinty, b. October 4, 2001, in Santa Cruz, Santa Cruz Co., CA. He is the son of Gerald Kirk McGinty Jr. (Kirk) and Kimberly Kirsten Terauds.

Kirk McGinty is the son of the author, and Kimberly "Kim" Terauds McGinty is the daughter of Juris Terauds (b. October 15, 1936, in Jelgava, Latvia) and Shirley Jean Henry (b. September 28, 1941, in Kankakee IL). Latvia is a land on the eastern shore of the Baltic Sea, and was formerly part of the Soviet Union. During the WWII years, Juris and his parents fled from the Russians, who were occupying the country. They left Latvia and first went to Poland. From there, they moved on to Czechoslovakia and then to Austria for one year. They lived in Germany until 1947. They seized an opportunity to immigrate to Canada as indentured servants and arrived there in 1947 living in Howick, Quebec, a town that is near Montreal. Juris attended college in the U.S. while still a Canadian and later became a U.S. citizen. He was a track star in school, specializing in the javelin. He later became a college professor and most recently operated a business that produces a unique type of exercise machine, many of which are exported to Japan.

Kimberly's paternal grandfather was Janis Hermanis Terauds, b. March 2, 1909, in Tukums, Latvia, d. November 12, 1995, in Canada. Her grandmother was Tatjana Odins, b. August 7, 1909, d. June 8, 1998, in Canada. Janis was a farmer in Latvia, and studied agronomy and horticulture. He was also the mayor of the county in which they lived. Janis and Tatjana retired in FL. Due to Tatjana's health issues, they moved back to Kingston, Nova Scotia where they both passed away.

Tatjana Odins father (Kimberly's paternal great-grandfather), was Gederts Odins, b. January 29, 1877, d. August 19, 1937, in Ruba, Latvia. His wife was Eizenija Goldbergs. Gederts was a farmer in Latvia when he qualified for entrance into a school in St. Petersburg, Russia. He excelled in this school and because of his high marks, was chosen to be tutor to the brother of Czar Nicholas II. Later, he was promoted to director of the Czar's school in St. Petersburg and remained there, even after the Czar and his family was killed in 1918. He returned to Latvia after 1924 and is said to have been killed by a bull in 1937.

Kimberly's maternal grandfather was Frank Albert Henry, born November 5, 1913, in IL and died April 15, 1995, in Deltona, Volusia Co., FL. His wife was Marjorie Ethyl McGee, born November 18, 1913, Fulton, IL and died, August 7, 2009, Deltona, Volusia Co., FL. Her maternal great-grandfather was William Franklin Henry, born 1885 in IL. His wife was Verna Eunice Schrader, born 1889 in IL. Her maternal great-great- grandparents were James K. Henry and Melinda Emeline Fanning. The parents of Marjorie E. McGee were John Wilson McGee, born in MD and Sarah A. Jackson, born in England. Sarah immigrated to America in 1888. Her parents were Benjamin and Francis Jackson, from England.

Her paternal great-grandfather was Augusts R.H.K. Stals, b. August 22, 1885, in Tukums, Latvia, d. January 24, 1936, in Tukums Latvia. The family changed their name from Stals to Terauds. Stals (Stahls) is the German word for steel. Under German rule, many Latvians had their names assigned by the government. At a later date, the Stals changed their name to the Latvian word for steel, which is Terauds. Her great grandmother was Anna Fridenbergs, b. March 2, 1883, in Janunpili, Latvia, d. ca. 1942 in Tukums, Latvia.

Kimberly's paternal great-great-grandfather was Janis Hermanis Stals, b. ca. 1853 and d. ca. 1902 in Tukums Latvia. Her great-great-grandmother was Eizenija Frolichs, b. ca. 1861 and d. 1917 in Tukums, Latvia.

A complete Terauds family history book, with much more detail, was compiled by Kim's father, Juris Terauds. Members of the immediate family received copies.

Generation No. 2

Gerald Kirk McGinty, Jr. "Kirk", b. March 16, 1967, in Tampa, Hillsborough Co., FL (photo p. 12). He is the son of Gerald K. McGinty Sr., and Carol Ann Simpson. He married Kimberly Kirsten

Terauds, b. July 15, 1968, on August 5, 1995.

Children of G. Kirk McGinty Jr., and Kimberly Kirsten Terauds are:

Macon Henry McGinty, b. October 4, 2001, Santa Cruz, Santa Cruz Co., CA.

Tate Maclean McGinty, b. August 1, 2003, Santa Cruz, Santa Cruz Co., CA.

Mark Carlos McGinty, b. September 10, 1975, in Greensboro, Guilford Co., NC (photo p. 12). He is the son of Gerald K. McGinty, Sr., and Sylvia Dolores Roque. He married Meridith Madelyn Catherine Vollmar, September 17, 2004, in Cincinnati, Hamilton Co., OH.

Children of Mark C. McGinty and Meridith Catherine Vollmar are:

Avery Inez McGinty, b. January 19, 2005, in Cincinnati, Hamilton Co., OH.

Generation No. 3

Gerald Kirk McGinty Sr., "Jerry", b. December 18, 1940, in Atlanta, Fulton Co., GA. He is the son of Wiley Patterson McGinty Jr., and Elizabeth Jordan Smith. The name Gerald is said to have come from the French, Gerard. His father was a French teacher at the time of his birth and liked this name. His middle name, Kirk, was the maiden name of his maternal great-great-grandmother, Harriet Lee Kirk. He married (1) Carol Ann Simpson, b. November 14, 1944, on June 6, 1964, at the Druid Hills Baptist Church in Atlanta, GA, Louie D. Newton, pastor (2) Sylvia Dolores Roque, b. November 26, 1941, on November 26, 1971, at the First Methodist Church in Brandon, FL, Ray Harrison, pastor.

Children of Gerald K. McGinty Sr., and Carol Ann Simpson:

Sandra Elaine McGinty, b. March 14, 1966, in Tampa, Hillsborough Co., FL (photo p. 12). She is the daughter of Gerald

K. McGinty Sr., and Carol Ann Simpson. She married Gregory Blake Scott, b. July 15, 1966, on June 15, 1992, in Destin, FL.

Gerald Kirk McGinty Jr., b. March 16, 1967, in Tampa, Hillsborough Co., FL. He is the son of Gerald K. McGinty Sr., and Carol Ann Simpson. He married Kimberly Kirsten Terauds, b. July 15, 1968, on August 5, 1995, in Del Mar, CA.

Child of Gerald K. McGinty Sr., and Sylvia Dolores Roque:

Mark Carlos McGinty, b. September 10, 1975, in Greensboro, Guilford Co., NC. He is the son of Gerald K. McGinty Sr., and Sylvia Dolores Roque. He married Meridith Vollmar, September 17, 2004, in Cincinnati, OH.

Sandra, Mark and Kirk with Maxwell
December 28, 1992, St. Paul, MN

The Life of Gerald K. McGinty Sr.

The following section is included for the benefit of my children so that they will know more about their McGinty and non-McGinty parents and grandparents.

Gerald K. "Jerry" McGinty was born at Piedmont Hospital in Atlanta, GA. This hospital stood on the area that is now the Turner Field parking lot in downtown Atlanta at 551 Capitol Ave. The hospital building was demolished when the Atlanta-Fulton Co. stadium was built in the late 1950's. At the time, his parents lived at 194 East Lake Dr.

**Four Generations. L to R: Great-grandmother Ida Elizabeth Rooks Miller, grandmother Ruby Blanche Miller (Momie) holding grandson, Gerald K. McGinty Sr. (Jerry) with his mother, Elizabeth Jordan Smith McGinty.
Photo ca. 1941**

Jerry attended East Lake Elementary School and Druid Hills High School. In his senior year, 1958, he was named to the Georgia All State high school football team. He then attended the University of Tennessee in Knoxville, TN. He served in the U.S. Army Reserves for six years, receiving an honorable discharge as a Staff Sergeant July 17, 1969. In 1960 he began a career with H.B. Fuller Co. starting in the manufacturing plant in Atlanta. In 1964, he accepted a sales position in Tampa, FL. He and his new wife, Carol Ann Simpson, relocated to Tampa, FL. His daughter, Sandra and son Kirk, Jr. were born at Tampa General Hospital. He and Carol divorced on February 26, 1971, and he married Sylvia Dolores Roque on November 26, 1971. She was a schoolteacher at the time and is a native of Tampa. She is a graduate of the University of Tampa. Jerry was then promoted to sales manager in Greensboro, N.C., and they moved there from Tampa in 1971.

He was raised as a Baptist, became a Methodist in FL and later converted to Catholic while living in Greensboro. He became a 4th Degree Knight of Columbus in 2013. His son, Mark, was born at Moses Cone Hospital in Greensboro. In 1978 Jerry was promoted to regional manager and relocated to Kansas City, KS. In 1981 he and the family were relocated to St. Paul, MN where he worked at the H.B. Fuller Co. world headquarters. He was appointed a corporate vice president and was responsible for the largest business segment in the company. He retired on January 1, 2001, after more than forty years service. A long term Rotarian, he was president of the White Bear Lake, MN club in 1995/96. During his career and after retirement he has traveled the world extensively. He is an avid fisherman and enjoys golf and researching McGinty family history.

Jerry McGinty
2008

Sylvia Dolores Roque, Jerry's wife (2), was born November 26, 1941, at Tampa General Hospital in Tampa, Hillsborough Co., FL. She is the daughter of Carlos Corral Roque and Camelia Alicia Perez. Her father, Carlos (Charlie) was born August 21, 1918, in Tampa, Hillsborough Co., FL. He died at the Baldomero Lopez Veterans Nursing Home in Lutz, Pasco Co., FL, August 11, 2007. Her mother, Camelia (Cam) was born February 25, 1916, in Key West, Monroe Co., FL. She died April 30, 2000, in Tampa, FL. Sylvia was their only child. Sylvia's middle name, Dolores, is taken from her maternal great-grandmother, Dolores Orta.

Carlos (Charlie) was born in the Ybor City section of Tampa. He came from a large family of ten children. He served with the U. S. Navy

Seabees during WWII. In April 1959 he moved his family from Ybor City to a new home at 2911 W. Braddock St., in West Tampa. Charlie had a long career as a commercial painter in Tampa. Camelia moved with her family from Key West to Tampa in 1935. She graduated from Hillsborough High School in 1936. She worked as a secretary in the office of the State Attorney for Hillsborough Co., FL for several years and was also an active hospital volunteer worker for over twenty years at St. Joseph's Hospital in Tampa.

Charlie's father was Jose Florentino Roque de Fernandez, b. February 24, 1882, in San Jose de Las Lajas, Havana, Cuba, d. November 24, 1950, in Tampa, FL. He was a cigar maker in Ybor City.

Jose Florentino Roque de Fernandez
Cuban passport, March 31, 1921

Charlie's mother was Urzula Margarita Corral, b. November 16, 1887, in Key West, FL, d. February 22, 1958, in Tampa, FL. Florentino and Urzula were married on March 21, 1903, in Tampa and produced ten children, Elisa (Piro), Angela (Songo), Florentino Jr. (Macho), Oscar (Pirolo), Evelio (Billy), Olimpia, Agustin, Carlos (Charlie), Hortensia (Molly) and Margarita. In 1919 because of a long cigar strike in Ybor City, the family left Tampa for Cuba, sailing on the *S.S. Cuba*, and opened a "buckeye" (small cigar factory) in Guanajar near Havana. When the strike was over, they all returned to Tampa in May of 1921.

Family of Florentino Roque

Florentino (top, second from left) and Ursula (seated, middle) with children (clockwise from Florentino) Angela (Songo), Florentino Jr. (Macho), Evelio (Billy), Agustin, Charlie, Olimpia, Oscar (Pirolo) and Elisa (Piro)

17

Charlie's paternal grandfather was Juan Maria Roque, b. unknown, d. unknown. In the 1910 Tampa census his son, Florentino says that he was born in Cuba. Family lore also says that the family originated in the Canary Islands. There is also a possibility that the Roque name is from the Basque region in Spain. His wife was Eusebia Orihuelas Fernandez. They had two children, Florentino and Maria. Charlie's maternal grandfather was Pablo Corral, b. 1863 Cuba, d. 1922 in Tampa, FL. His wife was Elisa Maria Urriola, b. unknown in Havana, Cuba, and d. unknown.

Camelia's father was Carlos Perez y Romero, b. November 4, 1885, in Cuba, d. December 7, 1955, in Tampa, FL. Her mother was Rosa Maria Ramos y Orta, b. February 16, 1887, in Regla, Cuba, and d. December 12, 1935, in Tampa, FL. The marriage certificate shows that they were married on July 1, 1907, in Cuba. They produced two sons, Raul and Anibal "Neno," and a daughter, Camelia.

Camelia's paternal grandfather was Felipe Perez, b. Mar. 1860, Cuba, d. 1914, Key West, FL. His wife was Asuncion Romero, b. Mar. 1864 Cuba, d. 17 Apr 1914, Key West, FL. Camelia's maternal grandfather was Genaro Ramos, b. Regla, (Havana) Cuba, d. unknown in Havana, Cuba. His wife was Dolores (Lolita) Orta, b. Regla, (Havana) Cuba ca. 1870, d. unknown in FL. Camelia's paternal great grandparents were Pedro Romero, who was born in Cuba and was residing in Key West in 1891 (bank records), and Anibal "Neno" Perez, also residing in Key West.

Carol Ann Simpson, Jerry's wife (1), is the daughter of Nace Elbert Simpson Jr., b. June 11, 1914, d. June 7, 2001, and Vera Frellie Howard, b. September 17, 1918, d. August 20, 2001. Nace Simpson, Jr. (N.E.) was born in Kirkwood, DeKalb Co., GA and Vera Howard was born in Anderson, Anderson Co., SC. They produced five children, Nace III (born December 31, 1941, in Meridian, MS), Carol Ann (born November 14, 1944, in Anderson, SC), Lynda Marie (born July 30, 1947, in Biloxi, MS), Betty Louise (born January 23, 1952, in Biloxi, MS) and Gaye Lynn (born July 9, 1954, in Norfolk, VA). Carol Ann married (2) Douglas Dale Etka and they have one daughter, Kristen Michelle, b. November 18, 1973. Nace, Jr. died of natural causes and Vera was killed shortly after his death in a tragic automobile accident in

Atlanta.

Nace attended Commercial High School, which was located on Pryor St. in Atlanta. He graduated in 1933. He spent close to fifty years in his career with the F. W. Woolworth Co. The family relocated to new cities many times. The last store that he managed was in Miami Beach, FL where he retired in 1985 and then lived in Miami Springs.

Nace told the following story of when he started with the company. He was an assistant manager and company rules said that you were not allowed to be married until you were a manager and had your own store. Therefore, he and Vera decided to be secretly married. The year was 1939. Vera rode the bus down from Anderson, SC to Ft. Lauderdale, FL where Nace was working as an assistant manager. They went to see the justice of the peace, but he had gone fishing. So they sat in a hot motel room and "just looked at each other" until the JP returned. They married, had dinner and Vera returned to Anderson, not letting anyone at Woolworth know what had happened until later, when he became a manager.

Nace Jr., was the son of Nace Simpson, Sr., b. February 26, 1882, in Gainesville, Habersham Co., GA, d. May 17, 1968, in Stone Mountain, GA. His mother was Callie Rucker, b. January 1, 1880, in White Sulphur Springs, Hall Co., GA, d. September 15, 1971, (age ninety-one) in Atlanta. They produced four children, Nace Jr., Glenn Marvin, Corwin Henry and Bertha Marie. They are both buried in Gainesville, GA at the Air Line Cemetery. Nace Sr. was a skilled carpenter and helped built some of the Woolworth stores. It is said that Nace Jr. (N.E.) got his job at Woolworth as a result of his father's connection with the large department store. Callie was a strong willed woman and would not let Nace Sr. smoke in the house. Later, he built a "smoking room" at their home on Boulevard Dr. in Atlanta. He had a big garden and raised prized tomatoes. They had chickens in the yard and plenty of fresh eggs.

Nace Jr.'s paternal grandfather was Raymond Calloway Simpson, b. July 11, 1845, in Hall Co., GA, d. January 8, 1931, in Hall Co. His maternal grandmother was Nevada Marie Vandiver, b. March 30, 1860, in Hall Co., GA, d. June 24, 1904, in Hall Co. They are both buried in the Hopewell Baptist Church Cemetery. Raymond spent his youth on the farm and then worked at his father's cabinet shop. At age seventeen, he enlisted in the Confederate Army and served for eighteen months under Gen. Joseph Johnston. After the war, he and his brother, Charles went to KS to work in the wheat fields. Raymond ruptured himself working in the fields and returned to GA after one year. He spent four years working on the farm of his mother's family and then moved to Atlanta where he worked in a general mercantile store at the southwest corner of Peachtree and Auburn St. During this time he met Asa Candler, one of the founders of the Coca Cola Company. Asa worked at the drug store across the street from where Raymond worked. During this time the formula for Coke was developed and patented. He also knew Mr. Rich (of the Rich's department stores, largest in Atlanta) who once offered him a position in the store.

His next venture was to start a commissary for the railroad. The commissary moved with the railroad crews. A family story recalls that Raymond would buy whiskey by the barrel to sell to the workers. He was supposed to pay tax on the whiskey sales but money was tight. When the tax collector came, Raymond would sell the whiskey and pay the collector the taxes that were due from the proceeds that day.

In 1878 after the railroads were completed, he married Nevada Vandiver and they moved back to Hall Co. They lived on her mother's farm for several years. Later, they moved to a farm in Gainesville, GA. They produced six children, Arthur Bradfield (1880), Nace Elbert (1882), Glenn Marvin (1884), India Augusta (1886), Raymond Calloway Jr. (1889) and LaUna Nevada (1892), all born in Hall Co. Nevada died here in 1904, and Raymond moved back to Atlanta. He married Molly Robinson in 1907. He lived on several farms in the Atlanta, Avondale area. Later, after 1913, Raymond and Molly separated and he spent his remaining years with his children who lived in MS (LaUna), Athens and Atlanta.

Nace Jr.'s great-grandfather was Miles Berry Simpson, b. 1822, d. 1892. Miles moved to GA with his father in the late 1830's. In 1843 he married Frances Bell and they had several children including Nace's grandfather, Raymond and Christopher Columbus (1849). He was a man of many talents being a farmer and also the Sheriff of Hall Co. He also was a cabinetmaker and had a cabinet shop. Frances died around 1851 and Nace married Margaret Grafton in 1852. They produced seven additional children. Margaret died in 1910. Later, in 1855 Miles was the executor of his father's estate.

Nace Jr.'s paternal great-great-grandfather was James T. Simpson, b. 1795 and d. 1855. James moved from SC to GA with his wife, Lei Pirkle Simpson and their family between 1830 and 1840. They settled in Hall Co. near Hopewell. They produced one son and four daughters. Lei lived with her son, Miles in her later years and died in 1894 at age ninety-seven.

Carol's mother, Vera Howard was the daughter of Samuel Grover Howard, b. April 27, 1888, in Hart Co., GA., d. January 6, 1950. Vera's mother was Frellie Atkins, b. January 27, 1894. Frellie Atkins was the daughter of J. Dunn Atkins and Martha J. Bailey. Martha Bailey is the daughter of John C. Bailey, b. 1826 in Lancaster Co., SC and Martha Sanders. John moved to GA at age sixteen. He also fought in the Civil War as a member of Co. C, 16th GA Reg. He died in 1916 at age ninety. His father was Richard Bailey and there is no further known information on the Bailey family. Martha J. Bailey's mother was Martha Sanders, daughter of Rev. Samuel B. Sanders.

Martha Sanders and John C. Bailey produced three sons and seven daughters. Martha's father, Rev. Samuel B. Sanders, was born in Elbert Co. (now Hart Co., GA) on June 22, 1808. He became a Baptist minister and was the pastor of several churches in GA. His wife was Ann Skelton and they produced seven sons and three daughters. Two of their sons were killed in the Civil War. Rev. Sanders' father was Elias Sanders, b. ca. 1775 and his mother was Mary Carter, b. ca. 1775. Elias moved to GA from MD while still a young boy. There is a deed on record showing that he was granted 250 acres there in 1808. It is said that the father of Elias was of English decent and that his wife was an Indian from the Plumer Tribe.

Wiley Patterson McGinty Jr.

(1910-2003)

Wiley Patterson McGinty Jr., b. September 10, 1910, in McGinty, AL, now part of Valley, Chambers Co., AL., d. June 16, 2003, in Atlanta, Fulton Co., GA. He is the son of Wiley Patterson McGinty Sr., and Mollie Hinton Redd. He married (1) Elizabeth Jordan Smith on December 20, 1939, at the Kirkwood Baptist Church in Atlanta, K. Owen White, pastor. She was born on November 20, 1918, in Newnan, Coweta Co., GA (Newnan Hospital), and died May 28, 1968, in Atlanta, GA. He married (2) Mrs. Jacquelin Flanders Satterfield on August 3, 1969. She was born on July 17, 1926, in Atlanta, GA, and died March 29, 2007, in Atlanta.

Children of Wiley Patterson McGinty Jr. and Elizabeth are:

Gerald Kirk McGinty Sr., b. December 18, 1940. He married (1) Carol Ann Simpson, (2) Sylvia Dolores Roque. See previous detail on his life.

Philip James McGinty, b. October 2, 1950, in Atlanta, GA. He married Betty Louise Stewart, b. October 17, 1953, on September 5, 1975. He was named Philip after his father's younger brother, Phillip Leon McGinty. His middle name, James, was the name of his grandfather, James W. Smith, Sr. They have three children, Andrea Laraine, b. March 7, 1978, Andrew Philip, b. October 18, 1981 and Megan Stewart, b. December 20, 1987. These children were all born in Atlanta, Fulton Co., GA.

Donald Jordan McGinty, b. May 24, 1955, in Atlanta, GA. He married (1) Robin Brooks in 1977 and (2) Barbara Anne Lane, b. December 26, 1959, on July 9, 1988. His middle name, Jordan, was his mother's middle name. Her grandmother was Lucy Wesley Jordan. They have two children, Fiona Lane, b. April 18, 1989, and Tessa Rose, b. April 17, 1992. Both children were born in San Francisco, San Francisco Co., CA.

The Life of Wiley P. McGinty Jr.

Wiley P. McGinty Jr., grew up in McGinty near River View which is now part of Valley, AL. He enrolled at Emory University in Atlanta, GA in 1928, completing his freshman year in 1929. In 1930 he moved to Atlanta permanently and took a position with Southern Mills, Inc., a textile manufacturer. The 1930 census shows him still living in his father's home and working in a cotton mill in the River View area. His sister, Maye, had married George D. Ray Sr., who was the plant manager of the Southern Mills operation in Roswell, GA. Wiley lived with them and attended Emory University from 1935 until 1938 while also working at Southern Mills. He graduated in 1938 with honors, including membership in the Phi Beta Kappa honorary fraternity.

Wiley married (1) Elizabeth Jordan Smith in 1939. From 1938 until 1941 he was a professor of French and English at Technological High School (Tech. High) in Atlanta. After this he was asked to return to Southern Mills where, during WWII he was involved in the manufacture of textiles for military use. He worked there until retirement in 1982 a career that spanned fifty-two years. His position at retirement was vice president and secretary. He served several sessions on the DeKalb County grand jury and was a member of the Atlanta Rotary Club for many years.

After Elizabeth's death he married (2) Jacquelin Flanders Satterfield in 1969. She was a widow, having lost her husband to cancer. Jackie is the daughter of James Morris Flanders, (1902-1984), and Rena Love McCorkle, (1904-1995). Jackie died March 27, 2007, in Atlanta. Wiley was a student of foreign languages. He had a collection of bibles and many other books from around the world, all printed in the local languages.

Elizabeth Jordan Smith McGinty
Wedding photo, 1939

He also enjoyed watching baseball and football games and doing the more difficult crossword puzzles because "the *New York Times* puzzle was too easy." In keeping with his strong Baptist heritage, most of his social life with Elizabeth revolved around the church. He died three months short of his ninety-third birthday on June 16, 2003, in Atlanta, Fulton Co., GA and was buried next to Elizabeth at Westview Cemetery in Atlanta.

Westview Cemetery, Atlanta, GA

Wiley's wife (1) Elizabeth Smith McGinty (she preferred to spell her name Eli̱sabeth) was the daughter of James Willis Smith Sr., b. Rome, GA, November 3, 1888, d. Atlanta, May 16, 1949. Her mother was Ruby Blanche Miller, b. April 27, 1895, in Franklin, Heard Co., GA, d. August 6, 1981, at the Baptist Village nursing home in Waycross, GA. She is buried next to her husband in the Westview Cemetery in Atlanta, GA (photo, opposite page). "Liz" was born in Franklin, GA at the home of her maternal grandparents, Rufus Milton Miller ("Tonny") and Ida Elizabeth Rooks Miller ("Ida"), on November 18, 1918. She has one brother, James W. "Jim" Smith Jr. (1924-2010), who was a Baptist missionary in Israel for over thirty years. The Millers had lived in Franklin for several generations.

Elizabeth's father, James Willis "Jim" Smith Sr., was the GA State Manager for the Modern Woodman of America from 1925 until he retired in 1945. He was a district manager from August 1, 1913, until 1925. His WWI draft card dated June 5, 1917, shows him as single and living in Augusta, GA. He shows four years of military service in the GA National Guard as a 1st Lieutenant. After marrying in December 1917 he moved from Augusta to Franklin where Elizabeth was born. Later, they lived in Columbus, Dublin, Decatur and finally, the East

Lake area of Atlanta, GA. He shows in the 1920 census as living in Dublin, Laurens Co., GA, and then in the 1930 census, pg. 24A, living in Decatur, DeKalb Co., GA. The Modern Woodmen was a fraternal insurance group and Jim traveled all over the state setting up offices that were called "camps." During this time, Jim knew several political leaders in GA including Sen. Richard Russell and Gov. Ed Rivers.

In 1937 he received an honorary appointment as Lieutenant Colonel, Aide-de-Camp, Governor's Staff from Gov. Rivers. Later in life he was employed by the Auto-Soler Co., a firm that made shoe repair machinery. He sold this equipment throughout the state, travelling in a 1939 Packard coupe. Later, he was employed by the Hathcock Insurance Co. in Atlanta. He said that he had graduated from Gordon Military Academy and had served in the GA National Guard. He was a staunch Methodist all of his life and a member of the Kirkwood Methodist church in Atlanta. His son, James Jr. related the following memory: "In my last conversation with Dad on the night before he died at Crawford Long hospital in Atlanta, he reminded me of a scripture verse that he often quoted: "A good name is rather to be chosen than great riches, and loving favor rather than silver and gold (Proverbs 22: 1 King James Version)."

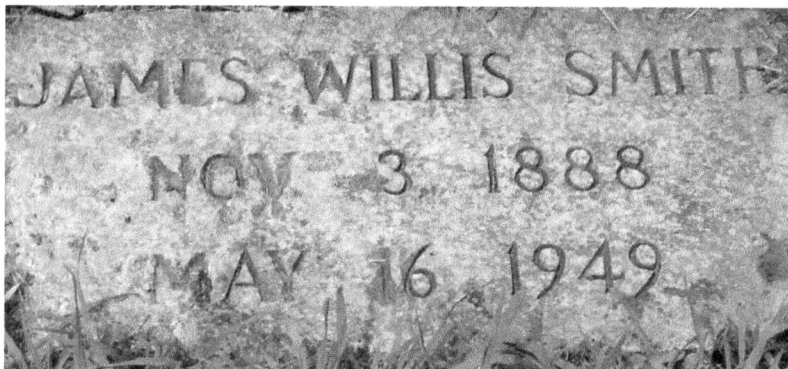

Westview Cemetery, Atlanta, GA

Elizabeth's mother, Blanche Miller was known by her family as Momie. She is said to have liked this name because one of the characters in her favorite book, *Little Women,* had a similar name.

Later in life she lived alone but loved being with her family and was always asking us over for dinner, even when the effort was taxing her greatly. She was kind and generous person and was loved by all of us. The marriage of Blanche and Bill Smith resulted in memberships in two different churches.

The Millers were ardent Baptists. Rufus Miller, the father of Blanche, was a charter member of the Franklin Baptist Church in Franklin, GA. As mentioned above, Bill Smith was a strong Methodist. His great-great-grandfather was Rev. Thomas Dunn, a Methodist minister who served as a chaplain in the American revolutionary war. Dunn was also an acquaintance of Francis Asbury, a pioneer Methodist in early GA and a personal friend of John Wesley. Bill would attend the Methodist church while the rest of the family attended the Baptist church with Blanche.

Their son, Rev. James Smith Jr., served as a chaplain in WWII and became a Baptist missionary, spending almost thirty-five years in Israel. After Jim Sr. passed away in 1949 Blanche continued to live at 2556 Tilson Dr. Her mother, Ida, had been living there with her since 1932. For awhile, her home was also the residence of Wiley, Elizabeth and grandsons Jerry and Phil. This is where I was raised and lived until 1953. Wiley then moved our family to our first owned home at 874 Artwood Rd., next to Fernbank Forest in Atlanta.

Blanche and Ida lived together until Ida passed away September 25, 1961, just two months shy of her ninetieth birthday. Blanche lived alone until the late 1960's. She took on boarders but eventually sold the home and moved to an apartment on Clifton Rd., near Emory University that was owned by the Wooten family. Her only daughter, Elizabeth, died in 1968 and her son, James Jr., was then living in Israel. It was best that she receive care at the Clairmont Oaks Retirement Home in Decatur. After a time, she was moved to the Baptist Village Nursing Home in Waycross, GA, where she died.

Ruby Blanche Miller
"Momie"

Westview Cemetery, Atlanta, GA

Elizabeth completed two years at Agnes Scott College in Decatur, GA and was employed by the First National Bank in Atlanta. Wiley met her at a party held by his first cousin, Lois Lennard Hanevold who was also one of Elizabeth's closest friends. They were married on December 20, 1939, at the Kirkwood Baptist Church. Elizabeth died of cancer May 28, 1968, at the early age of forty-nine. Elizabeth is remembered by all that knew her as a wonderful person. She was a member of the Druid Hills Baptist Church in Atlanta and devoted much of her time to serving the church. The long time pastor of this church, Rev. Louie D. Newton wrote the following about her: "Miss Elizabeth was one of the really great Christians I have ever known. There was something about her that one felt the moment he came within her presence – gentleness, assurance, and commitment. I shall always remember her for these rare and beautiful qualities." In June 1968, the church adopted a resolution memorializing the passing of Elizabeth McGinty. Elizabeth is buried next to her husband at the Westview Cemetery in Atlanta, GA.

Elizabeth's paternal grandparents were "Colonel" James Monroe Smith, b. Zebulon, Pike Co., GA, August 10, 1850, d. Barnesville, GA, July 22, 1921. He married Lucy Wesley Jordan, b. Monroe Co., GA, February 10, 1861, d. Barnesville, GA, September 29, 1902. They produced eight children. James Monroe Smith was a lawyer and the "Colonel" title came from his profession rather than from a military rank. In 1880 the young lawyer was serving in the Pike Co. superior court in Zebulon, GA. During this time, the census shows him rooming with a black family, the Maghums, in Zebulon. His connection to this family is unknown. During this same time, the 1880 census shows Lucy Jordan living with the family of R.Y. Beckham in Zebulon. Lucy had come up from her home in Bolingbroke, GA to attend school there. While in school, Lucy lived with her sister, Laura Jordan Beckham. Laura Jordan had married R.Y. Beckham who was clerk of the Pike Co. superior court and a colleague of James Smith. James and Lucy were married in 1882. Lucy died of complications giving birth when she was only forty years old. The surviving child was Lucy Jewell Smith. This death was a devastating blow to the Smith family. James then moved the family to Barnesville, GA. James and Lucy are buried at the Zebulon United Methodist Church in Pike Co., GA.

Elizabeth's paternal great-grandparents were Dr. Lorenzo Hope Hull Jordan and Susan B. Steger. Dr. Jordan was born August 18, 1825, in Oglethorpe Co., GA. Susan was born March 23, 1826, in Henry Co., GA. Shortly after her birth, her father, Robert Steger, moved his family to Pike Co., GA. Dr. Lorenzo and Susan were married October 10, 1845. They first lived in Fayette Co., GA and then moved to Bolingbroke, GA and built a home on Pea Ridge Rd. near the Salem Methodist Church. The 1850 census of Fayette Co., GA shows Lorenzo, age twenty-five, already an M.D. and living with his father, Willis A. Jordan. On the same 1850 census, but a few weeks later, Lorenzo is shown living in Monroe Co. with wife, Susan B. Like his father before him, he owned slaves.

The 1860 census of Monroe Co., GA shows them with their first three children and six slaves. They produced a total of six children. Dr. Jordan died June 9, 1865, at the early age of thirty-nine. Susan, pregnant with their last child, was appointed executor of his estate. She named this daughter Lorenzo Susan Jordan, later shortened to Rennie. The 1870 census of Monroe Co., GA shows Susan as a widow with all six children. The 1880 census shows Susan still living in Monroe Co., GA with three of her children. There is a deed dated December 28, 1888, showing the sale of a portion of the Lorenzo Jordan old home place by his heirs to Dean Howard, one of his daughters, (Monroe County Land Deeds, vol. X, pg. 186-187, Monroe Co. Courthouse, Forsyth, GA). Susan died November 26, 1902. They are both buried at the Salem Methodist Church Cemetery in Bolingbroke, Monroe Co., GA. Dr.

Jordan's gravestone is no longer readable but Susan's is still in fairly good shape.

Elizabeth's other paternal great-grandparents were Nevel Goodwin Smith and Rebecca Caroline Toland. Nevel was born June 13, 1809, in GA. Rebecca was born ca. 1820 in SC. Her parents were recent Irish immigrants to SC. Nevel and Rebecca were married August 8, 1838, in Monroe Co., GA. Nevel died in 1876 but Rebecca lived until after the turn of the century. Both are buried on the old Smith farm, now called Bush Cemetery near Zebulon, GA.

I think that the father of Nevel Smith was Lemuel Smith. Lemuel is shown in the 1830 and 1840 census of Monroe Co., GA. More research is needed but if this is correct, Lemuel would be Elizabeth's paternal great-great-grandfather.

Another set of Elizabeth's paternal great-great-grandparents were Willis Asbury Jordan and Sara Wesley Dunn. Willis was born in Oglethorpe Co., GA, November 8, 1801, and died April 22, 1877, in Spalding Co, GA. His middle name, Asbury, was taken from Francis Asbury, a pioneer Methodist who worked with John Wesley to bring this church to GA. Similarly, the middle name of his wife, Sarah Wesley Dunn, was taken from John Wesley. Willis was a Methodist minister. Sarah was born April 2, 1800, and died in April of 1879 also in Spalding Co. They produced thirteen children. Sarah's father, Rev. Thomas Dunn, served in the Revolutionary War as a private in the VA Continental Line.

Elizabeth's paternal great-great-great-grandfather, Edmond Jordan, was born (based on the 1800, 1820 and 1830 census age brackets) before 1755 in Halifax Township, Northampton Co., NC. His name is clearly spelled "Edmond" in all three of these census records, however, other records sometime show it spelled, "Edmund." Family legend says that he served in the VA militia during the Revolutionary War. He was supposedly wounded at the Battle of Princeton and as a result, was slightly crippled for the rest of his life. His service records have not been found. After the war, Edmond moved to GA. In 1786 Edmond appears in the Franklin Co., GA tax list with 400 acres and one slave (GA Archives). By 1787 Edmund had moved to Wilkes County, GA where he is shown on the tax list with 487 acres and two slaves (GA Archives). A 1790 deed shows him living on Mack's Creek in Wilkes County.

He married Mary Ridley Pope on April 16, 1791. Wilkes County tax records in 1792 and 1793 show him living on Dry Fork Creek near Lexington, GA. When part of Wilkes Co. became Oglethorpe Co. in 1795 Edmond's residence changed to Oglethorpe County. On the Oglethorpe Co. tax lists of 1799 and 1800 Edmond's land is shown adjacent to that of Lewis Pope, the father of Edmond's wife, Mary Ridley Pope. He shows in the 1800 census of Oglethorpe Co., GA., age bracket forty-five plus, pg. 12, living in Capt. Lee's dist., which was in GA military dist. 236, Grove Creek. Edmond and Mary had at least three children, two daughters named Jemima and Day Ridley, and one son, Willis A. Jordan.

The Jordan family was fairly prosperous in early GA. By the 1820 census of Oglethorpe Co., Edmund had accumulated thirty slaves. The 1827 land lottery confirms that he had seen military service. Interestingly, in his will, written in Oglethorpe Co., GA, November 12, 1836, Edmond wrote: "In grateful remembrance of the valuable services and great fidelity of my good servant Charles, my desire is that in the division of my negroes he may be permitted to choose where he will live and to whom he may belong." Willis A. Jordan served as executor of his will.

Willis A. Jordan was the oldest surviving son of Edmund and Polly. He attended the Meson Academy, a private school near Lexington, GA where he shows as a student in 1814. In 1822 Willis was commissioned to preach as a Methodist minister. Shortly after, he married Sarah Dunn in Oglethorpe Co., September 22, 1822. Although a preacher, Willis continued to own slaves and shows in the 1840 census of Monroe Co., GA with twenty-three. The 1850 slave census of Fayette Co., GA shows him with twenty-one. This shows how slavery was condoned and accepted at the time. Even preachers owned them. By 1860 Willis had accumulated real estate valued at $9,000 and personal property valued at $14,000. Of course, the war took its toll as the Confederacy collapsed. Willis saw his estate, located in western Spalding Co., GA, gradually divided up and sold off to satisfy creditors. He died in 1877 without leaving a will. A land survey map dated 1883 hangs in the Spalding Co. courthouse and shows the homestead of W.A. Jordan as being bankrupt.

The other set of paternal grandparents was Robert McLaurine Steger and Lucy Burton. Robert and Lucy were both born in

Cumberland Co., VA. They were married there on December 16, 1802.

In 1808 they moved from VA to the Abbeville District of SC. While living in SC, Robert served in the War of 1812 (pension application WC-3905). Around 1825, they moved to Henry Co., GA and settled land on Cotton River (Cotton Creek). Susan B. Steger was born there. They remained in Henry Co. for ten years, sold their land and moved to Pike Co., GA. Robert was prominent in antebellum Pike Co. politics. He served on the 1839 grand jury and was a delegate to the 1845 meeting in Barnesville, GA to nominate a Whig candidate for senator in the 26th district. An article about Robert's son Samuel, published in *Memories of Southern Arkansas*, pg. 374, dated 1890 mentions that Robert had "owned about thirty slaves." In his will, dated February 28, 1861, Robert states: "my desire is, after paying all my just debts and the legacies specified in the foregoing items of this will together with my negroes, for the rest of all my property to be kept by my wife Lucy W. Steger for her lifetime..." Robert died on August 24, 1863. Robert and Lucy are buried on the old Steger farm, now called Johnson Cemetery, near Zebulon, GA.

Robert's father was Samuel Steger. He was the husband of Agnes McLaurine of Powhatan, VA. Agnes's father, the Rev. Robert McLaurine, born ca. 1720 in Scotland, was commissioned in 1750 by the Church of England to establish the first Episcopal Church in the Colony of VA. He married Elizabeth Blaikley of Williamsburg, VA in 1753. She was the daughter of Catherine Blaikley, the famous midwife that delivered over 3000 babies in the area. Catherine is buried in the churchyard of Bruton Parish in Williamsburg. She is buried in a crypt with several of her grandchildren. Her inscription reads, "Mrs. Catherine Blaikley late of this city, Grandmother of the above named children. She departed this life the 25th day of October 1771 aged 75 years and upwards." This is the oldest known grave of our ancestors in America. She was my great-great-great-great-great-great-grandmother. Robert McLaurine died July 5, 1773. He was buried at the old Peterville Church in Cumberland Co., VA.

Elizabeth's grandparents on the maternal side were Rufus Milton "Tonny" Miller, b. April 6, 1863, in Franklin, Heard Co., GA, d. December 20, 1932, in Franklin, GA and Ida Elizabeth Lee Rooks, b. November 16, 1871, in Franklin, GA, d. September 25, 1961, in Atlanta. Elizabeth was, no doubt, named for her grandmother. Rufus and Ida produced four children. Flossie Lee was born in 1888. Ollie Cleo was born in 1891. The other children were my grandmother, Ruby Blanche (1895) and John Milton (1903-1971). Rufus and his family lived for a time in the Houston district of Heard Co. but had moved to Franklin by the 1920 census. Ida Miller was my great-grandmother. She lived with us late in her life at 2556 Tilson Dr. in Atlanta. Her funeral was held at the Kirkwood Baptist Church and she was buried with her husband at the Bevis Cemetery in Franklin, GA. Her favorite hymn, "How Great Thou Art", composed by Stuart K. Hine, was sung at the funeral. Her children, Flossie and Cleo died from influenza in the epidemic of 1919 ("Spanish Flu"). See the 1941 picture showing four generations, Ida, Blanche, Elizabeth and Gerald K., age one (pg. 13).

Ida's father was John William Rooks Jr.. He enlisted as a private in Co. I, 41st GA Inf., Army of TN (Heard's Rangers), March 4, 1862. He lived in Heard Co., GA. He was captured May 16, 1864, at Resaca, GA and sent to Rock Island POW camp where his brother Dennis had died a year earlier. Rock Island Prison was in Illinois. After the war, he took the required oath of allegiance to the U.S. on October 6, 1864, and then enlisted in the U.S. Army for frontier service. The Rooks family came from MD to GA in early 1800. Their name back in MD was spelled Ruark. Ida's mother was Harriet Lee Kirk (1836-1900). She shows in the 1900 census of Heard Co., GA, Houston district, pg. 25, living with her son, John W. Rooks III. Harriet's father was Wiley Jackson Kirk Sr., b. July 4, 1793, possibly in SC and later moved to GA. He shows in the 1850 census of Heard Co., GA, pg. 165, with a wife and seven children. He died there, November 28, 1877. His father was Jesse Kirk, born 1762 in VA.

Elizabeth's maternal great-grandparents were Thomas Miller, b. February 4, 1842, in Franklin, GA, d. June 9, 1921, in Franklin and (1) Mary Caroline "Callie" McDonald, b. June 6, 1842, d. May 8, 1902. (2) Lucy Montgomery. He married Mary at the beginning of the Civil War. Mary was the daughter of Hiram McDonald and Lucy "Lovey" Walden. Hiram served as Sheriff of Heard Co., GA. The Waldens are related to the James Mercer family whose son was Silas Mercer, noted Baptist minister in GA. His other son, Jacob, had a daughter, Rebecca that married a Walden. Their daughter was Lucy "Lovey" Walden, mentioned above. In *A Short History of Heard Co.,* by James Bonner, page 341, it states that Thomas enlisted as a private in Co. G, 4th Reg.,

GA State Troops, October 25, 1861. He mustered out in April 1862 and re-enlisted, May 12, 1862, in Co. K, 56th Reg., GA Inf. He was captured at Vicksburg on July 1, 1863, and returned home after the war. Thomas and Callie produced five children, Rufus Milton (1863), Walter Hiram (1880), Laura Ollie, Cora and William L. After Callie died of smallpox, he married Lucy Montgomery (date unknown) and they had one child, Tommie Lucile (1907).

Elizabeth's maternal great-great-grandparents were John Miller Jr., b. July 20, 1807, in VA, d. April 11, 1878, in Franklin, GA. and Talitha Cummie Hammond, b. ca. 1808 in GA, d. after 1880. Talitha shows her father on the 1880 Heard Co., GA census as being born in Ireland and her mother as born in SC. John Jr., was born in VA. His parents were John Sr. and Ailsey Miller, both born in VA. John Sr. died before 1830. Ailsey and two of her children drew successfully in the 1832 Cherokee land lotteries. John Jr. bought land in Oglethorpe in 1830. He also drew in the 1832 lottery and shows in the 1835-37 tax list of Oglethorpe Co., GA. He relocated to Heard Co. after 1838. In the 1840 census he is listed as living in Heard Co., GA. He shows in the 1850 Heard Co. census. In the 1860 census he is still in Heard Co. with eight slaves. His will is dated March 5, 1877. They produced a large family of ten children, Caroline (1831), Barbara Ann (1840), Thomas (1842), Rufus C. (no date), Elmira (1845), Joseph (1848), Frances "Frank" (no date), Willis (1850), William (1866) and Marshall (no date). John died in Heard Co. on April 11, 1878. Talitha died after 1880. Both are buried in the Miller Cemetery in Heard Co.

Wiley Patterson McGinty Sr.

(1865-1957)

Wiley Patterson McGinty Sr., b. January 22, 1865 in McGinty, AL, which is now part of Valley, Chambers Co., AL. He died March 30, 1957, in Atlanta, GA. He was the second son of William Pitts McGinty and Ann M. Moore.

**Wiley P. McGinty Sr. and wife Mollie Hinton Redd
Wedding photo, 1893**

He married (1) Mollie Hinton Redd, b. April 8, 1875, d. October 31, 1931, on December 14, 1893, in Chambers Co., AL, by James Weaver, JP. He married (2) Tinnie Mae Hunt, b. May 15, 1895, d. September 15, 1970, on November 23, 1932.

Children of Wiley P. McGinty Sr. and Mollie Hinton Redd:

Hilary Herbert McGinty, b. March 31, 1895, in McGinty, now part of Valley, Chambers Co., AL, d. January 3, 1990, in Cape Girardeau, MO. He married (1) Minerva (Minnie) Lou Finney (affectionately referred to as "Minnie Finney McGinty") on August 16, 1921, in Chambers Co., AL and (2) Julia Ethel Hitt Milliken (widow) on July 18, 1981. Their children were Martha Hinton, b. 1922, Charles, b. 1925 and Mary Lillian, b. 1931.

Notes on Hilary Herbert McGinty

Herbert was named after the first U.S. Cabinet member from the former Confederate States after the Civil War, Hilary Herbert. This Hilary Herbert was also the commanding officer of the Greenville, AL, troops during the war. Herbert attended school in Glass, AL, near his home in River View. He then became the school master there and taught for three years (1913-1915). He "got the calling" to be a minister and graduated from the Howard College in Birmingham, AL. He also attended summer school at Auburn University. He was ordained May 31, 1914, at the Bethlehem Baptist Church near River View. His first full time pastorate (1921-1926) was at the First Baptist Church in Guntersville, AL, on the Tennessee River.

From there the family moved to Asocial, AR and the Asocial Baptist Church. Herbert decided to go back to seminary for post-graduate training and in 1930 the family moved to Louisville, KY where he attended the Southern Baptist Theological Seminary and received his Ph.D. In 1932 the family moved to Lawrenceburg, KY where he was pastor of the Sand Springs Baptist Church. He was known as "Dr. McGinty." The family moved to Cape Girardeau, MO in October 1934 where he became pastor of the First Baptist Church. He was editor of the MO Baptist newspaper, *Word and Way*, for twenty years, beginning in 1948. In 1952 the MO Baptist headquarters were moved to Jefferson City and he relocated there. In 1973 he retired and relocated back to Cape Girardeau, MO. He was described by fellow editor W.G. Stracener of the *Florida Baptist Witness* as "One who had demonstrated the courage of his convictions, abiding loyalty and truth, compassion for lost souls, depth of concern for both civic and personal righteousness, fairness in judgment, clarity in speaking and writing, and a spirit of understanding and good cheer." Despite being born crippled, he led a very productive life. He mentioned in several letters that until he was physically unable, he was working on a history of the Missouri Baptist Church and had assembled quite a bit of research. Unfortunately it was never completed and was lost after his death.

Christine McGinty
Fairview Cemetery, Valley AL

<u>Christine McGinty</u>, b. May 22, 1896, in McGinty, AL, d. at birth. Her tombstone is inscribed, "Budded on Earth to Bloom in Heaven." She is buried in the McGinty plot at Fairview Cemetery, Valley, AL.

Maye McGinty

Maye Lillie McGinty, (Maye), b. January 13, 1898, in McGinty, AL, d. March 5, 1994, in Atlanta, GA. Rev. H. Herbert McGinty, her brother, married her to George Delorian Ray Sr. on December 26, 1916, in Chambers Co., AL. He was a plant manager for Southern Mills, Inc. in Roswell, GA. He was nicknamed "Pappy" by his fellow employees. Their only child was George Ray Jr., b. 1918 who was also an employee of Southern Mills and rose to the position of CEO. They are buried together at the Ray family cemetery in Hancock Co., GA.

Margaret McGinty

Annie Margaret McGinty, (Margaret), b. April 30, 1902, in McGinty, AL, d. February 25, 1995, in Marietta, GA. The 1920 census shows her as a schoolteacher in the public school system. During WWII, she was in charge of the War Service Center. This center facilitated communications between service personnel and their families. She married Milton C. Christie and by 1923 they were living on the large Christie "Plantation" in Plantersville, AL, which is near Talladega, AL. Later, because of his health problems, they moved to River View and he was employed for a time in the maintenance department at the Riverdale Mill. They lived in a house across River Rd. from her father, Wiley P. Sr. Her children and grandchildren called her "Mamie". Their children were sons Milton McGinty, b. 1924, Sim Patterson (1928-2003), Mollie Hinton (1931-1932) and Margaret Ann, b. 1930. Margaret is buried with Milton at Resthaven Memorial Gardens in Lanett, AL.

Ruth McGinty

__Nannie Ruth McGinty__, (Ruth), b. March 3, 1904, in McGinty, AL, d. April 24, 1994, in Conneaut, OH. She married William H. Anderson on May 7, 1925, in Chambers Co., AL. He was employed by the West Point post office for forty-seven years and became the assistant postmaster. He died in 1979. During WWI, she was a reporter for the local River View newsletter. In 1924 Ruth was attending State Normal College in Florence, AL. She later taught in the Fairfax, AL public schools. She was a member of the First Baptist church in West Point for sixty-seven years, singing in the choir and teaching Sunday school. During WWII, she worked as a lathe operator in an ammunition plant in West Point that made 20mm shells. After the war, she worked at two different jewelry stores in West Point and kept the books for the Bartlett Oldsmobile dealer. Their children were William Henry Jr. M.D., b. 1926, Wiley Stinson, b. 1927 and Ray Christie, b. 1934. She is buried next to Bill at the Pinewood Cemetery in West Point, GA.

Velta McGinty

Velta McGinty, (Velta), b. February 17, 1906, in McGinty, AL, d. February 26, 1996, in Union City, Fulton Co., GA. She married George Marvin Couch on December 24, 1926, in Chambers Co., AL. He was from Sharpsburg, GA, and was shown as a tobacco salesman in the 1930 census. His business was the stocking and maintaining of vending machines. Her name is said to originate from Theodore RooseVELT, 26th President of the United States, 1901-1909. Their only son was George Marvin "Pete" Jr., b. December 6, 1928, d. February 2006 in Newnan, GA. There is a Cenotaph, possibly for her, at the South Fulton Medical Center in East Point, GA. She is buried at Westview Cemetery in Atlanta

My Father, Wiley McGinty

Wiley Patterson McGinty Jr., (Wiley), b. September 10, 1910, in McGinty, AL, d. June 16, 2003, in Atlanta, Fulton Co., GA. He married (1) Elizabeth Jordan Smith and (2) (Mrs.) Jacquelin Flanders Satterfield. Their children were Gerald Kirk (b. 1940), Philip James (b. 1950) and Donald Jordan (b. 1955).

Phil McGinty

Phillip Leon McGinty, (Phil), b. August 30, 1912, in McGinty, AL, d. February 14, 1969, in Atlanta, GA. He married (1) Dorothy "Dot" Louise Hurt, and (2) Betty Cleo Cowart. His children by Dorothy were a son (stillborn) and Marilyn Hope (b. 1942). His children by Betty were Phillip Jr., b. July 8, 1968, and Lisa Melanie, b. June 11, 1967.

There is an unconfirmed family story, that "Phil" was named after a major league baseball player, Phillip Leon. Phil moved to Atlanta from Chambers Co., attended the University of Georgia night school, and eventually became president of Irvindale Farms, the largest dairy products company in Atlanta at the time. He loved to hunt quail and fish. He was an active Republican and received several letters from, and an invitation to John F. Kennedy's inauguration. Phil and Dot had two children. The first was a baby boy that passed away shortly after birth. Their daughter, Marilyn Hope McGinty Baker currently lives in Atlanta. After Dot passed away, he married Betty Cleo Cowart, April 30, 1966. They produced two children; Lisa Melanie and Phillip Leon Jr. Betty married Lee B. Kirkman, March 1, 1975, and as of this writing lives in Rome, GA. Phil is buried at Arlington Cemetery in Sandy Springs, GA.

Children of Wiley and Mollie Hinton Redd.
Seated: Herbert and Maye.
Standing, L to R: Wiley Jr., Margaret, Velta, Phil and Ruth.
Taken April 1, 1957, during the funeral of their father, Wiley Sr.

The Life of Wiley P. McGinty Sr.

It is my opinion that Wiley McGinty, known as an adult by many as "Mr. Wiley," was named after his Mother's brother, Wiley P.L. Moore. W.P.L Moore shows, age 16, in the 1860 census of Chambers Co., and again in the special Alabama census of 1866 as a Civil War casualty. Wiley McGinty was possibly named in remembrance of him. Wiley McGinty's mother, Ann Moore, was the daughter of Levin and Penelope Patterson Moore, early Chambers Co. pioneers. Penelope Patterson, Wiley's mother-in-law, was the daughter of Willie Patterson (b. October 15, 1775, Orange Co., NC, d. 1852, Jones Co., GA), and Anna Herndon (b. June 10, 1779, Orange Co., NC, d. 1853). Earlier McGinty researchers speculated that this name, Wiley Patterson, came from Willie Patterson, but that the "Willie" was changed to Wiley.

Wiley was the eighth of eleven children born to William Pitts McGinty and Ann M. Moore. He had three sisters and seven brothers. He was born and grew up on his father's 275-acre farm that was near the present day Fairview Cemetery in Valley, AL. At a much later date, this farm was sold to the Scales family. In late 1935 part of this original land was purchased by Rev. Basil B. McGinty who built a modern brick house on the old McGinty home site, which is still fronted by the original massive oak and cedar trees (see section on Basil McGinty). I visited the site in 2003 and the house was no longer occupied but still standing along with some of the ancient cedars and oaks on the grounds. The property was recently sold to another family.

Wiley was born in 1865 in the final days of the Civil War. The last Confederate fort to fall to the northern armies was Ft. Tyler in West Point, GA, very close to Wiley's birthplace. This battle actually ended eleven days after the surrender at Appomattox. After the war, the Valley was farm country with the property in the hands of a few large landowners. Wiley documented most of the farm locations, their owners and what happened to this land during his lifetime. In a 1941 article that he wrote titled *76 Years in the Valley*, he recalls that when he was born in 1865 this area was a farming community with all of the land in the hands of a few large landowners. The land where the River View village is now located was owned by Jim Campbell. The Riverdale mill was built here in 1866. Prior to this, the Campbell gristmill was on the site, about 100 yards from where the mill is located. Adjacent to this farm on the northwest was the Tyre Freeman place; and to the north was the Holly Weaver land. To the west of the Campbell place was the land owned by his grandfather, Levin Moore. Farther west in the direction of Fairfax, was the farm of his father, William Pitts McGinty. It is there that he was born. It is there that the McGinty cemetery (Fairview) is located. The next plot of land was owned by the famous Irish peach grower, John Parnell.

F. W. Shank(s) owned the next farm, and it is on this land that the Fairfax mill is located. This mill was built in 1915. Just east of the land where the mill is located was the Alex Jarrell (or Jarrett) property. Next was the Elish Trammel farm, on which the Langdale mill is located. This mill began operations in 1867. Prior to this, Trammel's gristmill was located on this property. Then came the Todd farm. Next to it was the Sharp land. Adjoining was the Tom Nolan place, and it is on this land that the Shawmut mill is located. This mill was built in 1908. In front of the Shawmut property was the Dave Robinson farm. Next was the Calloway farm, on which a large part of the Lanett mill was built in 1894. At the time, there was only one house in Lanett. Wiley was standing on this property, observing the initial grading for this new mill.

He started school in 1872 at the Center schoolhouse, located halfway between Langdale and River View. It was a one-teacher school and there were about forty students. He finished the tenth grade at Beulah, AL, and started working on the family farm. When he was twenty-one, he worked for Smith Brothers of River View. He worked at their cotton gin, planning mill and gristmill.

Wiley lived at a time when the economy of the entire Valley, AL area changed from a farming community to an industrial driven economy. With the coming of all the new cotton mills, people found secure employment without all the headaches and risks of farming.

After the Civil War, several cotton mills were built in the area, along the Chattahoochee River, which supplied the necessary water resources for power. Wiley witnessed this industrial revolution in the area. He was an excellent carpenter and helped construct some of the mills as foreman of the carpentry department at Batson Cook Co., in West Point. Around 1891 at age twenty-six, he constructed the family home at what was named McGinty Crossroads, where all of his children were later born and raised. His land was once the property of his grandfather, Levin Moore. He became an independent contractor, and built many homes in the small towns that now make up Valley, AL. Later in life he operated a general store at the crossroads. He was elected justice of the peace in 1896 and served in the position for forty-eight years. He was then a notary public until 1953.

He married Mollie Hinton Redd December 14, 1893. The consent letter from her father reads as follows: "River View, AL, Dec. 9, 1893. You are hereby authorized to issue marriage license for the marriage of W.P. McGinty to Mollie H. Redd of said county and state. Mollie H. Redd is my daughter and is under age but I hereby give my consent to the marriage. Respectfully, H.J. Redd."

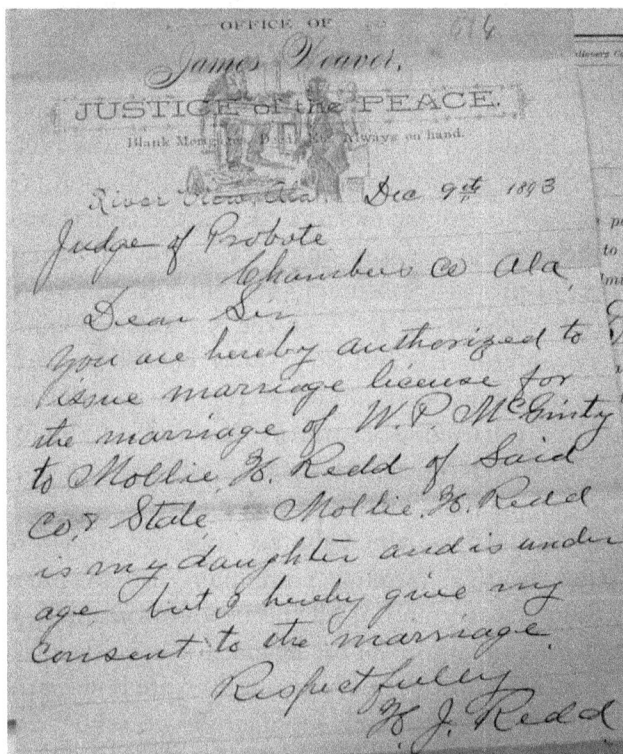

**Wiley and Mollie
Marriage Permission Letter from her Father
(Age of consent was twenty-one at this time)**

The 1900 census shows his name incorrectly as Wylie, age 35,

Bethlehem, Chambers Co., ED 16, house 116. He was appointed justice of the peace in Beat 13, by Gov. William Jelks in 1901 (*LaFayette Sun*, 9 Oct 1901). In 1910, he is shown on the federal census form as being responsible for taking and recording the census in Bethlehem, precinct 13 in Chambers Co. He is listed on the census form as the "Enumerator." The census index shows his name as Wily, age 45, ED 36, house 177/181.

In 1920 he helped construct the new River View Baptist church building and the census shows him as a farmer. He was a charter member of this church in 1897. He shows in the 1920 census as Wylie, age 54, Fairfax, Chambers Co., precinct 13, ED 36, house 283. There is an article in the March 19, 1924, *Lafayette Sun* social section that published almost everything of interest that happened in the area, showing that W. P. McGinty had purchased a new Ford automobile. I think that he still had this car when I used to visit him in the 1940's. It was then stored in a shed beside the house. In 1925 records show that his heirs sold the family home that he built in 1891. Wiley moved about a block down the street to a home at 1025 River Rd. Both of these homes were still standing in 2011.

In the book *Preacher's Kid* by Dr. Charles P. McGinty, who is the grandson of Wiley, he tells about the family reunions that were held at McGinty's Crossroads before 1930. Charles was the son of Rev. Herbert McGinty, Wiley's first child. They lived in KY at the time and would drive down to Chambers Co. in their 1929 Dodge. The family would drive down the graded dirt highway to the "Valley." Little mill towns of Lanett, Fairfax, Langdale and River View were clustered together along the Alabama side of the Chattahoochee River. Just across the river was West Point, Georgia, where Dad's sister, Ruth, lived with her husband, Bill Anderson, and her three boys (West Point is actually on both sides of the river). Bill worked at the post office. The main headquarters for this part of the annual trip was the old McGinty home while Dad's mother, Mollie Hinton Redd still lived. My grandfather, "Mr. Wiley," would have his little general store open when the family arrived. We children loved this, not only because of the atmosphere around the store and the interesting people there, but because Granddad would always give us a "soda," usually Nehi grape or Orange Crush. He had many black customers who lived in the shanties "on the line" just beyond the railroad tracks. They bought a lot of snuff and chewing tobacco. He also had cheese, canned goods and other staples.

"Mr. Wiley" was respected by the white and black citizens of this small community in the "Valley" because he was the justice of the peace. He actually held court out on the porch of his one-story, unpainted, frame dwelling. Preliminary hearings took place and people were bound over for trial in circuit court in Lafayette, AL, the county seat. Granddad, in his younger days, had been foreman of a moderate sized construction firm, and later built a number of small, inexpensive houses himself (ca. 1942). Many of these were sold (or rented) to Negroes along "the line." The line was a long row of frame dwellings (single story, three or four rooms) established about 100 feet back from the railroad track with trains going from River View to West Point, hauling product from the mills.

At family reunions, all of the McGintys would gather on Sunday. Uncle Phil was still living at home. Uncle Wiley (Jr.) would come down with Aunt Maye and Uncle George and cousin, George Ray Jr., from Atlanta. Aunt Margaret and her husband, Milton Christy, would come in from their farm with their three children. Aunt Ruth, her husband Bill, and their boys would be over from West Point and Aunt Velta's husband, Marvin Couch, would make it in with his Jewel Tea truck most of the time. On these occasions, there were always two black women, referred to as "Niggrahs" working in the kitchen, sometimes more. They were treated like the servants they were – no more spoken words than absolutely necessary. They were allowed to take some left over meal home with them. They walked everywhere they went, home, church, and back to work.

The newly released 1930 census shows Wiley at age sixty-five as a merchant in the grocery business. Molly, his wife is there. Wiley Jr., age nineteen, is shown living at home, and was a laborer in the cotton mill. Phillip L. is still at home. Mary Reese "Molly," his sister, is in the house along with his daughter, Velta and her husband, Marvin Couch Sr., and their son, Marvin Jr., are also shown there.

In March of 1930 he announced that he would run for the office of county tax assessor in the August 5 election (*Lafayette Sun*, March 19, 1930). He had voted the Democratic ticket for the past forty-five years, but under the new order of things, had failed to qualify as an "Al Smith Democrat." This split in the Democratic Party in 1928 is a story in itself and I will not go into detail here. He was not successful, being defeated by Walter Greene.

Wiley stayed pretty close to home, but did travel to Cape Girardeau, MO to visit son, Herbert in 1939. Late in life, he enjoyed weaving Afghans, rugs, place mats and hot pads by hand. His hearing was declining so he had the speaker from his television removed from the set and placed on a long cord that reached to his bed, close to his ear, so that he could hear the programs.

The sister of his first wife, Carrie Redd Lennard, knew him well and remarked that "He was frugal, hospitable, affectionate, industrious and at times imperious. He was a loving husband and father and a good manager of his affairs. He was very religious as were all his family."

Wiley Patterson McGinty Sr.
1865-1957. Photo, ca. 1940

He received many tributes in recognition of his outstanding life. *The Valley Daily Times/News* in 1953, on his eighty-eighth birthday said "He has spent his entire life here, ever exerting an influence for good, and it is to him and those like him that we owe a deep debt of gratitude. Mr. McGinty, throughout his life, has lived simply and sincerely, quietly and modestly, but always positively and helpfully as churchman, citizen, neighbor and friend. Since his retirement, Mr. McGinty has demonstrated in a magnificent manner the fine art of 'growing old gracefully.' Possessed of an alert mind, he keeps abreast of the radio and television sets. Of a bright, cheerful disposition, he is still an inspiration to his many friends."

In 1953 Wiley donated to the H. Grady Bradshaw Chambers County Library and Cobb Memorial Archives in Valley, AL, a man's dress coat that was made by his grandmother, Penelope Moore for his grandfather, Levin Moore. According to Wiley, the coat was made in about 1828. He related that the cotton lint was handpicked from the seed, carded, spun, copperas dyed and woven by hand. It is of the cut-a-way style with long tails. This is one of the oldest articles in the library collection. I have seen and photographed the coat (see pg. 104).

Already in his nineties, Wiley was moved to the Emory Convalescent Home in Atlanta, close to several of his children, and passed away peacefully in 1957 at the age of ninety-two. His funeral was held back at the River View Baptist Church, and he was buried with his family in the McGinty plot at the Fairview Cemetery in Valley, AL. In his will, written in 1944 he left his house to Tinnie Mae and divided his other assets equally between Tinnie Mae, Herbert, Maye, Margaret, Wiley, Jr., and Phillip. For some reason, Ruth and Velta were excluded from the will. However, after his death, when the will was probated in August 1957 they were included as heirs. There was also a codicil to the will, written in 1949 concerning a debt owed him by daughter, Margaret for $750. If not paid by his death, this amount was to be withheld from her share. Sons, Wiley, Jr. and Phillip were co-executors (Chambers Co. probate court, vol. 12, pg. 127-140).

Mollie Hinton Redd, Wiley's first wife and the mother of all their children, was born in Northport, Tuscaloosa Co., AL, April 8, 1875.

Mollie Hinton Redd

She was the fifth of fourteen children, five of which did not survive infancy. Her parents were Henry Jackson Redd and Margaret "Maggie" Jane Taylor. Henry was born November 17, 1848, near Tuscaloosa, AL. Maggie was born January 30, 1852, in Chambers Co. Henry and Maggie were married April 11, 1869, in Tuscaloosa Co., AL. Henry was a Primitive Baptist preacher and his early pastorates were in the area of Northport and Tuscaloosa. After 1889 he moved his family often, filling various preaching assignments. They lived in Taylors, MS and then Camp Hill and Opelika, AL. On April 25, 1892, their nineteen-year-old daughter, Jessie Duma Redd, was accidentally killed by a boxcar while walking to work at the cotton mill. In 1892/93 Henry moved the family to River View, AL. He served as pastor of the Ephesus Primitive Baptist church, of which several McGintys were founders and very active. The family rented space in the house owned by Wiley P. McGinty Sr. Mollie had been raised as a Primitive Baptist, whereas Wiley was a Missionary Baptist. I wonder how this difference worked itself out!

After Wiley and Mollie were married, Henry and the family moved to another residence in River View and they show there in the 1900 census (page 318, ED 16, house 307). His name appears misspelled in this census as "Reedd." His occupation is listed as a carpenter. Henry became the River View postmaster 13 February 1900. In 1904 Henry moved back to Birmingham (Jefferson Co.) where as "Elder Redd" he operated a shoe repair shop and finished out his days. The family shows there in the 1910 census (page 110, ED 71, house 65). His name appears misspelled in the census as "Reed." He died there, November 24, 1916. Maggie is shown in the 1920 census living in Birmingham with daughter, Belle Redd Inscho. She then moved to Nashville, TN and was living with daughter Carrie Redd Lennard when she died January 31, 1925. Henry and Maggie are buried together at the Woodlawn Cemetery in Birmingham.

Mollie's paternal grandparents were Josiah Jackson Redd Jr., and Narcissa McElroy. They were married January 21, 1848, in Bibb Co., AL and settled ten miles west of Tuscaloosa. They lived at what was called the "Jim Booth Place" not far from the headwaters of Big Creek that empties into the Warrior River. Their house was built on a high hill. In 1855 Josiah purchased 120 acres of land about one mile south of the Booth place and built a small home there. It was in the forest about one mile from the public road. It was constructed of split logs and had one door and no windows. The floor was made of twelve-inch wide, undressed wooden planks. The chimney was made of rocks and clay. This house served the family well during the war years. On March 31, 1862, Josiah enlisted as a private in the 41st Reg., AL Inf., Army of TN (Sipsey Guards). He sustained a serious shoulder/back wound at Chickamauga on September 20, 1863. He recovered but was crippled for life. On February 5, 1894, then living in Tuscaloosa, he applied for and was granted a war relief pension (#6410). The war years were not good for Narcissa and she died December 26, 1865. She was buried at the old Bethany Missionary Baptist Church in Tuscaloosa. Around 1866 Josiah married a war widow, Mrs. Ellen Glover Savage. Later, his son, Henry Redd often credited her with the long life of his father. When Josiah was eighty years old, he attended a Confederate veterans' picnic in Tuscaloosa. For some reason, the horses pulling his wagon spooked, reared up and threw Josiah out of the wagon. He was injured and died of complications three weeks later on September 2, 1906.

Mollie's paternal great-grandparents were Josiah Jackson Redd Sr., and Elizabeth Woods. They were from GA and settled in Bibb Co., AL, ca. 1827. They moved to Tuscaloosa in 1838 and then returned to Bibb

Co. in the 1860's and died there.

Mollie's maternal grandparents were John Duke Taylor and Sarah Ann Burdett. They were married on January 2, 1851, in Chambers Co., AL. John was born in Covington, Newton Co., GA, January 21, 1827. Sarah was born in DeKalb Co., GA in 1832. Margaret "Maggie" was their only child. Sometime before 1850 John Duke moved from Meriwether Co., GA to Randolph Co., AL with his father Thomas Taylor and mother Sarah Duke. They show there in the 1850 census. The marriage of John and Sarah was short lived. When Maggie was only seven, Sarah became blind and died in 1859. She is said to be buried near her mother, Isabel Davis Burdett, at the Macedonia Primitive Baptist Church near Lafayette, AL. In 2003 my brother Phil and I visited this cemetery and found the grave of Isabel Burdett. After searching the maintained portion of the cemetery, we found her gravesite, partially obscured by undergrowth. Her gravestone is a solid slab of grey slate, covered with moss.

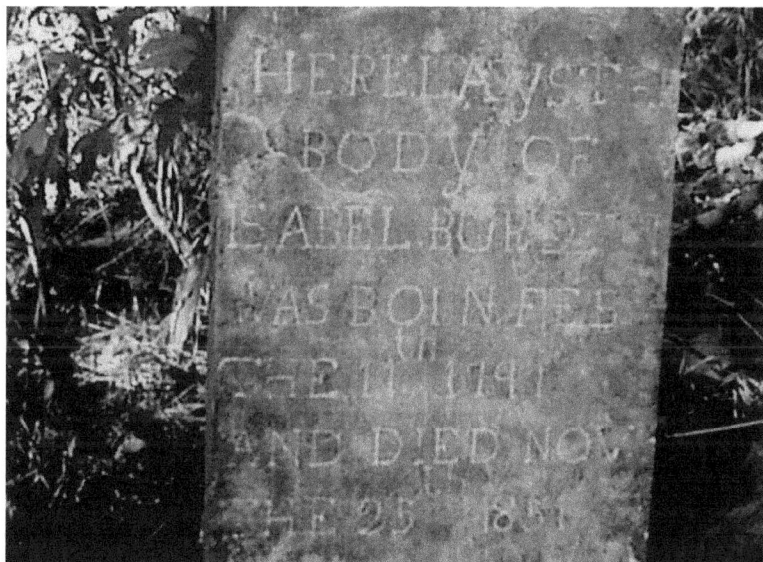

Isabel Davis Burdett
Macedonia Baptist Church Cemetery
Chambers Co., AL

The inscription reads: "Here lays the body of Isabel Burdett. Was born on February 11, 1791 and died November 25, 1851." This was quite a find for us as she is our great-great-great-grandmother.

After Sarah died, John sent Maggie to live with John T. and Margaret Rose Burdette Amos in Randolph Co., AL (census of 1860). Margaret Amos was a sister of Sara Burdett. At this time, John lived with the family of Daniel and Nancy Coggin(s) in Chambers Co., AL (census of 1860). Nancy was the sister of Sara Ann Burdett. Sometime later, John and his brother, William ("Billie") purchased a farm together in Coosa Co., AL. Maggie may have joined her father there. This farming venture ended when the war broke out. John Duke enlisted in March 1862 as a private in Co. G, 2nd AL Calvary and Maggie was sent to live with her grandparents, Thomas and Sarah Taylor, who were living in Cottondale, AL. During the war, it is said that John had his hat shot off and his horse shot out from under him, but he survived. His unit served as escort for Jefferson Davis from Greensboro, NC to GA. He surrendered with his unit at Forsyth, GA at the war's end in 1865. Later in life, in 1904, he applied for and received a disability pension while then living in Jefferson Co., AL (#14175). After the war, ca. 1866 John Duke married Mrs. Martha "Martie" Elmore Morgan and moved to Northport, AL. It was there in Tuscaloosa Co. that Maggie met Henry Redd.

John Duke Taylor was a member of the fraternal order, "Woodsmen of America," and his gravestone is said to symbolize a tree stump. He was a butcher and sold meats for years in Tuscaloosa. His motto was "The best meats at the lowest prices." He advertised regularly in the *Tuscaloosa Times*. John and Martha show in the 1900 census as living in Bessemer, AL, ED 121. At one time, he was in partnership with his son-in-law, Henry Jackson Redd who later became a minister. John Duke Taylor died September 11, 1904, and is buried along with Martha, at the Cedar Hill Cemetery in Bessemer, AL.

Mollie's maternal great-grandparents were Humphrey H. Burdett Sr. and Isabella Woodall (some say her name was Davis) who had moved from DeKalb Co., GA to Chambers Co., AL around 1837. Isabella died in 1851 and sometime after 1855 Humphrey moved to Randolph Co., AL (census of 1860). Humphrey Burdett served in the War of 1812. He entered service as a private on January 1, 1815, in the Pendleton District of SC. He was discharged on March 10, 1815, at

Sister Ferry, SC near Savannah, GA. Later, Belle Redd Inscho, sister of Mollie Redd McGinty, was accepted into the Daughters of the War of 1812 based on his service record.

Mollie's other maternal great grandparents were Thomas Taylor and Sarah Duke. Thomas was born ca. 1806 in SC. They were married in Covington, Newton Co., GA, November 7, 1824. By 1842 they were living in Newnan, Coweta Co., GA. By 1844 they had moved to Columbus, Muscogee Co., GA. They moved to Randolph Co., AL from GA sometime after 1849.

Mollie's maternal great-great-grandfather was John P. Taylor. He was born ca. 1780 in NC. He moved his family to GA. He lived near Newnan, Coweta Co., GA and died there, ca. 1867.

Mollie Redd McGinty died of a heart attack on October 31, 1931, at age fifty-eight. Her gravestone shows a death date of November 1, 1931, but the death certificate shows death occurring at 1:00am on October 31, 1931. She had suffered from high blood pressure for some time. She had been a beloved wife and companion, raising a large family who all turned out to be good citizens in their communities. Her epitaph was published in the *Lafayette Sun* and reproduced on the front page of the *Chattahoochee Valley Times* on November 11, 1931. It reads, "Mrs. W. P. McGinty Passes at Riverview Saturday, Oct. 31. Mrs. Mollie McGinty, age 58 years, died at her home in Riverview Saturday morning, October 31 at 1 o'clock, following a heart attack early last Friday night. The beloved Riverview woman had been suffering for some time with high blood pressure which resulted in the attack last Friday. Funeral services were held from the family residence last Sunday afternoon at three o'clock...the deceased was a member of the Baptist church and had lived a useful life in that community...internment was in the McGinty cemetery."

Wiley P. McGinty Jr., recalled that as part of her funeral service the pastor read from the last chapter of Proverbs, 31:10 - 31, *"A good wife who can find? She is far more precious than jewels...."* She was buried next to her husband in the McGinty plot at Fairview Cemetery in Valley, AL.

Mollie Hinton Redd McGinty
Fairview Cemetery, Valley, AL

Wiley married Tinnie Mae Hunt on November 23, 1932. Rev. Basil B. McGinty performed the ceremony at his residence. Tinnie Mae's father was George David Hunt, the "Grand Old Man" of the Congregational Christian Churches in AL. He served as pastor of Beulah Church for fifty years. Her mother was Winnie Ann Vickers. The 1910 census shows Tinnie Mae living with her parents in Tallapoosa Co., AL. The 1930 census shows her boarding with other River View teachers in the River View teacher's dorm, with Ann E. Fargason, manager, Beat 13, Chambers Co. A surviving hotel ledger shows that from June 1931 until January 1932 she had meals in the River View Hotel. Tinnie Mae taught in the area for years. She had received her home economics degree from Auburn University. Tinnie Mae was appointed postmaster of River View in 1943 replacing Manly M. Hunt who had been postmaster since 1905. She retired from this position on July 31, 1962. She loved to paint and some of her landscapes were proudly displayed in the homes of her nieces and nephews. In the 1950's Tinnie Mae and Wiley did some commendable McGinty family research, using the limited resources that were available to them at the time. Tinnie Mae was affectionately called "Mother" by

Tinnie Mae and Wiley, Sr.
Ca. 1950

some of Wiley's children, including my father, Wiley Jr. Tinnie Mae passed away on September 15, 1970. Her obituary appeared in *The Valley Times-News* on Wednesday, September 16, pg. 7.

Rites Thursday For Mrs. McGinty

Mrs. Tinnie Mae McGinty, 75, of Lanett died at 7:25 p.m. Tuesday at George H. Lanier Memorial Hospital, Langdale. She was the widow of the late W. P. McGinty.

Born in Tallapoosa County, May 17, 1895, Mrs. McGinty was a former resident of River View. She was a member of the First United Methodist Church of Lanett, and also was a former school teacher in River View. She retired from the River View Post Office as postmisstress several years ago.

Funeral will be Thursday at 3:30 p.m. at the First United Methodist Church of Lanett with the Rev. V. Peter Furio, church pastor, officiating. Burial will be in the Old River View Cemetery with Johnson-Brown Service Funeral Home, Langdale, in charge of arrangements.

Survivors include two brothers, James A. Hunt Sr., of Lanett, and George S. Hunt of Albany, Ga.; and one sister, Mrs. Iola Walker of Wadley, Ala.

Tinnie Mae Obituary

Tinnie Mae Hunt McGinty
Fairview Cemetery, Valley, AL

Her will, dated November 9, 1962, leaves her household goods to her nephew, Phillip Hunt and his wife.

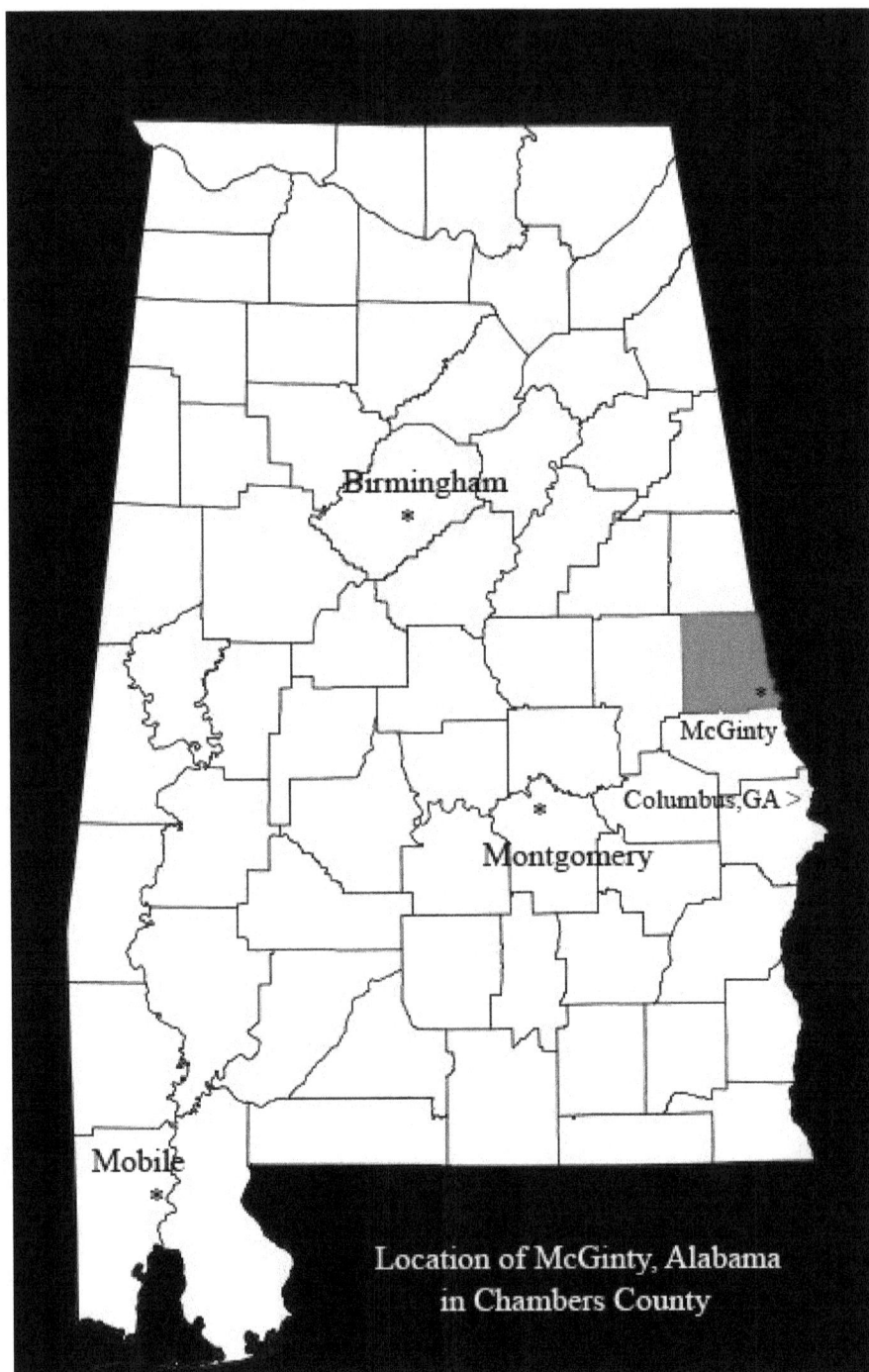

Location of McGinty, Alabama
in Chambers County

McGinty, Alabama

McGinty, AL, also referred to as McGinty Crossroads, McGinty Crossing and McGinty Station, appears today on the official AL state roadmap. It is located at the intersection of River Road and Columbus Road in what is now Valley, AL. This crossing is located very close to River View (originally spelled this way). Today, there is a paved bicycle path that crosses the intersection. This path was once the Chattahoochee Valley Railroad track that was built in 1897. It ran behind Wiley McGinty's property and on to West Point. Alabama maps show the CV railroad as early as 1909 with McGinty named as one of the regular stops on the railroad line. This confirms that this area was already named McGinty before that time.

The 1926 railroad schedule shows that on the weekends, you could board the train at McGinty in the morning and be in West Point in roughly thirty minutes. An afternoon train would take you back to McGinty. The tracks through McGinty were used until 1974. Wiley McGinty's grandfather, Levin Moore, originally owned 320 acres of land including the crossroads at what is now called McGinty, AL. When he died in 1855 the land passed to his wife, Penelope, and at her death, to her children, Ann and Malinda. Her son, Wiley P. Moore had died in the Civil War. Ann Moore was Wiley's mother.

It is not yet known exactly how and when Wiley got the land for his home, but it was part of the family estate. The first house that Wiley built was in 1891. It is still located at one of the corners at the crossroads. Wiley also operated a general store on one of the other corners of this intersection. Later in life, he moved a few blocks down from the crossroads to 1025 River Road. I visited the River Road house many times as a young boy and it was still occupied in 2011. The first school constructed from sawed lumber was also built on the northwest corner of the crossroads.

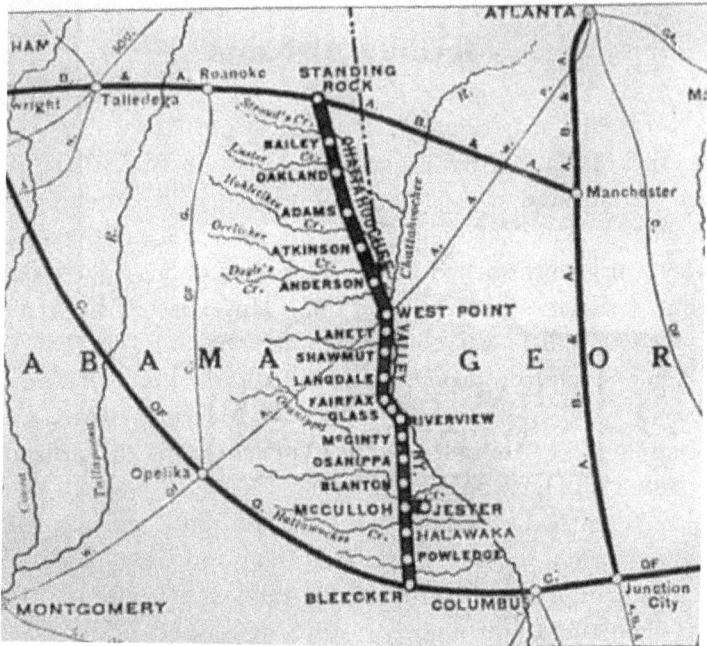

Chattahoochee Valley Railroad in 1916 showing McGinty, AL

Wiley was a prominent citizen, having been justice of the peace for forty-eight years. He also was a builder and constructed several small houses near the CV railroad track just south of the crossroads. It is thought that McGinty, AL was named partly for his presence at the crossing, and also for all the earlier McGintys that had lived in the immediate area. It is interesting to note in the 1940 census, the street where Wiley P. McGinty, Sr. was living is shown as McGinty Highway.

River View, Alabama

After the Civil War, when most of the south was in shambles, this area received some good news. A cotton mill was going to be built both at Campbell's gristmill and Trammell's mill further up the river. Confederate money was worthless, but a few men were fortunate enough to have the financial means to invest in these mills. The Huguley family was the primary investor. It is said that they had considerable cotton in their possession and were able to sell it to British buyers and ship it before it was conscripted by the North. During the war, cotton prices were over $1.00 lb. The Huguleys were said to be from northeast GA and SC and were familiar with the potential that cotton factories held. In 1853 George and Amos Huguley purchased 1,920 acres of land from Milton M. Marcus for $17,000. In 1865 they purchased an additional 143 acres from James Campbell for $2,430, which included three islands in the Chattahoochee River. Part of this land was in GA and is the site where the Riverdale mill was built in River View.

Prior to the coming of these textile mills, this entire area of Alabama was strictly agricultural and cotton was the most important crop. There were several gristmills for grinding corn and wheat, cotton gins and sawmills all using waterpower from the river and creeks to turn the mill wheels. After the war, when these large textile mills were built, the economy quickly converted to textile manufacturing as the chief industry and major employer. River View had one of the first large mills, named the Alabama-Georgia Manufacturing Co. The plant was given this name because it actually spanned the state line, with part of the plant in AL and the other in GA. The plant was four stories high, 50 feet wide and 250 feet long. The manufacturing of course fabrics such as Osanburg and single filling duck began here in 1866. Osanburg is an unbleached cotton cloth that was heavy and coarse. It was used for goods such as farmers clothing, overalls, sacking and bagging. Single filling duck was also a course fabric used for such things as tents, awnings, boat sails, tarpaulins and belts for machinery. One of the old-timers, D. W. "Uncle Dan" Simms, who arrived in River View in 1879 gives an excellent picture of life there around 1880 when my grandfather, Wiley P. Sr., was fifteen years old. He remembers that the

River View of 1880 had no school in the village, "But there was a little schoolhouse at the cross-roads (McGinty), where the railroad crosses the dirt road. This school was operated only three months in the year. After the public funds were exhausted, parents would pay one dollar a month for each child. There were very few families that could afford to pay this tuition."

Simms goes on to say that by 1880 the population in River View was about 175 with most of the people in town living on mill property and working in the mill (note that most of the early McGintys, prior to the mill being built, were farmers in the outlying areas around River View). Exceptions were older people and children under seven years of age. The mill used only waterpower from the river. There was no electricity, and it operated sixty-six hours per week. There was no sprinkler system. Water was kept in large barrels in each room in case of fire. The floors were made from pine boards and were full of splinters. The children went barefooted, so the foreman carried a sharp pocketknife to cut splinters out of their feet. Children were paid around 60 cents a day for the menial jobs that they could fill such as sweeping. Top pay for the more skilled weavers might be $6.50 per week. A colored man brought the drinking water in cedar buckets to the workers from a spring. Everyone drank from the same dipper. It would take the "water man" about three hours to make his rounds. The "hands" would get pretty thirsty, especially during the hot summer months. Cotton and other supplies for the mill were brought in from West Point by large mule drawn wagons (drays). Manufactured cloth goods were then returned to West Point on the same wagon (the railroad was built to the plant at a later date).

West Point was the shipping center for the entire area. Workers would go to West Point (seven miles away) on Saturday afternoon after they got out of work at 4:00pm. They would purchase their dry goods and groceries then carry their supplies home in their arms and across their backs. On Saturday afternoon and night, the road would be filled with friendly, happy, congenial people that knew little about the outside world. Columbus, GA was thirty miles away, an all day trip, and seemed like a faraway country.

The main forms of entertainment were swimming, fishing, marbles, town ball, fox and hounds, hunting and square dancing. Sometimes an entertainer would come to the village with something like a magic show. In 1880, there were no bicycles, no gasoline automobiles, no telephones, no short dresses, no bare legs, no powder and paint, no boy-and-girl going out at night alone, no girls smoking, no bobbed hair and no "mixed" swimming pools. No young man stayed at his girl's house after nine o'clock. None of the girls wore silk stockings; they were all cotton.

There were no cold drinks and no 'bought bread'. The farmers raised their own wheat and the flour was very dark, but very good. Lighting was from kerosene lamps and water from a well. People raised much of their own meat and poultry. Eggs sold at three dozen for twenty-five cents, butter was .10 to .12 cents per pound, and bacon was .04 to .05 cents per pound. Coffee sold for .10 cents per pound, it came in bulk, green, and the housewives had to parch and grind it. Flour was $4.00 per barrel. The women and girls made their own clothes or had help from the village dressmaker. Life was simple but good.

The last McGinty family living in River View is that of Douglas Clairfield McGinty, b. October 2, 1922. My brothers and I visited him in June 2003. He is the son of William Grover McGinty and Era Waller McGinty and the grandson of William Levin McGinty. Doug passed away, June 15, 2006. He worked in the local mill for eighteen years. Later, he repaired watches and for forty-five years, operated a television repair business, McGinty TV Repair. He could tell one interesting story after another about the old days in River View. His daughter, Teresa Ann McGinty Williams and her husband, Denny lived with Doug at 1205 California St. in River View. His death ended a McGinty legacy in the area that lasted over 170 years!

The Parnell Peach Farm

Another very interesting venture in the area was the John Howard Parnell cotton and peach farm. Parnell was a handsome young man from a very wealthy family in Avondale, Wicklow Co., Ireland and came to the area in 1867 to purchase himself a "plantation."

John Howard Parnell

I visited Avondale during a trip to Ireland in September 2003. It is now a national park of over 200 acres in a beautiful forest. The original

Parnell home, built in 1777 is open to the public. The 1870 and 1880 census of Chambers Co. (pg. 21/203) shows that he was born ca. 1845 and would have been about twenty-two years old at the time of his arrival. However, the book *Charles Stewart Parnell, A Memoir*, which he wrote around 1905 shows his birth date as 1843. His mother, Delia Tudor Stewart, an American, was the daughter of Admiral Charles Stewart, U.S. Navy, who had served in the Revolutionary War and the War of 1812 and was Captain of the *USS Constitution*, known as "Old Ironsides," from 1813-1815. He was also referred to as the "American Nelson." John Parnell's uncle, Charles Stewart, who lived in America, told him after the Civil War was over that great fortunes were to be made there, and advised him to come to America.

Parnell had just inherited some money and his uncle advised him that he had the chance to double it. He came and purchased 1,482 acres of land from Col. George W. Huguley on January 1, 1867, for $12,000 after seeing it advertised for sale in the New York newspapers (Deed Book 14, Page 768). As the story goes, he took a train from New York to West Point and met with Col. Huguley on the front porch of his home. As part of their negotiation, it is said that Parnell stacked gold coins on a table until Col. Huguley agreed that a fair price had been reached. This land was located on the old Columbus-Berlin road, about eight miles south of West Point, near Glass, AL. According to his book, he originally purchased this land for growing cotton. Later, he started a peach-growing venture on part of the property. His first home in the area was the log cabin once owned by Rev. Tyre Freeman, former pastor of the Primitive Baptist church. This home was located near McGinty Crossing. Sometime later, he purchased the larger Huguley home, which had four big columns on the front porch.

Both the 1870 and 1880 census shows that William "Billie" Merna, also from Ireland (spelled Mernagh in Ireland), was the supervisor of Parnell's farm, which was later named the Sunny South Peach Farm (some accounts called it Sunny Side). Merna is listed as age twenty-five and his wife, Maggie, age twenty in the 1870 census. Maggie was Parnell's housekeeper and they lived next door. They show four children in this census, all born in AL. They are credited with founding the first Catholic church in the area, with services held in their home. This church later became the Church of the Holy Family in Lanett. This Mernagh family came from Glenmalure, about eight miles from

Avondale. Merna and family stayed in the area after Parnell sold the farm. Merna worked for the Atlanta and West Point Railroad. They show in the Macon Co., AL census of 1900, pg. 196, with six children. There is also a Martin and sister Kate Linahan from Ireland listed in the 1880 census. They could have been involved in the Parnell business. They could also have been Maggie's parents.

An article in the *Savannah (GA) News*, dated April 22, 1883, reads as follows: "John H. Parnell, a brother of the famous Irish leader by that name, owns the largest peach farm in the world. It is situated about six miles below West Point. There are 125,000 peach trees in it, besides a large number or other kinds of fruit trees. They cover 700 acres. Mr. Parnell has planted 500 acres of young trees this year, and reports his business a paying one. This year's crop will be tolerably good, notwithstanding the freezes."

He is said to have ultimately planted up to 700 acres of peach trees, and after they started bearing fruit, shipped them to various markets by train. He was one of the first growers to ship peaches from the south to eastern cities (the peach industry was young, but already well established in Georgia by then). Shipping was a problem because the fruit ripened so rapidly that spoilage was a big issue. Some of the peaches were used locally to make brandy which was sold by the barrel to local customers. Parnell is said to have attempted peach cultivation methods that would produce a species combining the advantages of freestone and the clingstone varieties. Parnell was a man of culture and education and was a devoted chess player. He frequently went to the chess club in Atlanta for games. Later in life, he was a member of a chess team representing the British House of Commons against a team from the U.S. House of Representatives. The moves were played over the lines of the transatlantic cable, each move being telegraphed across the ocean. He also made frequent trips to New York and back to Ireland. He remained single while in AL.

In 1872 his brother, Charles Stewart Parnell, came over from Ireland, and visited him for three weeks. Charles was a famous Irish agitator that was later president of the Home Rule Conference and the Irish League. He was also a Member of Parliament. He was sometimes referred to as "the uncrowned king of Ireland." He visited John when he was younger, around twenty-five years old, and before his political career started (and being used to the life in metropolitan London) found it difficult to accept the "primitive" ways of early Alabama. He is said to have been shocked to find his brother living in a two-room log cabin and associating with the "common folks." However, it is said that while he was in Chambers Co., he enjoyed his contacts with the larger plantation owners. He shot quail, caught catfish and hunted fox. He tried to persuade his brother to return to Ireland, but John was in the middle of establishing his plantation and refused to return at that time.

Charles Stewart Parnell

After setbacks such as crop failures, Parnell sold his plantation to A.M. Eady & Co. on April 3, 1884, for $5,068 and left AL (Deed Book 19, Page 40). However, he continued to spend much time in America and had a fruit business and investments in other American fruit farms as late as 1891. An article in the February 17, 1892 *Lafayette Sun* reads, "Mr. Lanier of West Point now owns the once famous Parnell peach orchard and is having the trees cut down and the soil is being prepared for corn and cotton. So, the peach business, which brought many dollars to this community for a number of years, is a thing of the past. It was a great help to the needy in this country and Mr. John Parnell will be greatly missed by that class."

Today, the West Point Mfg. Co. stands on his original land. He died May 3, 1923, and his obituary in the *New York Times* reads, "Dublin, May 3 (Associated Press) John Howard Parnell, brother of Charles Stewart Parnell, the famous Irish statesman died today. He was born in 1843 and spent many years in the United States, engaged in fruit and cotton growing. From 1895 to 1920 he was Member of Parliament for South Meath. He was married to Olivia Isabella Smythe in 1907 and is survived by one son."

His obituary in the *Irish Times* reads: "Parnell, May 2, 1923, at his residence, Sion House, Glenageary, after three day's illness, John Howard Parnell, City Marshall. Deeply regretted by his sorrowing widow and relatives. Funeral private. No flowers by request." He sat in the House of Commons as a member from Meath, under his brother's leadership. Despite the failure of this early peach growing venture in Alabama, he is credited with being one of the pioneers of the peach industry that later flourished in the south. The soil and growing conditions were ideal. The lack of refrigeration at the time was the main obstacle to success. During his stay, he was a very influential and important citizen in the area.

On Wednesday, April 18, 2001, approximately forty members of the Parnell Society from Ireland visited Valley, AL, and were shown the land where John Parnells farm was located. The West Point Stevens Co. mill and warehouse now occupy this area. A row of peach trees was planted on the original land, along River Road, in front of the warehouse, in memory of the Parnells. This strip of land is named The John Parnell Memorial Park. When I visited this site in June 2003 there were already peaches on some of the trees.

Rev. Basil B. McGinty, son of William Levin McGinty, said that as a young girl, his mother, Laura Viola Spikes McGinty, picked peaches on the Parnell farm.

William Pitts McGinty

(1819-1901)

William Pitts McGinty, b. June 4, 1819, in Wilkinson Co., GA, d. January 1, 1901, in McGinty, Chambers Co., AL. He was the second son of George Washington McGinty and Tabitha Moore. He married (1) Mary Ann Freeman, November 30, 1843, in Chambers Co., by Moses Gunn, MG (marriage book 3, pg. 42) and (2) Ann M. Moore, April 8, 1846, in Harris Co., GA (pg. 34). Mary Ann Freeman was the daughter of Rev. Tyre Freeman and his first wife, Lucinthia Moore. The original consent letter from her father reads as follows: "I do curtify [sic] that William P. McGinty is at liberty to obtain licens [sic] to be weeded [sic] to my daughter Mary Ann Freeman. Consented to without objection, November 28, 1843, Signed, Tyre Freeman."

Tyre was the first pastor of the Ephesus Primitive Baptist church in McGinty, AL. He was born ca. 1826 in Jones Co., GA. The Freeman family was originally from Jones Co., GA and had relocated to this area around 1842. Tyre was a member of the Mt. Zion Baptist church in Jones Co., GA for several years before relocating to Chambers Co., AL. He was also active in the Ocmulgee Baptist Assn. meetings in GA and shows in their minutes up until 1843. Mary Ann possibly died during the birth of their first child, Lucynthia. William's second wife, Ann Moore was born March 3, 1830, in Jones Co., GA and died of acute bronchitis, February 5, 1898, in Chambers Co. They are both buried in the McGinty plot at Fairview Cemetery. Ann's father was Levin Moore, b. July 4, 1799, d. October 10, 1855. Levin was one of the earliest settlers in Chambers Co., arriving there with William's father Washington, around 1835. This is confirmed in the 1840 census. He was buried, on his property, in a family cemetery located south of McGinty's crossroads on the old Osanippa-Berlin road. This cemetery later became part of the property owner's junkyard. It is said that it contained other, unmarked gravesites, possibly including that of Penelope. The Rev. Basil B. McGinty had Levin's grave marker moved from this site to the McGinty plot at Fairview cemetery sometime after 1973.

Children of William Pitts McGinty and Mary Ann Freeman:

Lucintha Elvira McGinty, b. October 27, 1844 (confirmed by family bible) in McGinty, Chambers Co., AL, d. February 8, 1918, in Choudrant, Jackson Parish, LA. These dates are taken from her gravestone; however, her death certificate shows a birth date of October 23, 1845. It is interesting to note that her name is misspelled as "McGenist" on her gravestone. Her death certificate and gravestone confirm her middle name, Elvira. Her name has also been shown in other research as Cynthia, Lou Cynthia and Lucinthe. Her grandmother was named Lucynthia Moore, so she is most certainly named after her. However, she is listed in both the 1850 and 1860 AL census as Lucinthe. In the 1870 census she is listed as Cinthia and in the 1880 census, as Lucinthia. Her death certificate shows her as Lucinthy. Her father's family bible shows the spelling as Lucintha. She was married to William Henry Fallin on July 18, 1866, by James M. Hill, JP (photo below). They were married at the home of her father, William Pitts McGinty, and they lived to produce ten sons and one daughter.

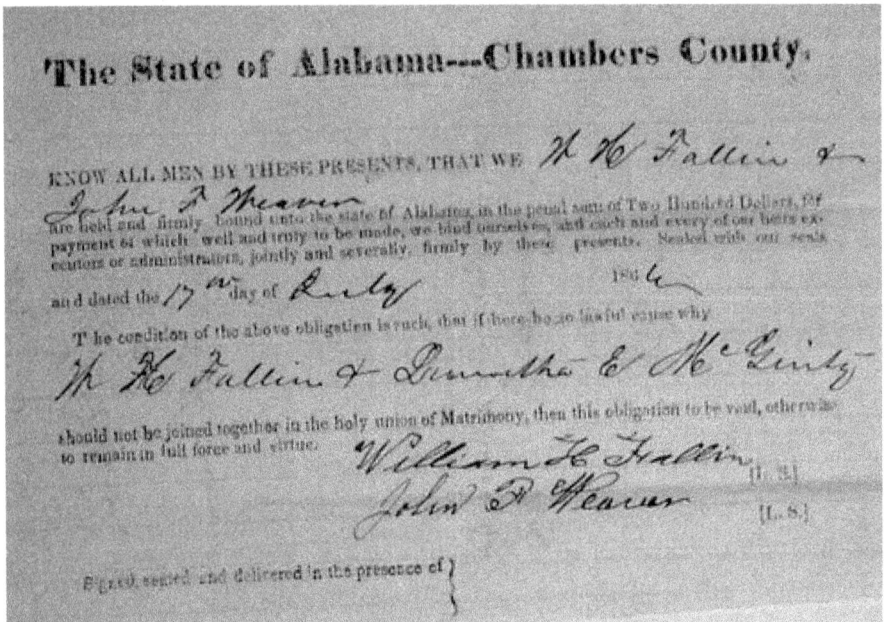

Lucintha and William Fallin Marriage License

Fallin was a farmer. In a letter written to her sister, Tabitha, March 10, 1867, she describes "Mr. Fallin" getting ready to plant his corn crop and how well their garden, with cabbage, peas, beans, "sallet" and Irish potatoes was doing. They show in the 1870 census, living in Tallapoosa Co., AL, next to several other Fallin families. They were still living in Tallapoosa Co., AL in 1879 and show in the 1880 census in Rome, AL. They moved to LA sometime after that and family lore says their trip was by train. They show in the 1900 census of Jackson Parish, LA with sons, Ira and Irvin and daughter Martha A. Holmes. They also show here in the 1910 census. William died March 13, 1921, in Epps, West Carroll Parish, LA. His CSA gravestone is inscribed with Co. D, 34th AL Infantry. The death date on his stone is March 27, 1921, which does not agree with his death certificate that shows the date-of-death as March 13, 1921. They are both buried at the Longstraw Cemetery in Lincoln Parish, LA (photo, next page).

Longstraw Cemetery
Lincoln Parish, LA

Children of William Pitts McGinty and Ann Moore:

James Madison McGinty, b. September 30, 1847, (confirmed by family bible) in McGinty, Chambers Co., AL, d. February 19, 1929, in Chambers Co., AL. This date is taken from his death certificate. However, his gravestone shows 1920 as the year of his death. There is a record listing him as one of the construction employees at the Riverdale mill that was built in 1866. He married Oliver J. Weaver (her name is spelled "Oliver" on her gravestone and also in the 1860 census) on March 15, 1872, in Chambers Co., AL., H.M. Higginbotham, pastor. She was born in 1835 in GA (confirmed by census records) and died June 24, 1913, in Chambers Co. Previous McGinty researchers show that her father was Tyre Weaver. Actually, her father was Holly Weaver (b. 1812) and her mother was Nancy Floyd. Holly was a farmer who had also moved to Chambers Co. from GA and who is shown in the 1860 census as owning the farm next to Washington McGinty. James was received into the Ephesus Church by experience, August 5, 1873. James wrote several entries in his parents' family bible. He also wrote his mother's epitaph. James is also shown as signing the oath of allegiance to the United States after the war during the reconstruction in 1866-67. James is shown as a farmer in the 1880 census. On December 26, 1898, he purchased eleven acres of his father's land at McGinty's Crossroads for $200 (deed book 28, pg. 113). There is an article in the *Lafayette Sun* dated December 26, 1923, saying, "J. M. McGinty, who has been a resident of this town for over seventy years, left Monday for his new home in Tallapoosa Co." Later, in 1924 we see him living there in Dadeville. James and Oliver are buried together in the McGinty plot at Fairview Cemetery. They produced no children.

**Fairview Cemetery
Valley, AL**

Theodosia Burr McGinty, b. April 24, 1849, (confirmed by 1850 and 1860 census and the family bible), in McGinty, Chambers Co., AL, d. 1877. Some census records and earlier research have shown that this child was a male named Theodore. However, both the 1860 and 1870 census clearly lists this child as a female. She is also shown as Miss Theodosia B. McGinty in the Ephesus Baptist church minutes, joining by experience, September 28, 1872. I have a letter that she wrote to her brother James Madison on January 15, 1872. At the time she was living in Tallapoosa Co., possibly with sister, Lucintha. She was single and talks about all the young people there and her sweetheart. She seems to be very happy. She includes a note to sister, Tabitha, asking her to send her summer dresses by way of Aunt Kizzy Freeman. I have nothing else on her life. According to the research done by her brother, Wiley P. McGinty Sr., she died in 1877. This date is not confirmed. She would have been only twenty-eight at the time of her death. She was most possibly named for Theodosia Burr, daughter of Aaron Burr, Vice President of the United States (1801-1805).

Tabitha Ann McGinty, b. May 24, 1851, (confirmed by family bible), in McGinty, Chambers Co., AL, d. June 12, 1924, in Chambers Co., AL. The Lee Co., AL census of 1870 shows her, age nineteen, living in the home of E. D. Pitts in Opelika, AL. I think that this is Epaminondas Dunn Pitts, born in Jones Co., GA in 1826. He was a well-known educator. In this census, Pitts is shown as a minister and teacher. She could have been attending school at this time, possibly at the Oak Bowery Female College that was founded in 1837. Oak Bowery, AL is about eight miles north of Opelika. She is shown here, joining the Ephesus Primitive Baptist Church, with her two sisters, and sister-in-law: "September 28th, 1872, The Church of Christ at Ephesus. After preaching by Brother A. B. Whatley, the church set in conference, first, invited visiting members of our order to seats with us. Second, Opened the doors of the church for the reception of members, when Mrs. Olivia (Oliver J. Weaver) McGinty, Miss Theodocia B. McGinty, Miss Tabitha A. McGinty & W. M. Moore came forward and were received by an experience of grace as we believe and when baptized into full fellowship with the church. Baptism administered tomorrow morning at 9 o'clock at Huguley's Mill, by Brother A. B. Whatley. The church agrees to commune and wash each other's feet tomorrow. The church having no further business, conference adjourned. A. B. Whatley, Moderator, J. H. Sanders, C.C."

The 1880 census of Chambers Co., AL shows her, age twenty-nine, living back in the home of her father. She married (1) Marshall Moseley Tomme on September 29, 1896, in Chambers Co., AL, by Elder Rees Prather. This was a late marriage as she was already forty-six years old. After their marriage, she transferred her church membership, by letter, from the Ephesus Primitive Baptist church in Chambers Co., AL to the Lebanon Primitive Baptist church in Troup Co., GA. Tomme was a deacon here and remained a member until 1902 when they moved to Chambers Co. They show in the 1900 census, living in West Point,

Troup Co., GA with no children of their own. However, three of his children by a previous marriage to Eliza Scott were living with them. Eliza had died in 1893. Tomme was a Civil War veteran, having served as a corporal in Co. E, 41st GA Inf. In December 1898 Tabitha purchased thirty acres in Section 32 from the family of William Pitts McGinty for $200 (deed book 28, pg., 41). In November 1901 Marshall purchased the original 120-acre William Pitts McGinty farm from the heirs for sixteen hundred dollars (deed book 28, pg. 336). Tomme is seen again at a 1910 family reunion in Troup Co., GA. His daughters by his first marriage were there. They were Miss Ella Tomme, Mary Simmons, Anna Pratt and Pamelia Taylor.

Tomme died October 18, 1918. After his death, Tabitha received a "Class C" Civil War pension for him. Tabitha married (2) James B.F. Lindsey on February 19, 1922. She had inherited the Tomme family home. She was not well at this time and an article in the February 20, 1924, *Lafayette Sun* mentions that she underwent an operation the past week and is improving rapidly. However, she died in June. Her estate was probated in July 1925. After her death, her Tomme home, which included two acres of land, was sold at public auction to T. J. Goggins for $1,300. She had named all of her brothers and sisters as heirs and they decided to handle the sale of her property in this manner. Apparently, she had no children of her own. Her husband, James B. F. Lindsey, was the administrator of her estate. He was born April 2, 1847, in GA and died on April 12, 1930, in Buffalo, Chambers Co., AL, which is about 3.5 miles north of Lafayette on Hwy. 431. He is shown as a prominent farmer and citizen. His epitaph reads: "The deceased was for many years actively identified with the life of the community in which he lived, but during late years he contented himself by staying near his home. He was a member of the Macedonia Baptist Church, and lived to rear a fine family of children under the influence of his church."

Lindsey shows in the 1860 census of Coosa Co., AL, age thirteen, living with a female, M.A. Lindsey. According to this census, she was born in SC. He and wife Malissa are shown in both the 1870 census of Heard Co., GA, and the 1880 census of AL. He is buried with his first wife, Malissa Caroline "Carrie" Jackson at the Macedonia Primitive Baptist church cemetery, which is located just east of the intersection of County Road 62 and 110 near Lafayette, AL.

Tabitha and first husband Marshall Tomme are buried in the McGinty plot at Fairview Cemetery, Valley, AL.

Tabitha McGinty Tomme Lindsay
Fairview Cemetery, Valley, AL

Nancy Laura McGinty, b. October 11, 1853, (date shown in family bible, but her original marriage license shows that she was born in 1856) in Roanoke, Randolph Co., AL, d. February 2, 1942, at Pine Grove, Tallapoosa Co. AL. Her parents show in the 1855 census of Chambers Co. and then in the 1860 census of Randolph Co. She was called Laura. She married Steven Cullen "Teab" Bass, November 26, 1878, in Chambers Co., AL, by J. H. Shirley, MG, at the residence of her father. Bass was born October 30, 1851, and died January 18, 1929. He was a farmer and also preached at the Ephesus Church. They produced seven children, three of which died in infancy. They moved to Dadeville, Tallapoosa Co., AL before 1880. The 1900 census shows them living in Tallapoosa Co. with four children whose names were Eula, James Arthur, Nancy Lillian and Ruby. The 1920 census shows them living in Tallapoosa Co., with one child, Ruby. Nancy Laura is buried next to her husband at the Sardis Methodist Church Cemetery in the Sardis Community, Tallapoosa Co., AL.

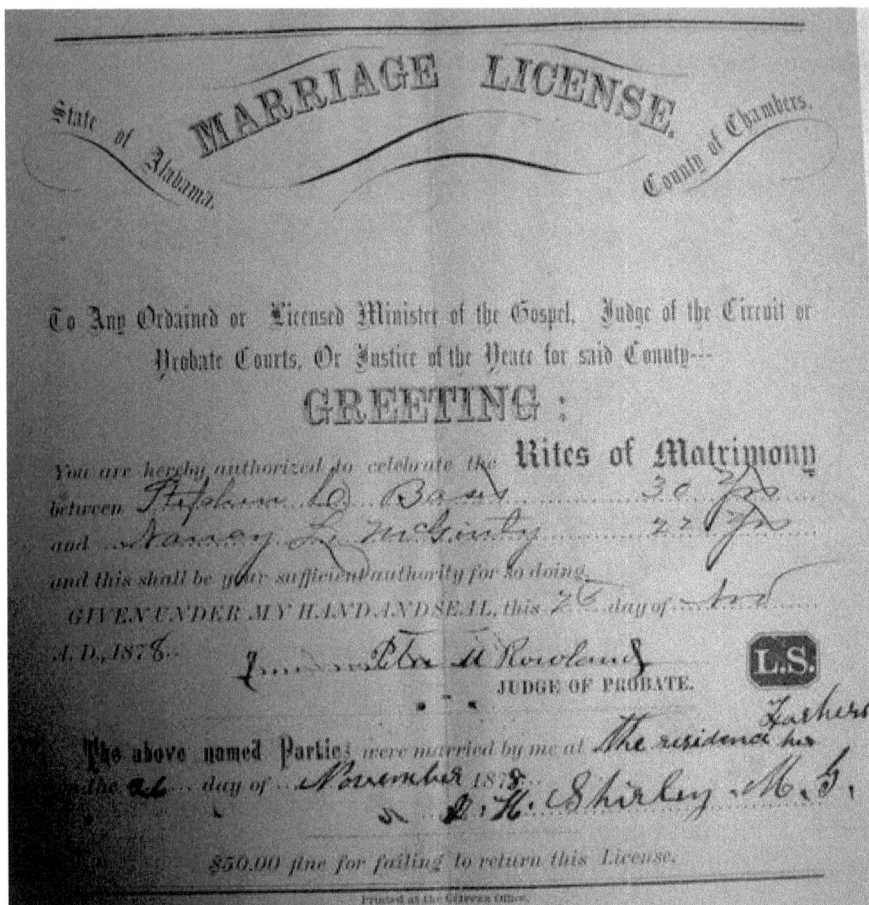

**Nancy Laura and Stephen Bass
Marriage License**

John Franklin McGinty, b. August 13, 1855, (confirmed by family bible) in Randolph Co., AL, d. December 2, 1930, in Chatsworth, GA. He married (1) Laura Viola "Lou" Spikes, February 25, 1885, in Chambers Co., AL, H. Wood, pastor, and (2) Mrs. Ella Capes Webb Long, April 14, 1925, in Lanett, AL. Laura died September 5, 1924, at the home of her son J. Roy McGinty Sr., in Chatsworth, GA and is buried at the Hillview Cemetery annex, section 5, lot 2, space 7, in LaGrange, GA. The inscription on her gravestone reads: "To the good there is no death. The stars go down and rise upon some foreign shore, all bright with heavens jeweled crown, they shine forever more." This plot also contains the grave of Emma C. "Cliffie" McGinty and her infant son J. B. Emma was the wife of J. F.'s son, John Roy McGinty. J. F.'s second wife is sometimes incorrectly shown as "Caper" Long. Their wedding announcement in the local newspaper shows her name as Mrs. Capes Long. Capes shows in the 1920 census of Murray Co., GA., age forty-five, living with her mother Jane Webb, also a widow.

"Mr. Frank" was born in Randolph Co., AL during the brief period that his father and mother farmed there. Around 1860 he moved with his parents to Chambers Co., where he lived for about forty years. There is a record showing that he was one of the construction employees for the Riverdale mill that was built in 1866. In 1900 he left Chambers Co. and lived in Lanett, Opelika, Birmingham and LaGrange, GA. The 1920 census shows him back in Chambers Co. as a merchant living with his wife, Laura and grandson, Frank A. After Laura's death, he married Ella Capes Webb Long. In 1924 he moved to Chatsworth, GA where he was elected mayor for three terms. He shows in the 1930 census as being retired and living with wife, Ella. He died later that year. He was buried next to Laura at the Hillview cemetery annex, section 5, lot 2, space 8, in LaGrange, GA. His plain grave marker has no inscription.

His epitaph in the December 4, 1930, edition of the *Calhoun Times* reads, "Mr. John Franklin McGinty, father of the editor of the *Calhoun Times*, died at his home in Chatsworth Tuesday morning at 8:30, after a brief illness. He was seventy-five years of age. Up to six years ago, Mr. McGinty spent practically all his life in Chambers Co., AL, with the exception of short terms of residence in Opelika and Birmingham, AL and West Point and LaGrange, GA. In 1924 he came to north Georgia and located in Chatsworth. Although a comparatively newcomer to the little city, he was three times elected mayor of Chatsworth, without opposition, retiring voluntarily at the end of his third term....he was a member of the primitive Baptist church for more than thirty years, and his religious faith was the rule of his everyday life....the neighbors among whom he spent his days found only words of praise for his exemplary life."

Another article in the March 26, 1931, *Calhoun Times*, written by his fellow church members, shows that he was a deacon and that he was "specially gifted mentally and spiritually, was a deep thinker -

impressive talker and endowed with great ability as a writer." *The Lafayette Sun* reported on December 3, 1930, that "Mr. J. F. McGinty, prominent and beloved citizen of Chatsworth, GA, died at his home in that city early Tuesday morning following a short illness. The deceased was seventy-five years of age and had lived a useful life in this section of the state."

He and Laura had three children, Rupert, John Roy and Roland M. Rupert went to Colorado and became the superintendent at the state horticultural and agricultural college, and later was a doctor, heading up of the horticultural department at Clemson College in SC. John Roy became a lawyer in Troup Co., GA and then was the editor of a newspaper in Calhoun and Chatsworth, GA for thirty years and is a member of the Newspaper Mans Hall of Fame. He also served as a Senator in GA in 1945 and was a member of the GA Legislature for two terms, 1939-40 and 1945-46. Roland became a linotype operator in Chicago and later moved to Atlanta, where he worked for the Atlanta Journal/Constitution as a proofreader.

John Franklin had a grandson (son of John Roy Sr.), Franklin Alexander McGinty, b. November 22, 1911, in Atlanta, GA, d. August 5, 1943.

Franklin Alexander McGinty

Frank was a musician and scholar. Music, books and the fine arts were his chief interests. He attended the old Chatsworth High School and graduated from the University of Georgia in 1941 as a member of the Phi Beta Kappa honorary fraternity. He taught for one year at Lavonia High School before entering the service. He was an accomplished organist and was offered, after his basic training, an opportunity to become assistant to the chaplain where he would have arranged the music for religious services for the sailors. He declined, saying that he "wanted to be where he could sink a submarine." Frank was a soundman (listened to sonar), third class in the U.S. Navy Reserves. He was killed in action aboard the *USS Plymouth* which was hit by a torpedo while on convoy duty as she prepared to depth charge the German submarine *U-566*. One account says that they were off Cape Charles about ninety miles east of Elizabeth City, NJ. An article in the *New York Times*, August 16, 1943, says they were off of the North Carolina coast. According to accounts, as she swung left to bear on the target, a violent underwater explosion occurred just abaft the bridge. She took a heavy list to port with her entire port side forward of amidships in flames. She sank quickly. Rough seas and sharks hampered rescue operations. An article in the New York Times, October 8, 1943, shows that a Coast Guard cutter rescued sixty of the approximately 160 members of the crew "from stormy waters."

Frank was posthumously awarded the Navy Cross on October 21, 1943. His citation reads: "For heroism and outstanding performance of duty during the sinking of the USS PLYMOUTH on August 5, 1943. Soundman McGinty attempted to rescue a man who was trapped in the flaming ship's armory. He was seen to enter the armory, but he also was trapped there and thus lost his life. Such action reflects great credit upon the Naval Service." Later in the war, a new destroyer escort, DE-365, the *USS McGinty*, was named in honor of him. His name is included on the monument, Tablets of the Missing, in Battery Park, New York City. This ship was built at the Consolidated Steel Corp. shipyard in Orange, TX. On August 5, 1944, the anniversary of his death, it was christened by his stepsister, Mrs. Perrillah Malone, who broke the traditional bottle of champagne over its bow. The ship was then launched and glided down the ramp into the Sabine River. His stepmother and father were in attendance at the ceremony along with his brother and several other dignitaries. This ship was active in WWII, first based at Pearl Harbor. She performed escort duty between Guam, Eniwetok and Ulithi, later making runs to Okinawa and Tokyo Bay. After the war, she returned to San Diego and was made part of the reserve fleet in 1947. In March 1951 she was brought back into active service in the Korean War where she received three battle stars. From May to July 1956 she participated in Operation Redwing at the pacific proving grounds. These were a series of at least seventeen nuclear detonations, testing various aspects of the weapons. The tests were held at the Eniwetok and Bikini atolls. The *USS McGinty's* role was in measuring radiation fall-out. At this time her homeport was at Pearl Harbor. In 1959 she was decommissioned and berthed at Portland, Oregon. Then in 1961 when the Berlin Wall went up, she was reactivated and traveled the Sea of Japan and South China Sea. She was then sent to South Vietnam to train their naval officers on how to patrol the coastal waters. Crewmembers who served on the ship say that she could out steam the newer DE's because she had two screws and most of them only had one. She was decommissioned for the final time in August 1962. In September 1968 she was taken off the Navy records and sold to American Ship Dismantlers of Portland, OR who cut it up for scrap. I have a *USS McGinty* Navy shoulder patch from one of the uniforms, and also an ash tray from the ship showing the ship's name. (Department of the Navy, Naval Historical Center, Washington Navy Yard, DC, and Dictionary of American Naval Fighting Ships, vol. IV and V.

For more details visit http://en.wikipedia.org/wiki/USS_McGinty

Thomas Jefferson McGinty, b. March 5, 1858, in McGinty, Chambers Co., AL, d., at birth, March 5, 1858 (confirmed by family bible).

William Levin McGinty, b. August 23, 1859, (confirmed by family bible) probably in Randolph Co., AL, d. October 19, 1937, at Bryce Hospital in Tuscaloosa, AL. He married Laura Virginia Echols, January 15, 1887, in Tallapoosa Co., AL, W. T. Rowe, pastor. Earlier research shows that William was born in a log cabin on the land where his father lived in Chambers Co. It seems more probable that he was born in Randolph Co., AL where his parents were living in 1859. He shows in the 1860 census of Randolph Co., at age one. His wife was born in 1866 and died in 1918. Her father, Thomas M. Echols (Eckles?) (1820-1898), was shot to death by a son-in-law, Richard Calhoun on September 30, 1898. Her mother was America Fuller (1824-1885) and both of her parents are buried in the cemetery at Camp Hill, AL. William and Laura are both buried in the McGinty plot at Fairview Cemetery. He is the father of Rev. Basil B. McGinty who contributed much to the McGinty family research. He was a tenant farmer, and from 1883 until 1900, he and his family rented a farm in old Dudleyville, Tallapoosa Co., AL. After the death of his father, William Pitts in 1901 he came back to Chambers Co. and farmed on the old McGinty lands. They had four children, Basil, George Carlton, Grover and Annie Sujette.

He shows as Willie McGinty in the 1910 census of Chambers Co., Precinct 13, pg. 172. With him are wife, Laura, sons Basil (19), Grover (16), Carlton (12), and daughter, Sujette (9).

His life took a tragic turn around 1913 when his mental condition began to deteriorate. On April 15, 1915, he was admitted to the Bruce Mental Hospital in Tuscaloosa, AL by court order (hospital file 14923). On May 18, 1915, there is a letter to the hospital from his wife, Laura V. McGinty expressing concern that he might be returned to River View. She would not feel safe around him unless he was in good health and was sound of mind and did not want him released to return home for fear for herself and her children. William tried to escape from Bryce Hospital shortly after he was admitted and sustained a fall that resulted in a fractured clavicle. There is a letter written to the hospital by his brother, John Franklin McGinty of LaGrange, GA on October 14, 1915, saying that none of his brothers and sisters had heard from him and were wondering what the prospects were of his return home. It says that his wife and children were averse to having him return. This was obviously a big family disagreement. His brothers and sisters did not agree with the position taken by his wife and children.

However, after being confined at Bryce for two years (until May 1917) he was allowed to return to River View and lived with his brother, James Madison McGinty. I do not know the circumstances that led to his release and return. His wife died shortly after this on January 4, 1918. He secured work with the railroad and later as a mill hand in the cotton mill. His condition grew worse, and he was re-admitted to Bryce Hospital, again by court order, on July 2, 1919, (hospital file 17808). In a July 29, 1919, letter to the hospital from his brother, James Madison McGinty, he expressed concern that William should not have been re-admitted. His brother insisted William was working and doing better and that his brothers and sisters wanted him to return and would take care of him. In a letter from brother John Franklin McGinty to the hospital dated April 28, 1921, he says that William was always peculiar and simple – in childhood, as a young man, and when he was married – and that his brothers and sisters feel that a great wrong had been done by placing him there. That his son (Basil) and daughter (Sujette) were determined to keep him "imprisoned" there. According to a November 22, 1924, letter to the hospital from son, Basil McGinty, when James Madison McGinty secured the release of William and brought him back to River View in 1917 James was in feeble health and mind and almost caused the death of his father due to lack of necessary food and medical attention. He said that William should continue to be confined at Bryce. William did remain at Bryce Hospital until his death on October 19, 1937. His remains were removed by a local funeral director and sent back to River View by train. Family members met the train when it arrived in West Point and William was buried with his wife in Fairview cemetery. Mr. Thomas Goggans, superintendent of the Riverdale Mill where Basil was employed, owned a new Hudson automobile that was loaned to the McGinty family for this occasion. All they had at the time was an old T-Model Ford.

Another interesting letter in the hospital file is from grandson (Mr.) Jewel C. McGinty dated October 29, 1940. Jewel was trying to join the Marines and asked Bryce Hospital to write him a letter stating that his grandfather's condition was not hereditary. Jewel was the son of George Carlton McGinty, one of William's sons.

I would like to give special recognition to my first cousin (once removed), the Rev. Basil Beasley McGinty, son of William Levin. He was keenly interested in our family history and contributed greatly to the McGinty story in the River View area.

Basil was born June 19, 1890. There is disagreement as to where he was born. Some records say that he was born in McGinty, Chambers Co., AL but, as shown above, other records show that his father and family were living in Dudleyville, Tallapoosa Co., AL until 1900 and then relocated to the farm owned by his grandfather, William Pitts McGinty in Chambers Co. Economic conditions at this time were such that Basil started working as a floor sweeper in the Riverdale cotton mill at age ten. He continued to work at the mill for fifty-six years, retiring in late 1955. At the time of his retirement, he was office manager, personnel director and paymaster. He studied in his spare time and earned his high school diploma later in life, after he was already a father. Despite his lack of formal education, he was known as one of the most learned men in the area and was also a fine speaker.

He was twice married, the first time to Etta B. Suggs of Thomaston, GA in 1910. They produced two children, Elmo Leon and Mildred Shanks. Elmo, born in 1911 joined the U.S. Navy in WWII and died in Seattle of heart disease in 1944. Elmo left two baby girls, Laura Jeannette and Mary Maxine. Jeannette became Ph.D. at the U. of AL. Mildred was born in 1915 and recently died in Mississippi. Wife, Etta died in 1922 and is buried in the First Christian Church cemetery in River View. In 1924 Basil married Mary Melissa Hand of Gold Hill,

Clay Co., AL. They produced two daughters, Mary Sue, born in 1927 and Jane Berry, born in 1933. Sue Newberry lives in Columbus, GA and Jane Alford lives in North Carolina. I am very fortunate to have acquired some of his original notes and research from his daughter, Sue Newberry.

Basil studied the Bible from a very young age. He used to tear out a page and take it to work with him so that he could study it when the boss wasn't looking. In 1914 he became an ordained minister at the Bethlehem Missionary Baptist Church. He began to serve rural churches as their pastor in addition to his full time position at the mill. These churches included Cusseta, Farmville, Rock Springs, Antioch and Waverly. He also served as moderator of the East Liberty Baptist association for seventeen years. Few men have been more successful as a pastor. He wrote a wonderful book, *History of the East Liberty Baptist Association*, and was a long time column writer in the Valley newspaper.

In late 1935 Basil purchased part of the old McGinty land from the heirs of the late H. W. Scales. The Scales family had purchased this land about twenty-five years earlier. This included the home site where his grandfather, William Pitts McGinty had lived. During 1936 he replaced the old house with a new, modern brick home on this same site. The supervisor of the new construction was my grandfather, Wiley P. McGinty Sr., who was in his seventies by then. Several interesting things were noted when the old house was torn down. There were three large sills, cut from solid logs with a broadax, and they were fourteen inches square. Two of them were twenty-six feet long and the other twenty-eight feet. The latter is interesting because it is solid resin pine or lightwood, solid from one end to the other. All of these sills were used in the construction of the new house. The house still stands today and Basil's daughter, Jane, now owns the property. The house has been unoccupied since Mary's death in 1994. Basil's notes show that he and Mary had to borrow $4,000 to finance the construction of the new house. He got a loan at 4% interest from Fred Finch. There was no formal mortgage, only a gentleman's agreement. To pay off the loan, Miss Mary bought some more milk cows and milked from five to seven of them every day for seven and one half years. Basil would deliver the milk on his way to work every morning. They paid off every dollar right on schedule. While Basil was frequently found in the house reading, studying and operating his ham radio (his handle was "Mac," and call letters, W4ZS), Miss Mary would be out in the field on her tractor, both doing what they enjoyed the most. I visited this house in June 2003. I was particularly impressed by the row of huge and very old cedar trees in front of the house. Because of their size and age, they would have been planted by William Pitts or perhaps were there even earlier. This site is steeped in McGinty history.

Basil died June 29, 1975, and wife Mary passed away August 21, 1994. They are buried, together with son Elmo, in the McGinty plot at Fairview cemetery, just down the road from their home.

In Memory

Rev. Basil McGinty

In this time of recognition and appreciation, we honor the memory of one who meant so much, to so many, for a long, long time.

The 36 Churches of the
East Liberty Baptist Association
of the Southern Baptist Convention

Fairview Cemetery
Valley, AL

Recognition from one of his churches in 1953 reads, "When God called B. B. McGinty to his gospel ministry, he seemed to have endowed him with a heart big enough and a love broad enough to include a greater field and a larger constituency than that afforded most ministers. No association of churches, or brotherhood of preachers, ever had a more faithful friend, leader, counselor and pastor than this brother-beloved." Basil McGinty was a loved and respected man.

George Washington McGinty, b. February 13, 1862, (confirmed by family bible, census and gravestone) in McGinty, Chambers Co., AL, d. September 13, 1947, in Camp Hill, Tallapoosa Co., AL (death certificate). He married Francis Emma Handley, December 18, 1889, in Tallapoosa Co., AL, William Lively, pastor. She was called Emma. They had five girls, Oriel N., Nancy Ozella, Rosa Emma, Georganna "Lala" and Lou Ella (1894-1898). He is shown in the 1900-1930 census as a farmer. Deeds show that he made a land purchase from R.A. Henderson in Section 15, Township 21, Range 24 containing 30.37 acres. He is buried, along with Frances, whose gravestone shows the death date of October 29, 1944, at the Camp Hill cemetery on Hwy. 50 in Camp Hill, AL. Death certificate shows cause of his death at age eighty-five was pneumonia, arteriosclerosis and heart disease.

Camp Hill Cemetery
Camp Hill, AL

Wiley Patterson McGinty Sr., b. January 22, 1865 (confirmed by family bible) in McGinty, Chambers Co., AL, d. March 30, 1957. He married (1) Mollie Hinton Redd, December 1, 1893, and (2) Tinnie Mae Hunt, November 2, 1932. They are all buried in the McGinty plot at Fairview Cemetery.

Mary Reese (Mollie) McGinty, b. September 8, 1868, (confirmed by the 1870, 1880 and 1900 census and family bible) in McGinty, Chambers Co., AL, d. February 5, 1941, in Chambers Co. Mollie never married and late in life lived with her niece, Nannie Ruth McGinty Anderson in West Point, GA. There was an Easter morning chimney fire in Mollie's room at the Anderson home, for which Ruth's husband, Bill Anderson Sr., asked fire chief Novatus L. Barker "<u>not</u> to sound the siren." This request was made because when the siren was blown in West Point, once for downtown, twice for the west side of the river and three times for the east side of the river, everybody in town would flock to the location to watch the action and Bill Anderson did not want a crowd to gather as it had the week before during another fire that was in the dining room. At that time, spectators were actually walking around inside the house and Mrs. Anderson had to run them out. This amusing story is confirmed by Wiley Anderson, son of Bill and Ruth Anderson who, as a young boy, was living at the house at the time of the fires. In December 1898 Molly purchased forty-seven acres in

Section 32 from the family of William Pitts McGinty (deed book 28, pg. 119). This land was adjacent to that owned by William Pitts and William Levin McGinty. Both the 1900 and 1920 census shows her living in the home of her brother, James Madison McGinty. She owned land in Chambers Co. in 1925. Her name is shown on a deed as adjacent to land that had been owned by William Pitts McGinty. The 1930 and 1940 census shows her living in the home of her brother, Wiley P. McGinty Sr. I have not yet confirmed her occupation, but have heard that she was a school teacher. In the 1900 census of Chambers Co., pg. 307, she was living with brother, James Madison McGinty. Her father was also living there. Mollie is buried in the McGinty plot at Fairview Cemetery. Her gravestone shows an incorrect birth date of 1875.

Miss Mary McGinty Of Riverview Dies Wednesday Morning

Miss Mary Reece McGinty, 71, member of one of the Valley's oldest and most prominent families, died at the Valley Hospital, Wednesday morning, following an illness of 12 weeks. Services will be held from the W. P. McGinty home in Riverview, Thursday afternoon, 2 o'clock, with the Rev. John W. Faulkner officiating, assisted by the Rev. Kelly Johnson.

The survivors are three brothers and one sister: G. W. McGinty, of Camp Hill; A. W. McGinty, of Birmingham; W. P. McGinty, of Riverview; and Mrs. T. Bass, of Dadeville.

Johnson and Company are in charge of arrangement.

Andrew Jackson McGinty, b. December 2, 1872 (confirmed by family bible), in McGinty, Chambers Co., AL, d. February 14, 1958, in Birmingham, Jefferson Co., AL. He married Sarah Fletcher Murphy (1879-1960) February 2, 1899, in Lee Co., AL and they produced four children, Andrew Wilton (1899-1970), Mary and Carey who were twins, born September 16, 1908, and Sarah Palestine (1912-2001). Andrew moved from Chambers Co. to Birmingham in 1907. He became a prominent grocer and member of the Bush Creek Primitive Baptist church. His wife, "Fletch" was a seamstress and operated a sewing store in Birmingham. He is buried, along with other members of his family, at the Elmwood Cemetery in Birmingham.

The Life of William Pitts McGinty

William Pitts, known to some as "Billie," moved to AL with his father, George Washington, when he was about fifteen years old. His birthplace was probably in Wilkinson Co., GA, because his father shows in the 1817 church records as living there and also in the 1820 census. Other sources say that he was born in Jones Co. and Upson Co. No death certificate or obituary has been located.

A possible explanation for the origin of his middle name, "Pitts," comes from the history of Jones Co., GA. Here we see that the Pitts family intermarried with the Moore family. His mother was Tabitha Moore. A certain Peyton Pitts was a county and state leader, living between Macon and Milledgeville. His son and grandson married Moore girls.

In 1863 at the height of the Civil War, he acquired a farm near McGinty's Crossroads. His son, Wiley P. McGinty Sr., said that he had in his possession the original deed to a parcel of this land and that it was signed by President Zachary Taylor and dated June 1, 1850. This document has not been located. However, various deeds showing the purchase and sale of this land have been traced back to the Creek Treaty of 1832. There is no evidence that his father, Washington McGinty ever lived on this land. William Pitts married Mary Ann Freeman, the daughter of Rev. Tyre Freeman (Chambers Co. marriage records, vol. 3, pg. 42) in 1843.

**William and Mary Ann Freemen
Permission from her Father**

Soon after her death, and prior to 1846 he married sixteen year old Ann M. Moore, daughter of Levin and Penelope Patterson Moore, early Chambers Co. pioneers. It is possibly from Penelope's father, Willie Patterson that the name Wiley and Patterson of Wiley Patterson McGinty Sr., originates. Ann Moore's brother, Wiley P. Moore, b. 1844, was actually the first to have the "Wiley" name.

Willie Patterson signed his will as Willie. The original is on file at the Jones Co., GA courthouse in Gray, GA, and I have seen it. The 1850 census of Jones Co., pg. 197, shows his name as Willie. Willie was very active at the Elim and Mt. Zion Baptist church in Jones Co., GA. He, along with son, Hearndon Patterson shows in the Ocmulgee Assn. Minutes as messengers to the annual meetings from these churches. Hearndon Patterson was elected clerk of this association in 1849 and was active until his death, ca. 1868. In 1839 the Ocmulgee Assn. split into two separate groups. Five of the original churches became "missionary" and the balance remained "primitive." Elim church was one that became "missionary." Willie Patterson left it and went with his son to the Mt. Zion "primitive" church.

It is interesting to note that William Pitts McGinty's second wife, Ann "Annie" Moore, was the daughter of Levin and Penelope Moore. Ann's father, Levin Moore, was the son of Ephriam and Nancy Moore. William Pitts' father, Washington McGinty, married Tabitha Moore who was also the daughter of Ephriam Moore. Tabitha was the mother of William Pitts. Therefore, William Pitts and his wife, Ann Moore were first cousins. Levin died in 1855 and the 1860 census of Chambers Co. shows Penelope Moore, age fifty-four, as a widow and farmer. A sixteen year old Wiley P. is living with her along with married daughter, Malinda Olive, age twenty-five and her child, one year old Mary L. Olive. She owned four slaves (pg. 17, slave schedule) and had real estate valued at $2,500 and personal worth of $7,575. Also of interest is that her next door neighbor in 1860 was the widow, Kisiah (Morris) Freeman, wife of Tyre Freeman.

Prior to his death, Levin owned 310 acres of land, which included the area that is now McGinty, AL. The Columbus Rd. cut thru the middle of it, from north to south. The location of his grave, and probably other family members, is known, and was visited and photographed by my brother, Phil McGinty, in September 2006. At the time of the census, these Moores lived in what was known as the Ossanippa district. Penelope's death date and burial site are unknown, but it is very possible that she was buried with her husband in this family plot on their property. Penelope Patterson Moore, was the daughter of Willie Patterson and Anna Hearndon of Jones Co., GA. Willie Patterson was born in NC, ca. 1775. Anna was born, ca. 1780 (1850 census, Jones Co., GA, pg. 197). Her grandfather was Capt. Mark Patterson who was from NC.

After Penelope's death which was prior to 1870, the 310 acres of Moore land somehow got into the hands and title of Robert A. McGinty. In court proceedings, daughters Ann and Malinda are shown as the high bidders for the land in May 1873 ($900). Then, in November 1884 (deed book 19, pg. 139), Ann and Malinda agreed to split up the land with Ann getting the land west of the Columbus Rd, and Malinda getting the land east of this road.

Because the area around the Moore gravesite had fallen into disrepair, Rev. Basil B. McGinty moved Levin's grave marker, but not his remains, from the old Moore family plot off the Columbus Rd. to the McGinty plot in the Fairview cemetery. This move could have actually been done by his wife, Mary, as one of Basil's last wishes before his death.

Concerning the son, there are five cards in his Confederate file. He is listed as W. P. L. Moore on all of the cards. He enlisted in Co. K, 34th Alabama Infantry at age 18 at Loachapoka, AL on May 23, 1862, for three years, or the war. By Oct/Nov 1862 he was in the hospital at Munfordville (KY), admitted on Sept 13. On February 12, 1864, he appears on a claim of deceased officers and soldiers from Alabama which was filed for settlement in the office of the Confederate States Auditor for the War Department. The claim was made by "Penelope Moore, Mo". The "Mo" obviously stands for Mother. The Alabama Special Census of 1866 confirms that Wiley was a war casualty.

Malinda married O.W. D. Olive. He died September 12, 1890, and she died sometime before him. O.W. D. served the CSA as a corporal in Co. A, 45th AL Inf. They are both buried at the Oak Hill cemetery in Union Springs, Bullock Co., AL.

Dress coat, handmade ca. 1828 by Penelope Moore for her husband, Levin Moore. It was donated to the Cobb Archives in Valley, AL, by Wiley McGinty Sr. in 1953 and is displayed by Sandra Scott, Wiley's great granddaughter, April 12, 2000

In the census of 1840 William is living with his parents, Washington and Elizabeth McGinty on their farm in Chambers Co. It is unclear where this farm was located. Some of his brothers and sisters are shown as being born in the Osanippa, AL area.

William is shown on the 1850 census in Chambers Co. (pg. 369) at age thirty-one, living with his wife, Ann and children; Lucinthe, 5, James M., 2 and Theodore, 1 (listed as a male). I have located one deed dated February 19, 1850, showing the sale of a parcel of land by William and Ann to Holly Weaver for $112.50. Holly Weaver was a Confederate veteran and lost an arm in the war. Later, he was the tax collector in Chambers Co.

The Chambers Co. agricultural census of 1850 gives a complete picture of William's farming operation. It shows the following:

Acres of land – Improved	50
Acres of land – Unimproved	35
Cash value of farm	$300
Value of farming machinery and implements	$85
Horses	1
Milk cows	2
Working oxen	2
Other cattle	1
Swine	26
Value of livestock	$100
Wheat, bushels of	11
Indian corn, bushels of	200
Wool	20 lbs.
Ginned cotton, bales of 400 lbs. each	9
Peas and beans, bushels of	50
Sweet potatoes, bushels of	800 lbs.
Butter, pounds of	100 lbs.
Value of homemade mfg.	$25
Value of animals slaughtered	$75

In the special Chambers Co., AL census of 1855 (pg. 38), he is shown with seven whites and no slaves in his household. At this time he shows five children who would have been, Lucynthia, James Madison, Tabitha, Nancy Laura and Theodosia.

He was in transit between the census of 1855 and 1860 and is shown in the 1860 census as living in the Buchanan area of Randolph Co., AL (pg. 156), age forty-one with his wife, Ann, age thirty and children; Lucintha, 16, James M., 12, Theodosia, 11(now correctly listed as a female), Tabitha A., 9, Nancy L., 7, John F., 5 and William L., 1.

Daughter, Nancy Laura, is shown as being born in Roanoke, Randolph Co., in 1853. Sometime around 1859 and before the 1860 census, he relocated his family from Chambers Co. to an area around Buchanan, which was about twelve miles north of Roanoke, AL. Their move to Randolph Co. is recorded in the minutes of the Ephesus Church, where they were dismissed November 12, 1859. According to the U.S. Postal Dept. archives, Buchanan had a U.S. Post Office box from 1857-1866. Old maps show Buchanan as being south of Potash and Big Springs about half way between them and level with Tin Shop. The Randolph Co. courthouse burned in the late 1890's and property records were lost, making it impossible to trace his land purchased and sold in this area. The 1860 agricultural census record of Randolph Co., AL was located in the University of NC archives. William is shown in the Buchanan area, pg. 49 and 50. His farming operation was recorded as follows:

Improved land, acres	80
Unimproved land, acres	102
Cash value of farm	$1000
Value of farming implements	$250
Horses	1
Asses and mules	2
Milk cows	1
Working oxen	2
Sheep	4
Swine	15
Value of livestock	$800
Indian Corn, bushels of	300
Ginned cotton, bales @ 400 lbs. ea.	9
Peas and beans, bushels of	50
Irish potatoes, bushels of	3
Sweet potatoes, bushels of	20
Value of orchard products	$5
Butter, lbs. of	100
Beeswax, lbs. of	5
Honey, lbs. of	100
Value of homemade manufactures	$30
Value of animals slaughtered	$240

The nine bales of cotton (3600 lbs.) are the most valuable item. During the Civil War, cotton prices jumped to over $1.25 per pound. Returning to Chambers Co., he purchased several parcels of land on November 2, 1863, that totaled 275 acres. The price was $2,000, (Confederate money). This land included the property later purchased by Basil B. McGinty (see section on Basil), where William's home was located. The Bethlehem Missionary Baptist church and cemetery is shown on the deed as owning five acres within this plot. The present Fairview cemetery is located on the site of this early church. This church was founded in 1835 and the building was located on this property until 1870 when it was moved to Fairfax.

William Pitts purchased this land from Elizabeth Wright of Harris Co., GA (recorded in Chambers Co. deed book 18, pg. 615/616). She had purchased it from John and Elizabeth Standard on December 20, 1858 (deed book 13, pg. 303). The Standards purchased part of this land from Tim and Terry Collins on August 28, 1852 (deed book 11, pg. 345). The Collins had purchased it from Cherry and Wallace on March 19, 1852 (deed book 10, pg. 496). James A. Cherry purchased the portion in section 29 from William Dougherty on December 21, 1840. Dougherty had purchased it on July 31, 1840, from a Creek Indian Chief. John Williams originally purchased the portion in section 32, June 29, 1840, also from a Creek Chief. After the Creek Treaty in 1832 ninety of their Chiefs were awarded one half of a section each to either live on for five years or sell. The 160 acres of this land in section twenty-nine was awarded to Chief Cho-full-war. Eighty acres of the land in section 32 was awarded to Chief Ko-wok-koo-oh-e-har-jo (confirmed by the Alabama Tract Book, pg. 239, located at the Chambers Co. courthouse and an 1832 map of Chambers Co. at the Cobb Archives in Valley, AL).

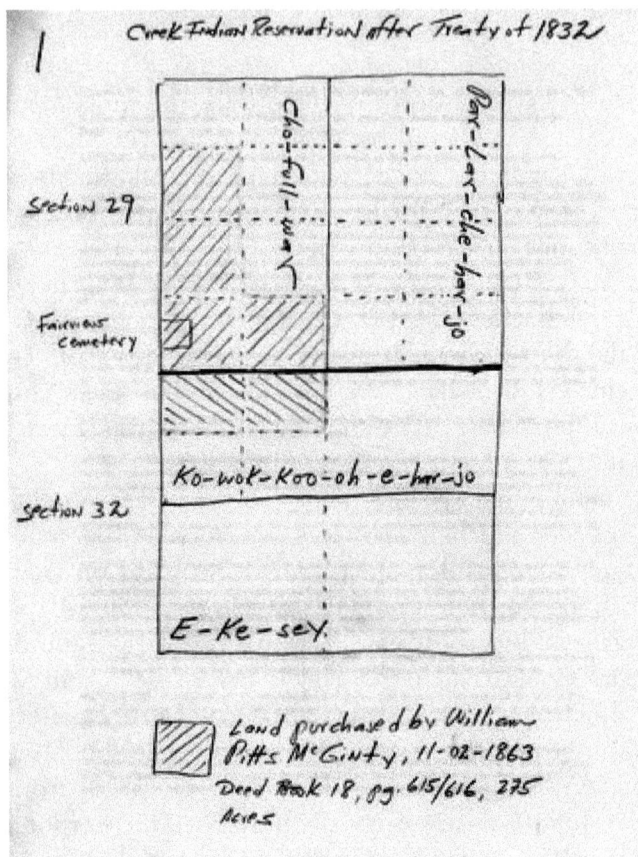

**William Pitts Land Showing the Original Grants to
Creek Indian Chiefs in the 1832 Treaty**

Bethlehem Missionary Baptist Church was at one time located on the land now occupied by the cemetery (this church was founded in October 1835 and admitted to the Liberty Baptist Association in September 1837). Until 1846 this was the only Baptist church in the Valley. In 1870 this church was relocated to Fairfax village (Glass). This church was always strongly missionary. In 1846 there was a split in the church and the faction known as the Primitive Baptists withdrew fellowship from the faction known as the Missionary Baptist. The Primitive Baptists started their own church known as the Ephesus Primitive Baptist Church (founded August 21, 1846). The first pastor was Tyre Freeman and William Pitts's father, Washington McGinty, was a charter member. William Pitts was also a member here in the 1850's, and shows as moderator in the church minutes. Tyre Freeman is shown in the Ocmulgee Baptist Assn. minutes of 1839-41 as a member of the Mt. Zion Baptist Church in Jones Co. GA. He moved to Chambers Co., AL before 1842 and purchased property there. The records also show that a number of the members' slaves were also admitted to the church. Some of our McGinty ancestors remained missionary and some became primitive Baptists.

William Pitts lived on this land until his death in 1901. The property was then sold by his heirs to his son-in-law, M. M. Tomme, in November 1901 (deed book 28, pg. 336).

Civil War records in the National Archives show W. P. McGinty as a private in Capt. H.F. Dunston's 4th Alabama Reserves. This unit included about eighty men from the area. This company subsequently became Co. E, 4th Reg., AL Reserves. William Pitts mustered into this unit August 5, 1864, at Opelika, AL. His enlistment documents give us his description as forty-five years old, five feet ten inches tall, blue eyes, dark hair and fair complexion. His service records do not show his active duty in this unit. However, at the time there was a crisis in Mobile which was under attack by Adm. Farragut and all available AL reserves were ordered to report there. The 4th AL was on post in Mobile by November 20, 1864. On February 7, 1865, they were ordered to Montgomery to help defend that area and arrived on February 20, 1865. 150 were present for duty and according to the CSA records, they were "very much disorganized." I have an original letter that he wrote to his wife early in his enlistment. It reads, "Mrs. A.M. McGinty my wife. This will inform you that we are at West Point and we don't know how long we are to stay here. I want you to send us something to cook in. I reckon a frying pan will suit us well. July 20, 1864, W.P. McGinty."

There is a record listing him as one of the construction workers at the Riverdale mill that was constructed in River View in 1866. The 1870 census (pg. 215) finds him in Chambers Co. at age fifty-one with his wife, Ann, and children James Madison, 22, Theodosia, 20, Laura Nancy, 18, John Franklin, 15, William Levin, 11, George, 9, Wiley P., 6, and Mary Reece "Molly," 2. His daughter, Tabitha, 19, shows in the Lee Co., AL census, living in the home of E. D. Pitts.

In 1880 at age sixty-one, the census shows him with his wife Ann and all of the children in the 1870 census with the addition of Andrew J., age eight. It also shows Tabitha A., age twenty-nine, again living in his house.

Ann Moore McGinty died in 1898 of acute bronchitis and her son, James Madison McGinty wrote her epitaph, which was published in the *Gospel Messenger* in July 1898, Vol. 20, No. 7, pg. 326. It reads as follows:

"With a heart full of sorrow and deep affliction, I write to inform our relatives, brethren, and sisters of the death of our dear mother. Mrs. Ann M. McGinty, who died at her home near River View, Chambers Co., AL, Feb. 5, 1898, sixty-eight years old less twenty-six days. She was the daughter of Levin and Penelope Moore. She was born in Jones Co., GA in the year 1830 and in early life moved with her parents to Chambers Co., AL; and on the eleventh day of April 1846, she was married to W. P. McGinty, and to this union was born eleven children, nine of whom, with her aged husband, mourn her death. She was a faithful and true wife, a kind and good mother, always ready to administer to the wants of her family. She was a great sufferer for a number of years, but bore her afflictions with great fortitude. She was a strong believer in the doctrine of salvation by grace, having joined the Primitive Baptist church at Ephesus, Chambers Co., AL, in the year 1846 which church sustains a great loss."

"Dearest mother, thou hast left us;
Here our loss we deeply feel:
But 'tis God that hath bereft us –
He can all our sorrows heal.
Yet again we hope to meet thee
When the day of life is fled,
And in heaven with joy to greet thee,
Where no farewell tear is shed."

J. M. McGinty

Ann Moore McGinty,
Fairview Cemetery, Valley, AL

William Pitts is shown in the 1900 Chambers Co., AL census, pg. 307, at age eighty, living with his son, James Madison McGinty. He died in January 1901 and was buried in the McGinty plot at Fairview Cemetery with Ann.

William Pitts McGinty,
Fairview Cemetery, Valley, AL

Note that his gravestone is inscribed W. P. McGinty Sr. This is interesting since there was no William Pitts Jr. Apparently, the custom at the time said that since his initials were W. P., the same as his son, Wiley Patterson Sr., he was referred to as W. P. Sr.

His son, Wiley P. McGinty Sr., was the agent for his heirs and after his death, published the following article in the October 9, 1901, edition of the *Lafayette Alabama Sun*: "By agreement among the heirs, I will offer for sale at the highest and best bidder for cash on Saturday,

November 2, 1901, the following described lands, property of Wm. P. McGinty, deceased, 130 acres in Beat 13, Chambers Co., AL, and one and a half miles west of River View, AL, 70 acres under cultivation, 60 acres original woods, one 5 room dwelling, tenant house, stables, outhouse, etc. Lands well watered. Sale on premises."

The interrogatory that was taken at the time when his son, William Levin was admitted to Bryce hospital gives us a somewhat slanted picture of William Pitts McGinty and Ann Moore McGinty. It reads: "Father, William P. McGinty; deceased; farmer; born in GA; stood well (in community); considered peculiar and was insane; used tobacco and whiskey moderately; he and his wife were second cousins (this was an error, they were actually first cousins); he was forty years old when patient was born; suffered with sick headaches; died of la grippe (influenza) at the age of eighty-one. His people all lived to be old – his sisters lived to be about eighty-five. Mother, Ann M. McGinty; born in GA; died of acute bronchitis at the age of sixty-eight years. Moral standing good; used snuff; generally healthy; condition of health good before patients birth at which time she was thirty years old."

This is purely speculation, but the fact that his father, William Pitts and mother, Ann Moore was first cousins could have caused genetic problems that led to William's condition. The mention here of William Pitts being "insane" is probably a bit misleading. We do not know what the definition of insane was at the time. William Pitts certainly lived a full life and was a successful farmer who raised a large family.

In October 2003 the original family bible of William Pitts was located in Smyrna, GA. It was in the possession of Shannon McGinty Bartlett who is a descendant of John Franklin McGinty, son of William Pitts. The bible was passed down to John Franklin and on to his son, Rowland and is now in the possession of Shannon. She sent me the bible and I have researched it. The bible contains the birth dates of all the children. There were some errors in earlier research, which have now been corrected. There were several letters and other documents between the pages that have been transcribed. This bible was a major discovery.

The bible is a large book measuring 9x11 inches and is 3.5 inches thick. It contains 768 pages covering the Old and New Testaments. The bible was originally bound with embossed brown leather and is now in extremely fragile condition. Pages one and two are missing. It was published between 1851-1852 by Alden, Beardsley & Co. in Auburn, NY and Wanzer, Beardsley & Co. in Rochester, NY. This was a popular bible at the time and identical bibles have been located in the possession of other families.

There is a page titled Family Record listing all of the children of William Pitts McGinty and their birth dates as follows:

> Lucintha Elvira McGinty was born October 27, 1844
> James Madison McGinty was born September 30, 1847
> Theodosia Burr McGinty was born April 24, 1849
> Tabitha Ann McGinty was born May 24, 1851
> Wiley P. McGinty was born January 22, 1865
> Nancy Laura McGinty was born October 11, 1853
> John Franklin McGinty was born August 13, 1855
> Thomas Jefferson McGinty was born March 5, 1858
> Wm. L. McGinty was born August 23, 1859
> G.W. McGinty was born February 13, 1862
> Mary Reese McGinty was born September 8, 1868
> Andrew J. McGinty was born December 2, 1872

There is also an entry showing that Thomas Jefferson McGinty died at birth on March 5, 1858.

There was also a page showing marriages but it has been removed. There is a small portion of this page remaining with a notation in the margin that "James Madison McGinty written this (month unreadable) 2nd, 1867." To the right of this notation there is a W and below this is written Ann and below this you can see an F. This is the first entry at the top left corner of this page and no doubt records the marriage of William Pitts McGinty to his first wife, Mary Ann Freeman.

Several letters and other notes were found between the pages of this bible. They include:

➤ A letter from T. B. (Theodosia Burr) McGinty written to her brother, James Madison McGinty, January 15, 1872. She was living in Tallapoosa Co., AL at the time.

➤ A letter from G. W. (George Washington McGinty Jr.) and wife M.A. (Mary Adeline Davis) to his brothers and sisters dated September 11, 1862. It was written from his home in Morehouse Parish, LA and addressed to his brother, P.H. (Pinckney Harrington) McGinty.

➤ A letter from L. E. (Lucinthia Elvira McGinty) Fallin to her sister T.A. (Tabitha Ann) McGinty written March 10, 1867. It was written from her home in Tallapoosa Co., AL.

➤ A listing of items, names of purchasers and proceeds from what appears to be an estate sale in Chambers Co. dated January 3, 1870. James, W.P. and Washington McGinty are shown purchasing many items. This could have been the estate of Penelope Moore, wife of Levin Moore.

➤ A small note to Miss Tabitha McGinty "at home" dated August 6, 1874. There are no words here, just some numbers.

➤ A receipt to W. P. McGinty for payment of $50 to a Mr. Mcanelly(?) dated January 5, 1865. It is signed by J.A. McGinty. This is probably James A. McGinty (1846-1885), son of Robert A. McGinty, the brother of William Pitts McGinty.

➤ A summons from the State of Alabama, Chambers Co., for William P. McGinty to appear in court and give testimony for the State in the case of The State of Alabama vs. William K. Fredrick. It is dated April 7, 1866. I was not able to locate this case file at the courthouse.

➤ A small slip of paper with letters of the alphabet written over and over by J. M. McGinty (James Madison) as he practiced learning to write the A, B, C's.

➤ There is a Family Record sheet showing the birth and marriage John Franklin McGinty and the birth of his three sons, Rupert, J. Roy and Rowland. This page is **not** part of the bible. This page is much larger than the bible pages. It was inserted into the bible by the John Franklin McGinty family.

> There is a poem written "For a Friend" with a heart drawn on the reverse. It appears to have been written to someone with the initials M.T. P.

> A small envelope addressed to Miss (?) Hand(?) "by the politeness or Mr. (?)." The envelope is empty.

> A pressed flower about four inches long of unknown variety.

The inside cover of the bible contains a few names scribbled by some of the McGinty children. Mollie Mc, Theodosia, William and some other unidentified marks are there. Across the top of this page is a pencil entry that reads, "Recd of W E Pulmer $31.60 Feb 5 1876 corn from J.M. Mc 14 ½ bushels."

The information contained in the bible clarifies some of the prior research. Tabitha is shown as being born in 1851 but previous research shows 1850. Mary Reese "Mollie" McGinty is shown as being born in 1868 but her gravestone shows a birth date of 1875. Also, the bible entry shows Reese where previous research shows the spelling as Reece.

This is an extremely important discovery in McGinty research. Consider that this bible was used by the entire family of William Pitts and was in their home before the Civil War and for many years thereafter. Because of its size, and their strong religious orientation, it would have occupied a prominent place in the home. His children grew up with this bible. Some of the items found in the bible show that it was also used for filing other important papers.

Shannon and I recently donated the bible to the Cobb Archives, Bradshaw Library in Valley, Al and it is one of their most prized possessions.

George Washington McGinty

(1786-1874)

George Washington McGinty, b. ca. 1786 in Wilkes Co., GA, died March 14, 1874, while visiting in Randolph Co., AL. Probate records in Chambers Co. have proved his death date. He was the son of Robert McGinty and Deborah Jackson. He married (1) Nancy Thompson in 1810, (2) Tabitha Moore, August 12, 1813, (3) Naomi Elvira ? around 1824 (there is an unconfirmed record showing that Naomi was born in 1805), and (4) Mrs. Elizabeth (Betty or Betsy) Harrington Northrop, April 22, 1838, in Chambers Co., AL, by Samuel Roth, pastor. She was a widow.

Children of George Washington McGinty and Tabitha Moore:

Benjamin Franklin McGinty, b. 3 Apr 1823 in GA, d. 20 Dec 1902 in Cullman Co., AL. Married Rebecca A. Sappington 20 Oct 1868 in Macon Co., GA. Was living in Russell Co., AL in 1850 census. Owned a tavern in old Berlin, AL, 1852. Was living in Troy, Pike Co., AL in 1860. Was living in Pulaski GA 1870 as a mill owner. He shows as an heir in his father's probate 1874. 1880 he is living in Bibb Co, GA. Was postmaster in Cullman Co, AL 1884 and 1896. Was living in Bayleton, Cullman Co., AL 1900.

Nancy B. McGinty, b. February 15, 1815, in what is now Macon, Bibb Co., GA (Bibb Co. was formed in 1822 from parts of Jones, Monroe, Twiggs and Houston Co), d. January 25, 1891, Meansville, Pike Co., GA (dates confirmed from her gravestone). She married John Means (1812-1896), in Pike Co., September 26, 1833, David Wood, M.G. They met during the time that her father and family lived in this area near Meansville, Pike Co., GA, which is west of Barnesville, GA. When her father left the area and moved to Chambers Co., AL, he sold part of his land to John and Nancy. They raised a large family of at least nine children all of who were said to be "reliable and prominent citizens."

117

**John Means and Nancy
Barnesville, Pike Co., GA**

Their children were: Lillie, James W., Emily A., Mary S., Sarah Elizabeth, Virginia A.M., Marietta A., John Francis Sr. and Benjamin H. The 1860 census of Pike Co., GA shows that John was a large property owner and had a good-sized farming operation. His personal worth is listed at $13,000. This census shows that the Joseph E. Howard family also lived on his property. He was the husband of Emily A. Means. John also operated the first circular sawmill in middle Georgia about 1866. He also owned a large planing mill and furniture factory in Barnesville.

He was much interested in education and the John Means Institute in Meansville was named after him (*History of Lamar County*, pg. 376, Mrs. Augusta Lambdin, 1932). Nancy's obituary, which was published in the *Barnesville-News-Gazette* issue of January 29, 1891, reads as follows: "Mrs. Nancy Means, wife of Mr. John Means of Meansville died last Sunday night after an illness of about ten days of pneumonia. She was nearly ninety years of age at the time of her death (*note: this was an error. She was actually seventy-five*). Mrs. Means was a consistent member of the Ebenezer M.E. Church and lived a true Christian life. Her husband and she were among the original members of Fincher's Church, this county, moving their church membership to Ebenezer Church directly after the war. She was a good neighbor, and loved by all who knew her, and leaves a husband and several children to mourn her death. One of her sons, the Hon. J. W. Means, represented this county in the legislature of 1888-9, previous to that he was a county commissioner and is a man who has proven true to every trust. Her remains were interred at Ebenezer Methodist church cemetery, which is located in Lamar Co. (formerly Pike Co.), on Hwy 18 between Zebulon, GA and Barnesville, GA. A good woman has passed away."

Her marker shows a hand, with the index finger pointing upward (photo, next page).

**Buried together at Ebenezer Methodist Church
Lamar Co., GA**
Photos courtesy of Lynn B. Cunningham

John married a Lucinda "Lou" Foster on October 4th, 1891 and died February 28, 1896. He is buried next to Nancy at the Ebenezer Methodist Church Cemetery and his inscription shows the Masonic sign and reads, "Blessed are the pure in heart for they shall see God" (photo). His epitaph in the Pike County Journal, Zebulon, Pike County, Georgia, Mar. 6, 1896, reads, "The Journal is sorry to note the death of Mr. John Means, which occurred at his home near Meansville last Friday morning. He was 84 years of age and general prostration was the cause of his death. Mr. Means was a man who was respected and esteemed wherever he was known. He was honest and honorable in all transactions with his fellow man, and in his death the county has lost one of its best and purest men."

Note: There is a **Nancy B. McGinty** showing in Chambers Co. records who is easily confused with Nancy McGinty Means, daughter of George Washington McGinty. Coincidentally, they both have the same middle initial. This Nancy shows in both the 1850 and 1855 special census of AL and also in the 1850 and 1860 Federal census of AL as a head-of-household farmer born in GA. She is thought to have been married to James Cooper McGinty (Jr.?), the son of James and Temperance McGinty (see complete research on pg. 170-172). If correct, her maiden name would be Nancy Griswold. There is a James McGinty in the 1830 census of Wilkes Co., GA, pg. 294, age bracket twenty-thirty. This is thought to be him. James was married to (1) Phebe Martin in 1829. They had two children including a son, John B., b. March 1, 1833. Phebe died in 1837. He married (2) Nancy B. Griswold on July 13, 1837, and they had five children. These included Emily Francis (1838), Rebecca Cannon (1840), James Alexander Cato (1843), Joshua Soule Wilson and Mary Jane (1848).

William Pitts McGinty, b. June 4, 1819, in Wilkinson Co., GA, d. January 1, 1901, in Chambers Co. AL. He married (1) Mary Ann Freeman, November 30, 1843, and after her death (2) Ann Moore, April 8, 1846.

Robert Alexander McGinty, b. March 8, 1821, in GA, d. January 10, 1892, Tallapoosa Co., AL. He married Jane Elizabeth Sharman, (b. November 14, 1827, in GA), on April 3, 1845, in Russell Co., AL. He moved to Chambers Co. and shows transferring his membership to the Ephesus Church by letter on November 24, 1849. On November 25, 1851, he purchased 120 acres in section 19 of Chambers Co., which joined the land of his father in section 18. This land was located in present day Fairfax (deed book 10, pg. 474). The 1860 census of Chambers Co., shows them with children, James A., Adnie, Robert, Calvin, Frances, Sarah J., and Mary (So. Div., Oakbowery P.O., M653, roll 4, pg. 997). In this census, he is shown with a good-sized farming operation, with property worth $3,000 and personal worth reported at $5,000. He is shown on the same page as his uncle and aunt, James and Temperance McGinty and their daughter-in-law, Nancy. His farming operation is shown in the 1860 agricultural census of Chambers Co. (pg. 27) and includes 100 acres of improved land and an additional 283 acres of unimproved land. Some of the larger items include production of 350 bushels of corn and twenty swine. Son, James Alexander, joined the CSA reserves at age seventeen and later served as a Sgt. in the 63rd AL Infantry. This unit was sent to Mobile where he was hospitalized. He was captured in Blakely, AL, Apr. 9, 1865, and paroled in Meridian, MS, May 11, 1865. After the war, Robert signed the oath of allegiance to the United States during the reconstruction period of 1866-67. The 1870 census shows them with eight children. The other children were Jesse, Adnie Tabitha, Calvin Edorous, Frances (Fannie), Sarah (Sallie), Mary Ellen (Mollie), who married Almon Clay Wyatt, Martha (Mattie), Robert W., William F., George P., and John Lee. The 1900 census shows his wife Jane living with her son, William Franklin McGinty, in Camp Hill, Tallapoosa Co., AL. Jane died July 19, 1903, and both are buried in the Fargason-Wyatt Cemetery, down the road from the Sandy Creek church, outside of Camp Hill, Tallapoosa Co., AL. I visited this area in Feb. 2004. His middle initial is shown as E (Elexander?).

Children of Washington McGinty and assumed wife Naomi Elvira

Naomi Elvira McGinty (II), b. 1826 in GA (confirmed by the 1850 census), d. unknown. She shows in the minutes of the Ephesus Primitive Baptist Church in Chambers Co., August 21, 1846, as a charter member along with her father. She married John M. Davis, March 21, 1848, in Chambers Co.; Tyre Freeman MG was the pastor. The original consent letter from her father reads as follows: "March 14,

1848, this is to certify that Mr. John M. Davis and Naomi Elvira McGinty intends uniting in wedlock. The bride is my daughter and I have no objection to their union nor know of any from any quarter. Yours respectfully, Washington McGinty." The 1850 census of Chambers Co., 19th dist., shows John, a farmer, age twenty-six and Naomi, age twenty-four, with a one-month-old daughter, Sarah J. Davis (pg. 367/773).

Some researchers say that her mother was Naomi Moore, sister of Tabitha, but there is no documented proof to date. However, her step-grandson, Wiley P. McGinty Sr., said that his step-grandmother's name was Naomi Elvira McGinty. We do know that she was from Illinois. This is confirmed in the 1880 census records by two of her children, Washington Jr. and Narcissa. I have not found her family in the 1860 census or any other records after 1850.

Marriage of Naomi and John Davis

George Washington McGinty Jr., b. 1828 in GA, probably in either Pike or Wilkinson Co., d. 1907 in Morehouse Parish, LA. He married (1) Mary Adeline Davis (b. January 1832 d. June 27, 1877) when they lived in GA and they show in Pike Co., GA in the Bluff Springs-Weaver Communities after 1853. He moved to LA before 1860. The 1860 census of Iberville Parish, LA (Plaquemine), pg. 67/287, shows his occupation as overseer, with wife, Mary A., age twenty-nine and a son, George W. (III), age three. In a letter that he wrote to his brothers and sisters back in Chambers Co., AL on September 11, 1862, he describes his life and farming operation. "I have about thirty-five acres in corn and about the same in cotton…one and a half acres in potatoes and a calf pasture…five hands at work and I supply them with everything but their clothes and shoes…we live on the edge of the Mississippi overflow, about thirty miles from Grand Lake (this is across the state line in AR)…our drinking water comes from a cistern that I built in four days with $25 in lumber…cleared land can be bought here for $15-$20 per acre and wooded land for $2 to $10 per acre…we have plenty of game including turkey and wild boar…I have four good dogs and a splendid old shotgun…we have one boy and two girls." Morehouse Parish deeds, G/208-210, show that he purchased this land December 2, 1861. It consisted of 253 acres which was the north 1/2 of section 24, township 23N, Range 8E. The land was purchased from James McDowell for $3,793.80 ($15.00 per acre). McDowell had obtained part of his land from U.S. Govt. land grants in 1859. The McGinty cemetery is on this land, and is located on State Hwy. 835 (Kilborn Hwy.) and Monroe Tubbs Rd. The McDowell families were their neighbors and several are buried in the McGinty cemetery.

They had at least three children, George, III (b. February 16, 1857, d. January 1, 1896). He is buried in the McGinty cemetery. His gravestone shows his name misspelled as McGenty, and also shows him incorrectly as George Jr. The other two children were Sarah Adeline (b. ca. 1865) and Mary Elizabeth (b. January 28, 1861, d. January 28, 1928). Mary married Thomas Marshall McDowell. Both of them are buried in the McGinty cemetery. George III also shows in the 1880 census, age twenty-three, married to Nettie with one daughter, Elizabeth A., four months old.

The 1870 census shows George Jr., age forty-three, in Morehouse

Parish, LA with wife, Mary, George III, Sarah, Mary and a black girl, Ann, age fifteen. Wife, Mary died June 27, 1877, at age forty-five. Later in life, George Jr. married (2) Julia Lawrence. She was the daughter of John and Mary Lawrence and they all show in the census of 1850 (pg. 398). Based on the 1900 census, she was born in LA, July 1840. Her gravestone shows a birth date of July 24, 1841. She died January 25, 1906, and is buried in the McGinty cemetery. Several other Sawyers are also buried there.

They show two children in the 1880 census (pg. 473C), Lizzie (Mary Elizabeth) and Adeline (Sarah Adeline) along with a stepdaughter, Alice Jersey, age seven. I do not yet know how the Jersey name fits here. Lizzie married Thomas McDowell and they show in the 1920 census. Also, in this 1880 census, George Jr. and Elenora Narcissa show their mother's birthplace as Illinois. He shows in the 1900 census, age seventy-two with Julia, age fifty-nine. Living with him are four grandchildren, Roberta, Callie, Minnie and a grandson named William Washington "Willie" Beard. His daughter Sarah Adeline had married Charles Christian Beard. A letter from his nephew, John Franklin McGinty, written in 1930 confirms that he went to LA and lived in Morehouse Parish, LA, until he died in 1907. He is buried there at the McGinty cemetery in McGinty, LA, very close to the state line between LA and AR. His uncle, Thomas McGinty came to this area of LA several years before George Jr. arrived and could have been instrumental in getting George to move there. There is a gravestone for George Jr. in the small McGinty cemetery that was placed there in the recent past. It includes a long inscription showing his marriages and relatives. Some of the information on the stone was taken from old McGinty research and is incorrect.

It appears that the McGinty surname for this branch ended with George III. He was an only son and produced only daughters.

McGinty Cemetery, Morehouse Parish, LA

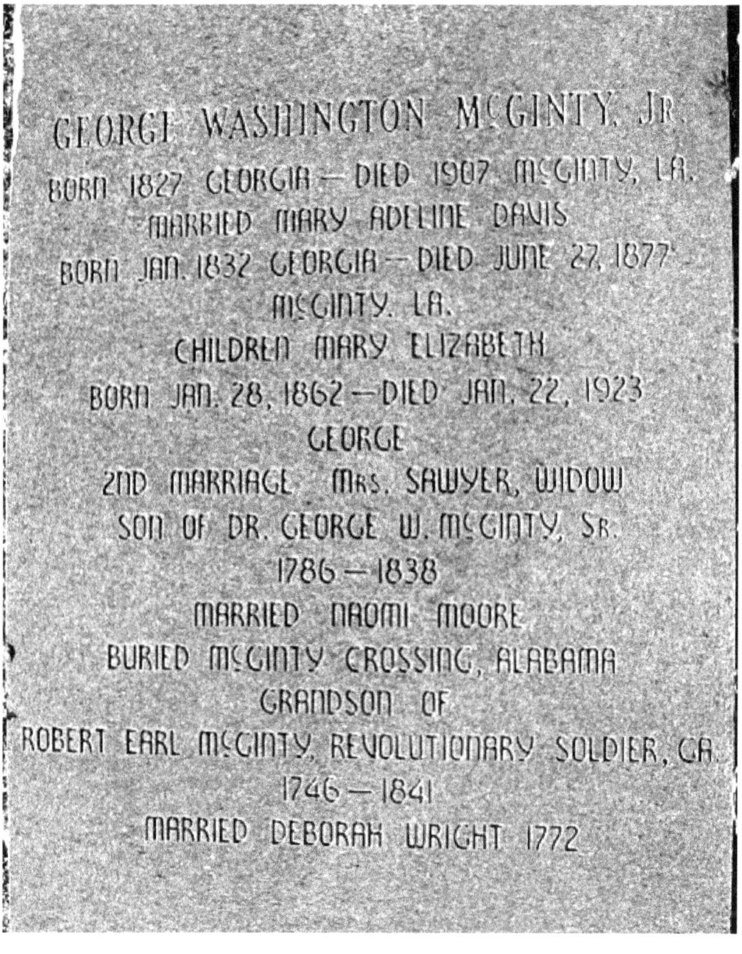

McGinty Cemetery, Morehouse Parish, LA

Elizabeth S. McGinty, b. 1830 in GA, (confirmed by the 1850 census), d. unknown, but probably before 1852. She married Benjamin Franklin Carpenter (son of Jesse Carpenter) July 2, 1850, in Chambers Co. AL, by John W. Chambers, JP. This marriage is recorded in Chambers Co. marriage book 4, pg. 259. Her father, Washington McGinty, is shown as giving his consent. She shows as Carpenter's wife in the 1850 census of Chambers Co. at age twenty. Apparently, she died and Carpenter then married her sister, Elenora Narcissa McGinty in 1852.

"This is to inform you that Francis Carpenter and Elizabeth McGinty intend in uniting in wedlock and that my consent is given. Yours Truly, Washington McGinty."

The State of Alabama, Chambers County
Personally appeared before me, Samuel Pearson, Judge of Probate for the County and State aforesaid. Franklin Carpenter, who being first duly sworn, disposith and saith on oath that Washington McGinty signed the annexed certificate on the day of its date and for the purpose therein named.
Sworn to and subscribed before me,

Samuel Pearson, Judge of the Probate.
Franklin Carpenter (sig)

Where upon the following license was issued:

The State of Alabama, Chambers County.
To any ordained Minister of the Gospel, Judge of the County Court or Circuit Court Judge or Justice of the Peace in and for the said County – Greetings.

You are hearby authorized to celebrate the Rite of Matrimony between Franklin Carpenter and Elizabeth S. McGinty, and this shall be your sufficient authority for so doing.
Given under my hand and seal this 29th day of June, A.D. one thousand eight hundred and fifty and of American Independence, the 75th year.

Samuel Pearson, Judge of Probate

I certify that I celebrated the Rites of Matrimony between Franklin Carpenter and Elizabeth S. McGinty on the 2nd day of July, A.D. 1850

John W. Chambers, J.P.

Marriage of Elizabeth and Benjamin F. Carpenter, 1850

Elenora Narcissa McGinty, b. 1831 in Pike Co., GA, when her father was then living near Barnesville, GA (confirmed by the 1850 census and CSA pension records), d. January 15, 1909, in Troup Co., GA. After moving to Chambers Co., she shows in these church records: "Saturday, the 22nd July 1848. The Primitive Baptist church at Ephesus in conference. Brother T. Freeman, moderator. Opened the door of the church for the reception of members. Miss Narcissa McGinty related her experience and was received in the fellowship of the church."

She married Benjamin Franklin Carpenter, in Chambers Co., March 5, 1852. The pastor was W. D. Harrington, M.G., who was the brother of her stepmother Elizabeth Harrington. The original consent letter from her father reads as follows: "To the legal authority of said county you are hear by notified that Franklin Carpenter and Elenora Narcissa McGinty hath entered into a covenant of matrimony and that I have no objection to their union. The said E.N. McGinty is my daughter. Yours truly, Washington McGinty, March the 3rd 1852." Her husband went by the name of Frank or sometimes Franklin. He was born in NC in 1828 and came to Chambers Co. with his parents when he was about twenty years old. Franklin and Narcissa later moved to LA where Franklin was occupied as an overseer. It is possible that he was employed by Richard King who was a large landowner and farmer. Franklin's home is shown next door to King in the 1860 LA census. This census of Caldwell Parish, LA confirms Franklin, age thirty, occupation, overseer. Narcissa is shown with him, age twenty-two, along with children, N. Elizabeth age five and William, age one. Franklin Carpenter enlisted in Co. K, 37th AL Inf. Reg., May 1, 1862, which was organized at Auburn, AL. His brother, Mahone, also served in this unit and survived the war. Franklin died July 4, 1862, in Columbus, MS from an infection in his leg while on picket duty (National Archives, M374, roll 8). Narcissa filed claim for regress on August 7, 1862. His death was not verified until July 26, 1864.

Their other children were Benjamin Franklin Jr. (b. May 1860 in LA, as shown in the 1880 and 1900 Chambers Co. census. However, the 1920 and 1930 census of Muscogee Co., GA show that he was born in 1863) and Gilbert "Gill" Washington Gilmore (b. November 1, 1862, d. July 5, 1913). In the 1870 census of Pulaski Co., GA, pg. 96, both of these boys are living in the home of Benjamin Franklin McGinty, a mill owner, and the uncle of their mother. They are both buried at the Hillview cemetery annex, LaGrange, GA.

Franklin died before his father, Jesse Carpenter. The petition for the settlement of Jesse's estate names Franklin's wife, Narcissa and her children as heirs (Pike Co., AL, general estate book 14, pg. 228-269). It reads as follows: "August 3, 1869. The heirs of Franklin Carpenter, deceased, to wit Narcissa Carpenter, widow of said Franklin and over the age of twenty-one and residing in Chambers Co., AL – her four minor children, Elizabeth, over fourteen years of age, William under fourteen years of age, Benjamin under fourteen years of age and George W. Carpenter under fourteen years of age residing with their said mother Narcissa Carpenter."

In 1870 Narcissa, age thirty-eight, was back in Chambers Co., AL, living in the home of her father, George Washington McGinty who was eighty-four at the time. Her daughter, Elizabeth, age fifteen and son William, age eleven, were living with her. I do not know why Benjamin Jr. is not also listed here.

The 1880 census is very interesting because Narcissa is listed twice. The first entry shows Narcissa Carpenter, age forty-seven with son, William, age twenty, both living in the home of her other son, Gilbert "Gill" and his wife, Sarah. The second entry shows Elenora N. Carpenter, age forty-eight with son William, age twenty-one (working in a cotton mill). It is in this census that we first see the birthplace of her mother, Naomi as being in Illinois.

By 1888 Narcissa was living in Troup Co., GA. She filed for and received a lifetime confederate widow's pension beginning in 1891. After her death in 1909 her grandson, Olin Adams, applied for her burial benefits of $60. It is unknown at this time where she is buried.

Doriann D. McGinty, b. 24 November 1833, in GA, (confirmed by the 1850 Chambers Co., AL and 1900 Parker Co., TX census and her gravestone), d., 5 May 1906, Hooker, Texas Co., OK. She married, (1) James Sterling Howard in Chambers Co., November 22, 1849. Jesse Carpenter, J.P., performed the marriage (marriage book 4, pg. 179/180). The original consent letter from her father reads as follows (next page):

Doriann and James Howard marriage,
permission from her father

Alabama, Chambers County, Nov 21 – 1849.
To Mr. Samuel Pearson or the legal authority, you are hereby informed that
James Howard and Doriann D. McGinty has agreed to unite in weedlock
[sic] and my consent given to the same said. D.D. McGinty is my daughter.
Your compliance will oblige your servant.

Washington McGinty

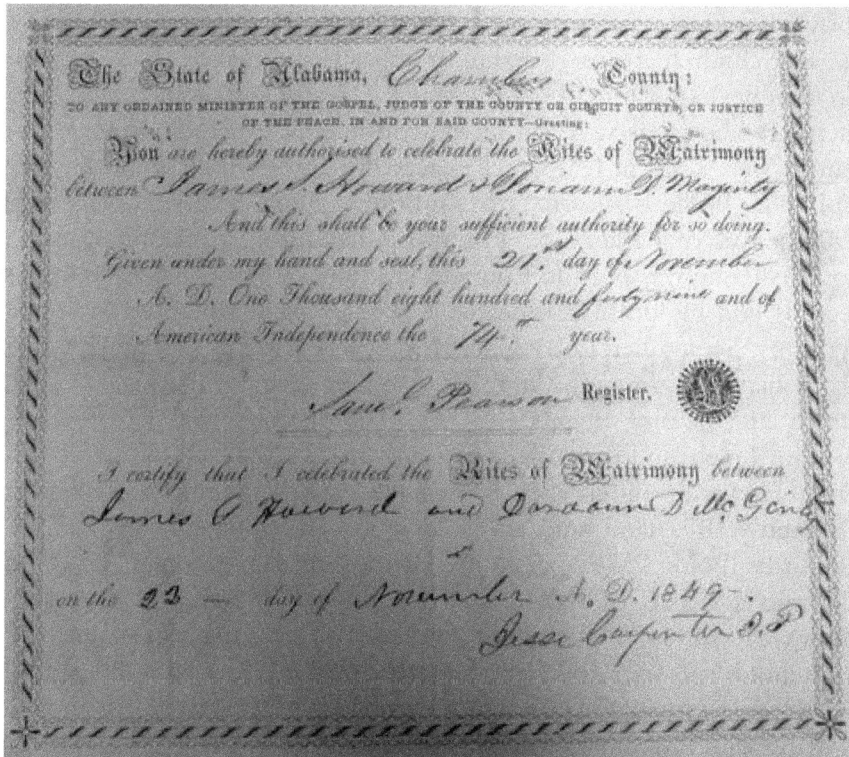

Doriann and James Howard
Marriage License

They show in the 1850 census of Chambers Co., pg. 367, James age looks like twenty-three and Dora, age sixteen. They are living next door to Franklin Carpenter and his wife Elisabeth who was Dora's sister. The special census of 1855 shows them living next door to her father, Washington McGinty, with two children under the age of twenty-one. Her obituary says that she joined the Chambers Co. church in 1866. They moved to LA and by 1869 were in AR. They do not show in the 1870 census. Howard died in 1873 (based on her obituary, place unknown) and she returned to AL. She is shown in a document dated 1874 as an heir to her father's estate. There is a Lee Co. deed dated May 20, 1879, showing her purchasing a ½ acre lot (#36) from the Ingersoll family. Ingersoll was a big land holder in the area and subdivided some of his land into smaller parcels for the mill workers. She then shows in the 1880 census of Lee Co., AL, pg. 231B, as head of household, age forty-six, widow. Occupation: "keeping house."

Her children are also listed in this census as Amanda L., 20, Frances E. "Fannie," 18, Emma L., 17, Willie A., 15 and Benjamin F., 12. All of them are shown as working in the cotton mill. Amanda, Frances and Emma were born in LA, which places the parents there between 1861 and 1863. Willie is shown as being born in 1865 in GA, however, the 1900 census of Parker Co., TX, shows her born in July 1865, in LA. Son Benjamin was born in Emmet, AR, July 5, 1869 (1900-1930 census records and his death certificate). Daughter Emma married James M. Williams, September 1, 1881, in Muskogee Co., GA. Doriann married (2) William E. Hughes, March 27, 1883, in Brownville, Lee Co., AL, which later became Phenix City, AL. The marriage was performed by William Lively and the marriage license reads, "Married by me at Mrs. Dora Howard's (house in), Brownville." They continued to live on Doriann's 1879 land, and she sold it in a deed dated 1889 to L.W. Edwards (book A-10, pg. 468). Hughes died September 19, 1895. Doriann and part of her family then moved to Agnes, TX and she shows in the 1900 census of Parker Co., pg. 141 A, as head-of-household, age sixty-six. Her son, Benjamin F. Howard is living with her. Her daughter, Willie A., who married Frank Boland in AR in 1890 is living with them in a rented house. Benjamin F. is then found in the 1910-1930 censuses living with wife, Emma and family in Texas Co., OK. Willie is found with Frank in the 1910 census of Pushmataha Co., OK. Frances "Fannie," married Dempsey Allen Jeffus, January 2, 1898, and shows with him in the 1900 census of Parker Co., TX. She died in 1933 and I have her death certificate. It is interesting to note that in this 1900 census, Doriann shows that her mother was born in SC. While it is true that her father married Elizabeth Northrop, who was from SC, in 1838 her actual mother (according to two of her brothers and sisters) was Naomi Elvira, born in Illinois. In the 1900 census, Doriann shows that she had eight children and that six were surviving at the time of the census. Only six of her children have been identified and they were all born after 1860. A son, Augustus lived in Nevada Co., AR and was married there in 1871. Since she married Howard in 1849 the other three children were born to them before 1860. The 1855 special census of AL shows them with two children under the age of twenty-one. This accounts for two of them and the third must have been born between 1855 and 1860. Their names are as yet unknown. Dora is buried in block 1, lot 24, at the Hooker Cemetery, Hooker, Texas Co., OK. Her gravestone reads, "Our Mother at Rest."

Hooker Cemetery, Hooker, Oklahoma
Photo courtesy of Linda Holbert

Her obituary, written by Rev. John J. Willis and published in the *Hooker Advance*, May 11, 1906, page five, reads as follows:

Taken to her Reward

Mrs. D. A. Hughes of Fernwood, this county, died Saturday, May 5, 1906, at her home. Mrs. Hughes was married to J. S. Howard in 1849: he died in 1873. She was again married to W. E. Hughes, who died Sept. 19, 1895. She was the mother of eight children, five girls and three boys, five of whom are still living to mourn the departure of a loving mother. She was for many years a living example of the faith she professed in Christ, having united with the Missionary Baptist church in Chambers county, Alabama in the year of 1866, and has ever since lived the life of a child redeemed from sin: her life's work was for the betterment of humanity and praising God. She came to Beaver County the 29th day of November, 1905, and built a home near Fernwood, this county, with hopes of the success of the future of this country. She passed away in the presence of two of her children and a host of loving friends on Saturday night, May 5, 1906, and was therefore 72 years, 5 months and 12 days old. She was interred in the Hooker Cemetery on Monday, May 7th, at 3 p. m.; the funeral services were conducted by the writer (lesson, 9th psalm-text, Job 14-14) at the cemetery, with a few friends and relatives present.

> *She was old, she passed the line*
> *Of years three score and ten.*
> *She was true and kept in mind*
> *that life on earth would end.*
> *Prepared she waited for the summons,*
> *come!*
> *To meet her God above*
> *In that, the bright celestial home,*
> *Where god and all are perfect love.*

Here are the children of George Washington McGinty and Elizabeth C. Harrington Northrop (b. February 8, 1805, d. April 29, 1891): Elizabeth (Betty or Betsy) was the daughter of Jeptha Harrington, a wealthy citizen in the area. Jeptha was shown with thirty-three slaves in the census of 1840.

Pinckney Harrington McGinty, b. July 6, 1839, Osanippa, Chambers Co., AL, d. January 14, 1918, in Lee Co., AL, according to his death certificate or January 8 according to his gravestone. He married Celia Toland Pitts on September 8, 1860, in Chambers Co., AL, by his uncle, William D. Harrington, MG (marriage book 5, pg. 594). They were married at the residence of her father, William Pitts.

Celia was b. January 2, 1839, in AL and d. February 18, 1915, in AL. They are both buried in the Beulah Baptist Cemetery, Lee Co., AL. They produced six children, Permelia Elizabeth, b. 1861, James Thaddeus, b. 1866 William Washington, b. 1871, Nannie E., b. ca. 1873, Oscar Lee, b. 1874 and John Luther, b. 1877 (Lee Co., AL was formed from Chambers and other adjoining counties, December 5, 1866, and was named for Gen. Robert E. Lee).

On Pinckney Harrington McGinty and the 14th AL Infantry: Pinckney or "Uncle Pink" as his nephews and nieces called him was one of three McGintys that enlisted as a private in Co. A of the 14th AL Volunteer Infantry Regiment.

Pinckney H. McGinty

His enlistment date is shown as April 7, 1862, in Yorktown, VA. This date is after the 14th had already moved to VA. It is possible that he actually enlisted at an earlier date with the other two McGinty boys, and that the date of April 7, 1862, is actually the date when the 14th AL was accepted into the Confederate army. At this time, his uncle Capt. William Darwin Harrington was the commanding officer of Co. A. He had been commissioned May 9, 1861. Capt. Harrington was the son of Jeptha Harrington and the brother of Elizabeth Harrington McGinty, wife of Pinckney's father, George Washington McGinty. Capt. Harrington resigned from the unit on August 2, 1862, for reason unknown. The Harrington family came to Chambers Co. in 1836 and joined the Bethlehem Baptist church. William Harrington, a minister, was ordained there in 1839 and served several churches in the area, both before and after the war. He died June 17, 1871, at age fifty-one. This regiment was known as the "Cusseta Grays"; named for Cusseta, AL (pronounced Cu-seet-a) which is the district where he lived in the 1860 census. Before the war, he had probably inherited his father's rather large farming operation and shows real estate worth $2,500 and a personal estate of $10,000.

The 14th AL infantry regiment, in which Pinckney, James and Joshua McGinty were members, was organized at Auburn, AL in 1861. It was raised under the call of the Confederacy for volunteers to serve three years or for the duration of the war. The unit was ordered to Richmond, VA, in October 1861. From there, they moved to Evansport, VA, where the real service began. In January 1862 the unit was transferred back to Richmond to recover from health problems described as "camp sickness." Then in March 1862 orders were received to move to Yorktown.

They fought with distinction at Williamsburg, May 5, 1862. At Seven Pines and during the seven-day fight with McClellan before Richmond, the company suffered severely in killed and wounded. At the opening of the seven-day fight at the end of June 1862 the company had forty-seven men for duty. During the seven-day fight, the surgeon sent eight men to the hospital. Thirty-eight were killed or wounded, leaving only one man, W. A. Prather, to answer roll call. The company went from this fight and through the battles of Second Manassas, Sharpesburg and Booneboro without any commissioned officers.

In 1863 the company was in all the important battles of the Army of Northern Virginia. It was part of the small force that fought at Salem Church, driving General Sedgewick across the river, and preventing his flank movement towards Richmond. At Gettysburg and Deep Mine,

Co. A did its part. During the fall of 1864 and into 1865 until the retreat from Petersburg, the company fought daily. In January and February 1865 the company was in several engagements on the right of Lee's army. The duties from January till the surrender at Appomattox were very difficult and said to "try men's constitutions as well as their souls." At Appomattox, Company "A" surrendered her arms and afterward took the oath of allegiance to the country. *[This from the records of Stephen Hodge, 3rd Sergeant. Elected to 1st Lieutenant, October 8, 1862, and promoted to Captain, June 2, 1864. He was still living in AL in 1901].*

It is interesting to note that James Judge Havis was elected 1st Lt. in Co. A. He was one of the builders of the Riverdale mill in River View after the war in 1866 and his name shows on the cornerstone. Havis was postmaster at Oakbowery, AL in 1858 and owned a store there. He was also a surveyor in 1840 and built a home near McGinty Crossroads.

Pinckney was captured April 6, 1865, near High Springs, VA, as Lee's army retreated from Petersburg and was imprisoned in Newport News, VA. He was released July 2, 1865. According to his personal statement, he participated in twenty-one battles from Yorktown to the siege of Petersburg. He also claimed to have taken care of Robert E. Lee's horse, Traveler, at some point during the war. The 14th AL was always near to Lee, and he is said to have been very fond of his "Alabama Boys." As long as Pinckney lived, he kept a framed picture of Lee's horse near him. After Lee died in 1870 Traveler was taken on tour through the South for the veterans to gaze at once more. Pinckney told many "war stories" to his family. He would laugh and say "how we made those Yankees run with our Rebel Yell." His records are in the National Archives (M374, roll 30).

The Lee Co. courthouse records show this entry for CSA veterans living in the county on 1907, "#132. Pinckney H. McGinty, Cusseta, AL. RD 1 b. July 6, 1839, near Langdale, (Chambers Co) AL. Private on April 7, 1862 at Yorktown, VA in Co A, 14 AL Regt until April 6, 1865. Captured near High Bridge, VA. Carried to prison at New Port News, VA and released July 2, 1865. Participated in 21 battles from Yorktown to wind up outside the siege of Petersburg."

It is interesting to note that, according to war records in the National Archives, there were over fifty McGinty men who fought in the Civil War, both for the North and the South. By 1860 there were

McGintys located in many parts of the country.

Pinckney joined the Beulah Baptist Church in Beulah, AL, July 19, 1873, "by letter." There is a deed showing his purchase of land from W.J.H. Carlton on April 4, 1874, *Chambers Co. Deed Book 8, page 311.* Pinckney was also a dentist after the war and had an office with a "barber pole" which identified a dentist office at this time. This occupation is confirmed by his obituary in the January 9, 1918, issue of *The LaFayette Sun*: "News was received here yesterday afternoon of the death of Dr. P. H. McGinty, which occurred at his home near Beulah yesterday morning. The funeral will be held at the home today and the remains interred in the Beulah Cemetery. Dr. McGinty was the father of Mrs. Sam Newman of Rock Springs," Wife Celia's obituary in the *Opelika News*, February 19, 1915, also confirms his occupation, where she is shown as Mrs. Dr. P. H. McGinty.

On July 1, 1911, at age seventy-two, Pinckney made an application for Relief of Confederate Soldiers under the act of the AL general assembly passed April 24, 1911. The application claims that he was wounded at Yorktown and at the Second Battle of Manassas and that he was unable to make a living because of age and infirmities. On his application, he shows ownership of 70½ acres of land and personal property worth $397. Family history says that he died at the home of son, Oscar Lee McGinty in Opelika, AL, which is probably correct because the attending physician shown on his death certificate, Dr. Haralson, is shown as being from Cusseta, AL. Cause of death was pneumonia.

OPELIKA, ALA. NEWS
PINKNEY H. MCGINTY
TUESDAY—JAN—8—1918

News was received here this morning of the death at the home of his son, O. L. McGinty in Beat 13, of P. H. McGinty, aged 79 years.

Mr. McGinty had ben ill several weeks and his death is ascribed as the result of rheuamtism and natural causes. He was born in Chambers county July 6, 1839, but had lived most of his life in the Beat 13 community. In 1860 he was married to Miss Cella Tolen Pitts. The deceased was a prominent farmer and was well known in Masonic circles. He was a member of the Missionary Baptist church.

Mr. McGinty is survived by two daughters, Mrs. W. S. Newman of LaFayette, and Mrs. J. A. Bledsoe of Pine Hill, Ala., and three sons, O. J. McGinty and W. W. McGinty of Beat 13, and J. L. McGinty of Beulah.

The funeral service will be held tomorrow, January 9, at the Beulah Baptist church and will be conducted by Rev. Cobbld. Interment in Beulah cemetery.

Pinckney McGinty Obituary

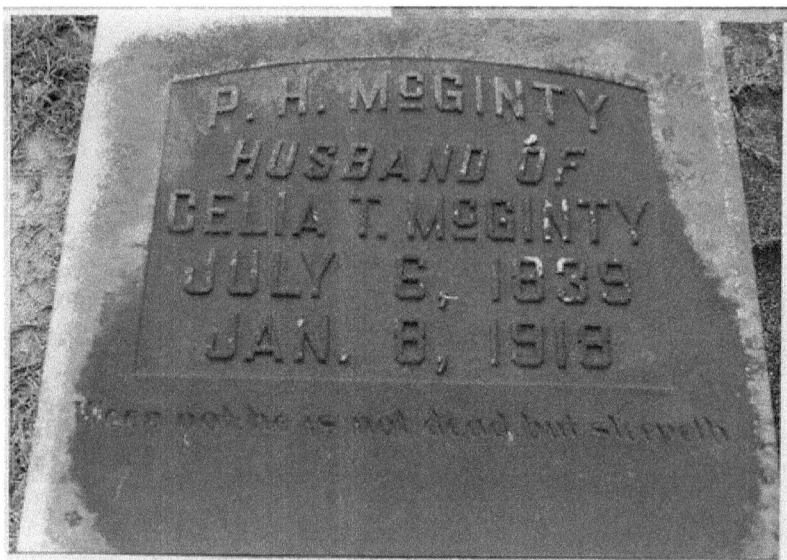

Beulah Baptist Church, Beulah, Lee Co., AL

James B. McGinty, b. 1841, Osanippa District, Chambers Co., AL, d. May 15, 1862, in Richmond, VA. James enlisted as a private in Co. A of the 14 AL Volunteer Infantry Regiment on September 9, 1861. He was twenty years old. James was admitted to Chimborazo Hospital No. 3 in Richmond, VA, May 10, 1862, with "remittent fever" (malaria). He died five days later. (*His military records are in the National Archives, M374, roll 30*).

Missouri Artimissie "Adnie" McGinty, b. May 18, 1845 (confirmed in the 1880 and 1900 census), Osanippa, Chambers Co., AL, d. February 22, 1907, (confirmed by her gravestone). She first married a Foster, after 1860 and before 1866. He could have died in the war. She then married Bluford Washington Webb, January 22, 1867. The 1850 Chambers Co. census shows him at age three. The 1860 census of Chambers Co. (pg. 41) shows him as age twelve. However, the 1870 Chambers Co. census (pg. 55) shows that he was born in 1850. This is confirmed again in the 1880 and 1900 census of Beulah, Lee Co., AL (sheet 1) which shows his birth date as July 1850. If he was born in 1850 he was only seventeen when he married twenty-two year old Missouri. He was the brother of John Andrew Jackson Webb who

142

married Missouri's sister, Salina. The Webb family had come to AL from Harris Co., GA. The 1870 census shows them living in Beat 1, Chambers Co. (pg. 55). He is shown at age twenty and she at age twenty-five. They had one child. The 1880 census shows them living in Beulah, Lee Co. with four children, Mary, Alonzo, Ada and Pinckney. The 1900 census of Lee Co. shows three children, Pink, John L. and Willie. It shows that there were a total of seven children and that six were still living. Bluford is listed as a farmer in both censuses. Page 59/60 of the Chambers Co., AL marriage book shows the marriage of B.W. Webb to (Mrs.) Missouri A. Foster, January 22, 1867, by David Williams, JP. She would have been twenty-two at the time. Based on this Foster name, she would have been a widow when Webb married her. She is buried in the Beulah Baptist Church cemetery, Beulah, AL.

Buried at Beulah Baptist Church, Beulah, Lee Co., AL

No record has been found showing when and where Bluford died and is buried. After Missouri's death, Bluford married (Mrs.) Minnie Griffin James, 27 Jun 1908, in Troup Co., GA.

Salina Ann McGinty, **"Lynie,"** b. May 8, 1848, Osanippa, Chambers Co., AL, d. March 21, 1932, (confirmed by her gravestone and death certificate) in Camp Hill, AL. She married John Andrew Jackson Webb (1844-1917), March 7, 1867, in Lee Co., AL, by William E. Hudmon, JP. They produced seven children, John James (1871), Nancy Elizabeth (1876), Dora Bell (1878), Robert Grady (1881), Annie Missouria (1884), Frona Adeline (1889) and Emily (1891). After John's death, Salina applied for his Civil War widow's pension. John Webb was the brother of Bluford Webb who married Salina's sister, Missouri. Both couples were married within three month of each other in 1867.

Salina McGinty

**Salina Ann McGinty and John Webb
Grandchildren, Lila on R and Ruby on L
Photo courtesy of Penny P. Sorrell**

Salina (pronounced "Sa-Line-ey") married John Andrew Jackson Webb, a Confederate Army veteran. After the war, they were married in her father Washington's home and settled down to farming and raising a family in Chambers Co., AL. When Salina was a young girl living in her father's house, she had a personal slave. After she was married she said that, "she was her own slave." She was a fun-loving girl and once got "churched" or censored by the church for buck dancing, which she loved to do. After she and her sister apologized, they were forgiven. They had a bad crop one-year and John A. almost lost the farm. He put all of his children to work in the Langdale cotton mill. When they got the bills paid off, they all quit and went back to the farm. Later in her life, when Salina was a grandmother, she lived with daughter, Emily.

She did the cooking for the family. One night she made green beans for supper. Everyone thought that they were the best green beans they had ever tasted. Later in the evening, Salina was missing a dishrag and it was found at the bottom of the pot that the beans had been cooked in. They never let Granny cook again! This information is from an interview with her granddaughter, Birdie Lumkin Sorrell in 1999. The 1900 AL census shows her living in the Beulah, AL area with four children. It also shows that of their seven children, one had already died. The 1930 census of Chambers Co., precinct 13, page 36 B, shows her living in the household of her son, Grady Webb. She died at age eighty-four in Tallapoosa Co., AL. Salina and John are buried together at the Pentecost Methodist Church cemetery, in Reeltown, AL. John had passed away October 15, 1917, at age seventy-three. Salina's mother, Elizabeth Harrington McGinty, age seventy-five, was living with John and Salina in the 1880 census.

Salina Ann McGinty and John Webb
Pentecost Methodist Church, Reeltown, AL
Photo courtesy of Penny P. Sorrell

Note: Naomi Elvira, possible wife of Washington, does not show by name on any known records that directly link her to Washington. She could have been related to Tabitha Moore. The 1880 census records of two children, George Washington, Jr. and Narcissa say that she was born in Illinois. It is interesting to note that one of the children by this possible wife was named Naomi Elvira McGinty. Was she named for her mother? Also, as mentioned before, her step-grandson, Wiley P. McGinty Sr., (1865-1957) said that his step-grandmother, was named Naomi Elvira McGinty. It is also possible that Naomi was not a Moore and was from another family.

The Life of George Washington McGinty

He was known as "Washington," the sixth son of Robert McGinty and Deborah Jackson. The first written record is his baptism on August 31, 1805, at the Island Creek Baptist church in Hancock Co. An article published in the *Farmer's Gazette*, vol. IV, no. 198, Saturday, August 29, 1807, Sparta, GA. shows the presentations by the Grand Jury of Hancock Co., where they list "all public wrongs which have transpired within our knowledge in our County....." Washington is shown with several other people as retailing spirituous liquors without a license. On November 26, 1808, at age twenty-one or twenty-two, he was issued a passport by the Governor of GA to travel through the Creek Indian nation. His father, Rev. Robert McGinty was also issued a passport for the same purpose in 1810 (*Passports Issued by Governors of Georgia, 1785-1809*, by Mary G. Bryan). By this time his father, Robert was very active in forming various Baptist churches and other association work in GA and traveled on a regular basis. It is probable that Washington accompanied him on occasion.

Washington's first marriage license was with Nancy Thompson. On October 26, 1810, this license (Bann) was issued in Hancock Co., GA for Washington to marry Nancy (*Colonial Georgia Marriage Records*, and FHL microfilm #222074, pg. 18).

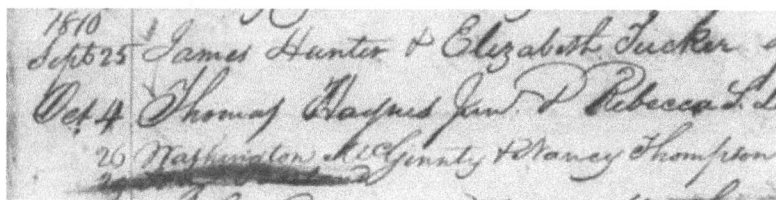

**Washington and Nancy Thompson,
Hancock Co. Marriage Book, pg. 18**

However, no record has yet been found showing the actual marriage. Also, on September 1, 1810, the minutes of the Island Creek Baptist Church have an entry showing that "application was made by Brother Washington McGinty for a letter for Sister Nancy," and that it was granted (FHL microfilm #0220537). Also of note is that the pastor of this church was a Benjamin Thompson, who was probably the father or possibly brother of Nancy. Something happened to Nancy prior to 1813. There is no record of them having children. The tax list of 1810 shows him owning property in Baldwin Co.

The *Georgia Journal* of December 9, 1812, shows that a new division of GA Militia was formed which included men from several counties. Washington is listed as a drafted member.

He married Tabitha Moore, daughter of Ephraim Moore Sr., and his wife, Nancy (last name unknown) on August 12, 1813, in Baldwin Co., GA. Tabitha was born, ca. 1795-97 (for her to be at least sixteen she would have had to be born before 1797), exact location unknown. Her grandfather was Isaac Moore who was from Somerset Co., MD and died there ca. 1788. Tabitha shows in the 1820 census and must have died shortly thereafter, ca. 1821 in GA. He is shown in the 1813 Baldwin Co., tax list as living in Capt. Thomas' District.

**Washington and Tabitha Marriage,
Baldwin Co. Marriage Book, pg. 326-327**

A lifelong Baptist, Washington was often at odds with fellow church members. In 1812 a difficulty arose with Pastor Benjamin Thompson. Washington asked that the Island Creek Church assist in resolving the problem and the church minutes reflect that it led to disagreement with the Bethel Church and that it had to be finally resolved by the Georgia Association. It seems that Washington owned a slave named Fanny and her child named Ambrose. The slaves supposedly ran away from Washington and went to the home of Benjamin Thompson. Thompson refused to return them. After filing a lawsuit against Thompson, Washington was successful and the slaves were apparently returned. His father, Rev. Robert McGinty also got involved in this dispute with the Bethel Church and was accused of several things but was later acquitted. The June 25, 1814, minutes of Island Creek Baptist Church in Hancock Co., GA (reel 303, Tarver Library, Mercer Univ., Macon, GA), show that Washington was investigated for "drunkingnes [sic], swearing and a neglect of attending to the church." He was thought to be ripe for excommunication, which was accordingly done without a decanting vote. Over two years later, on August 10, 1816, he was restored to membership having "admitted the correctness of the charges" for his expulsion.

On January 11, 1817, he requested and was granted dismissal from Island Creek by letter and joined the Ramah Primitive Baptist Church in Wilkinson Co., GA. Both he and Tabitha show on the membership roll. The Ramah Church was founded in 1809. Like other Baptist churches of the day, Ramah was involved in the dispute over Indian reform, missions and the encouragement to abolish slavery. When the church separated over these issues, Ramah became associated with the newly formed denomination, the Primitive Baptist. Thomas McGinty, (b. September 29, 1784), brother of Washington, is listed as one of the founders. I visited this church in January 2002. It is located on Hwy 57, two tenths of a mile east of the intersection with Hwy 18.

In 1818 at the age of thirty-two, Washington was activated to serve in the Seminole Indian War in FL for six months. He served in the Company commanded by Capt. David Childs (confirmed on his Bounty Land Application). There were actually three Seminole wars, and he served in the first one. It was short, beginning in December 1817 when Gen. Andrew Jackson received orders to move into the area of Spanish-owned FL where fierce Seminole Indians, some discontented Creek (referred to as Red Stick Creeks) and groups of escaped slaves and vagabonds had been raiding settlements north of the FL/GA border. Jackson's army of backwoodsmen fighters, which included Washington, pursued them into northwest FL all the way to Pensacola. The war was over in 1818. Washington served for fourteen days and was honorably discharged on April 7, 1818, at Irwinton, GA.

On November 11, 1850, when he was sixty-four years old, he made a declaration for the purpose of obtaining Bounty Land under a recent "Act Granting Bounty Land to certain Officers and Soldiers who have been engaged in military service of the United States," passed on September 28, 1850. He received the above forty acres Bounty Warrant.

On October 27, 1855, at age sixty-nine, he applied for additional bounty land under the act approved on March 3, 1855. He was granted an additional 120 acres for a total of 160 acres. He never exercised this warrant and actually owned the property. In this application, he says that he is sixty-nine years old. If correct, he was born in 1786.

He is shown on the 1820 census in Wilkinson Co., GA, along with his father and several of his brothers (pg. 392-393). There are three males under ten, sons Franklin, Robert A. (slight discrepancy here because later in life, Robert shows as being born in 1821), and William Pitts, and one male between twenty-six and forty-five, which is him. There is one female under ten, daughter Nancy, and one female sixteen to twenty-six, his second wife, Tabitha. There are two people listed as engaged in agriculture. The GA land lottery of 1821 shows him living in Wilkinson Co., GA in Brooks' military district. He drew land in Henry Co., GA. and between 1822 and 1823 he relocated his family to the new Pike Co., GA.

Pike Co. was formed December 9, 1822. Washington is shown in *The History of Pike County, 1822-1932* by Lizzie Mitchell, as a member of the first Pike Co. grand jury in September 1823. On June 5, 1824, he purchased 202½ acres in Pike Co. from Philip Pittman for $150. This was lot 14 in district 7 (Pike Co. mortgages, vol. G, pg. 364, GA Archives, Atlanta). This parcel of land originated in the land lottery of 1821 when it was part of Monroe Co. The minutes of the Flint River Baptist Assn., show that he was a member of the Antioch Baptist Church in Pike Co., which was constituted, September 13, 1823. Records show that this church was located six miles south of Barnesville. The 1824 Flint River Association minutes, (located at the

Tarver library, Mercer Univ., Macon, GA, reel 1081) show that Washington and Andrew Hood (pastor in 1828) were delegates from Antioch to the first meeting where the association was founded at Rocky Creek Meeting House in Monroe Co., GA, October 16-18, 1824.

As we know, his father, Robert McGinty, was a founder of the Ocmulgee Association and still very active in 1824. The Ocmulgee Assn. was the "mother" of the Flint River Assn., and fourteen churches from Ocmulgee, including the New Providence church where his father was pastor, along with six new churches composed the original charter. His father, Robert lived close by, south of Forsyth in Monroe Co. Washington and his father, Robert were both present at this initial meeting. Washington, along with Andrew Hood, is also shown as messenger to the Ocmulgee annual meeting at the Murder Creek Meeting House, Sept. 4-7, 1824, where plans were made to form the new Flint River Assn. On December 15, 1824, Upson Co. was formed from this portion of Pike Co. Later church records show Antioch in Upson Co. Washington, along with William R. Moore, show as the delegates from Antioch to the Flint River Assn. Meeting, October 15-18, 1825. The 1826 association minutes are missing. In 1827-1828 Antioch was still part of the association but the Flint River Assn. minutes of October 1828 show that a new association was to be formed, the Echoconna, which included the Antioch church in Upson Co. This new association was formed in 1829 (Jack Tarver Library, Mercer Univ., reel 1069 and 1081). In 1838 the church, choosing to remain "missionary," joined the Rehoboth Baptist Assn.

It is assumed, but not yet confirmed, that he married Naomi Elvira (possibly Moore), around 1824. Their first child was also named Naomi Elvira. We do know from 1880 census records that her children show that she was born in Illinois.

He shows in the Pike Co. tax list from 1825 thru 1835. He actually lived on the 202½ acres of land in district 7, lot 14. His land in Pike Co. was near current Barnesville, GA in what is now Lamar Co. (formed in 1920). His oldest daughter, Nancy, met John Means while they lived here and they were married in 1833. She did not go to AL with her father's family. The 1825-27 tax list also shows him owning 202½ acres in Henry Co., district 3, lot 52. This land was obtained by him in the 1821 land lottery. He sold this land to Wm. Lavender on December 11, 1828, for $325. He is shown in the 1830 census, living in Pike Co., GA, along with his father and several brothers (pg. 129-130). In this census, he is shown with five males, including himself at age forty to fifty, four females, including his wife, age twenty to thirty, and two slaves. This wife would have been born between 1800 and 1810 confirming that it was not Tabitha, but wife number three (Naomi Elvira).

On January 9, 1835, after he had relocated to Chambers Co., AL, he sold 100 acres of his land on lot 14, district 7, to his son-in-law, John Means for $200. John Means is shown in the records acting as his agent (Pike Co. mortgages, vol. F, pg. 488, GA Archives, Atlanta). In the tax list of 1835 he also owned 202½ acres in Twiggs Co., district 27, lot 117, 202½ acres in Heard Co., district 11, lot 53 and 40 acres in Cobb Co., district 19, lot 522.

Between 1833 and '34 Washington moved his family to Chambers Co., AL, named for Dr. Henry Chambers, a surgeon and politician. This part of eastern AL now comprised of Chambers, Randolph, Tallapoosa, Lee, Macon and Russell counties was owned and occupied by the Creek Indians up until 1832 and was almost unbroken wilderness. Up until this time, only a few hardy pioneers had ventured into the land occupied by the red men and they had come since AL was admitted to the Union in 1819. On March 24, 1832, at Cusseta, GA (spelled "Cussetaw" at the time) the Indians signed a treaty by which they ceded these lands to the United States. A tide of immigration began to flow into the new territory, now called "New Alabama." This movement began in the spring of 1832 and continued for several years. The government had the land surveyed as rapidly as possible, and it was completed by 1834. When the Alabama General Assembly met in its 1832-33 session, it organized the new counties mentioned above.

Washington was the first McGinty to move into what was called the "New Alabama" territory. According to the census, all of his children who were born in Chambers Co. were born in the Osanippa area, which is just south of today's River View and McGinty. His first cousin, Alexander McGinty, son of John McGinty II, was already in AL having arrived in Perry Co., in 1823. There is also a record of Alexander purchasing 60.27 acres of land in Perry Co. from the federal government under land patent 26397 on May 20, 1837. President Martin Van Buren signed this patent document. Perry Co. was formed and settled before Chambers Co.

The original survey documents on file at the U.S. Bureau of Land Management show the first owners of the Creek lands around River View/McGinty. William Dougherty, a wealthy land speculator and later attorney in Athens, Clarke Co., GA, is shown in numerous land transactions. He and several other speculators gained huge tracts of land at the expense of the Creek chiefs who had been given land for 5 years after the treaty. Dougherty shows in the 1850-1870 census of GA. In the 1840 census, he was living in Troup Co., GA, just across the line from Chambers Co. He became a noted GA attorney and is buried at Oaklawn Cemetery in Atlanta (1805-1872).

On April 28, 1838, Washington married the widow, Elizabeth C. (Betty) Harrington Northrop (born 1805), daughter of Jepta Harrington in Chambers Co., AL. The marriage record shows that they were married, "with the consent of Jepta Harrington, the father of Elizabeth Northrop, a widow." They were married by Samuel Rotch, JP (*Chambers Co. marriage records, book 1, pg. 166*). Jepta was a wealthy citizen and is shown as owning thirty-three slaves in the 1840 Chambers Co., AL, census. Elizabeth's former husband was Amos Northrop, and they had been married ca. 1832. The Harrington family was from Union Co., SC, and was one of the earliest settlers, having arrived in Chambers Co. in 1836. The 1830 census of Union Co., SC (pg. 211) shows Jeptethah (sp?) Harrington's family and next to him is listed Amos Northrop with two males including himself, age bracket 20-40, and three females including his wife, in age bracket 20-30.

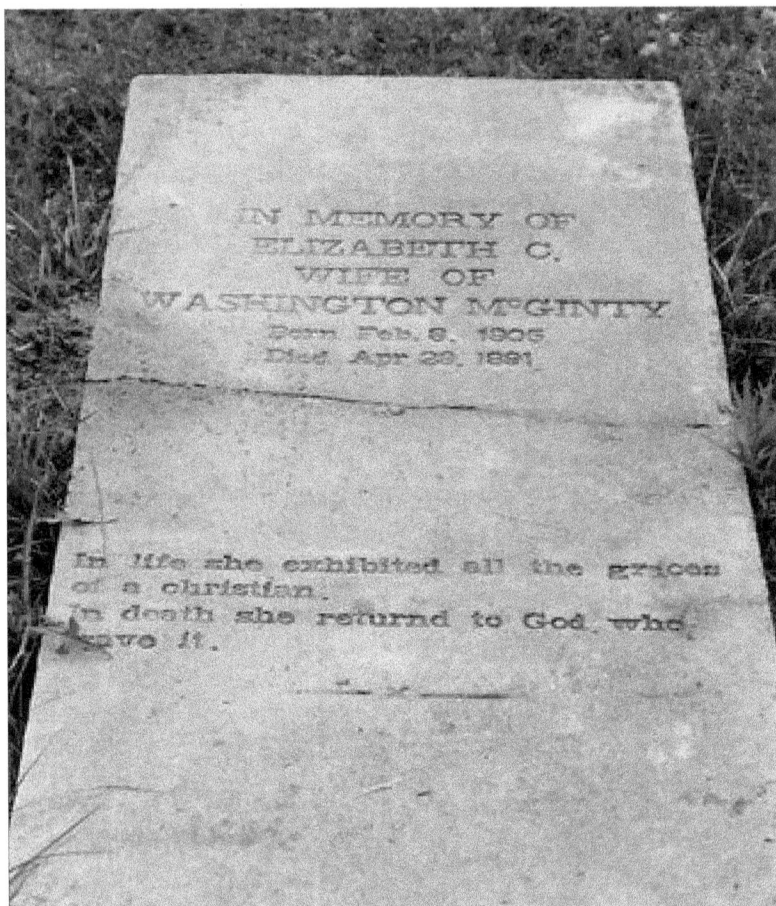

Elizabeth Harrington McGinty
Beulah Baptist Church, Beulah, Lee Co., AL

A successful planter, Washington is shown in the 1840 census in Chambers Co., AL, with seven white males and nine white females in his household along with ten slaves (pg. 190). Levin Moore and Jeptha Harrington are shown on the same census page. He was not the biological father of some of these children because there are too many. Some might have come to the marriage with his fourth wife, or there were other circumstances. A letter written by his grandson, John Franklin McGinty in 1930 and published in *A Twig of the McGinty Family Tree* by Garnie McGinty, says that Washington was married four times and also that he was a "cancer doctor of some fame, and very successful in the treatment of that disease." In those days, a person might be a self appointed "doctor or dentist" without formal training.

The Chambers Co. tax book dated 1842 which is located at the AL Archives in Montgomery, shows him with 160 acres of class three land located in Beat 8, Bluffton/Lanett (pg. 73), and three slaves over ten years old. Bluffton was the name for Lanett before it was incorporated.

Chambers Co. deed book 6, pg. 125 shows a purchase of 80 acres by Washington and James A. Cherry on July 10, 1843. This land was in the current Langdale area. It was purchased from the estate of Joseph Neil (last name difficult to read) and was the east ½ of the southwest ¼ of Section 18, Township 21, Range 29.

On August 21, 1846, Washington is listed as a charter member of the Ephesus Primitive Baptist Church. In 1850 the Ephesus Church records show that Washington was charged with accusing Tyre Freeman and Levin Moore, commissioners of the township school fund, of dealing unjustly with him in the distribution of school funds. After "laboring with him according to the order of the Gospel," the church excommunicated Washington for refusing to give satisfaction.

Washington is shown on the 1850 census of Chambers Co., AL as a sixty-three year old farmer with wife, Elizabeth, age forty-five (born in S.C.), Narcissa E., 19 (born in GA); Pinckney, 10, James, 8, Missoura A., 6, and Salina A., 2. His real value is shown as $2,000 and he owned six slaves (1850 census of slave inhabitants, pg. 501).

He is shown as a patron for the school year 1849/50 in Twsp. 21, Range 29. Also listed as patrons are Levin Moore, Tyre Freeman, Jesse Carpenter, Samuel Rotch and Holly Weaver.

In March of 1853 a document shows that Washington sold some land in Berlin, Chambers Co., AL area to Brokaw and Clemmens for $500. He shows in the special Chambers Co. state census of 1855 with a total household of six whites and one slave. He is shown again in the 1860 census as a farmer at age seventy-four, living with wife Elizabeth, age fifty-six, and four children, Pinckney, 21; James, 19; Missouri, 16; and Salina, 12. He owned two female slaves, age 47 and 30 (slave schedule, pg. 18) and his worth is shown as $1,500. Of note, his neighbors were the Holly Weaver family. One of the Weaver daughters, Oliver, married his grandson, James Madison McGinty.

The Chambers Co. agricultural censuses of both 1850 and 1860 give a complete record of his farming operation and the change over that ten year period, available on the following page.

McGinty Farming Operation

	1850	1860
Acres of land – improved	120	130
Acres of land – unimproved	80	90
Cash value of farm	$1200	$1500
Value of farming implements/mach.	$150	$300
Horses	2	2
Asses and mules	1	1
Milk cows	4	5
Working oxen	2	6
Other cattle	10	4
Sheep	10	0
Swine	30	25
Value of livestock	$520	$745
Wheat (bushels)	15	0
Indian Corn (bushels)	700	700
Oats (bushels)	75	0
Ginned cotton, bales of 400 lbs. each	3	16
Peas and beans (bushels)	5	12
Irish potatoes (bushels)	0	10
Sweet potatoes (bushels)	20	40
Butter (lbs.)	150	200
Beeswax (lbs.)	0	30
Honey (lbs.)	0	200
Value of animals slaughtered	$45	$300

These appear to be his best years. After the South was defeated in the Civil War, there were many changes for the farmers such as Washington as a new way of life emerged.

He did not serve in the Civil War because of advanced age but he is shown as signing an oath of allegiance to the United States after the war for the reconstruction period in 1866-67 (this document is in the Cobb Archives, Valley, AL). The signing of this oath was required of the more prominent citizens.

He is shown in the 1870 Chambers Co., AL census (pg. 215) at age eighty-four, as head of the household. Living with him is daughter,

Narcissa Carpenter and her two children, Elizabeth "Lizzie" and William. Narcissa's husband Franklin Carpenter died in 1869. Washington was no longer living with his wife, Elizabeth, at this time. She was living with her son, Pinckney.

According to probate court records, he died March 14, 1874, while residing in Chambers Co., AL. No obituary has been found. He left no formal Will or testament. According to a document dated March 30, 1874, concerning his estate settlement, he still owned the 160 acre Bounty Warrant for serving in the military, and his overall estate was valued at $300. In this document, his heirs were listed as his widow, Elizabeth, and children, Nancy Means, Robert McGinty, William McGinty, Frank McGinty, George W. McGinty, Narcissa Carpenter, Dora Ann Howard, Pinckney H. McGinty, Missouri A. Webb and Salina A.Webb. The administrator of his estate was son-in-law, John A. Webb. Wife, Elizabeth is shown as declining to be the administrator.

The 1880 census shows his wife, Elizabeth, age seventy-five, living with her daughter, Salina and son-in-law, John A. Webb. Elizabeth died in 1891 and is buried at the Beulah Baptist Church cemetery in Lee Co., AL.

Washington's death was related by his grandson, Wiley P. McGinty Sr. who was quoted as saying that when Wiley was nine years old, Washington actually died while visiting someone up in Randolph Co., AL. Wiley remembered the mule pulled wagon, bringing Washington's body back to Chambers Co. for burial and that he was buried under a cedar tree in what is now Fairview Cemetery.

George Washington McGinty
Fairview Cemetery, Valley, AL

The gravesite remained unmarked until 1986 when Mary Hand McGinty, widow of Rev. Basil B. McGinty, who was a grandson of Washington, in keeping with Basil's final wishes after his death, put a marker on the spot where Washington is thought to have been buried under the cedar tree. When I visited the site years ago, the stump of the old cedar was still there.

Robert McGinty

(ca. 1750-1841)

Robert McGinty, b., ca.1755 based on the 1830 Monroe Co., GA, census which shows him in the age bracket between seventy and eighty, and the 1840 census of Monroe Co., where he is living with son, William, showing him in the age bracket between eighty and ninety. He could have been born in either Ireland or PA, depending on when his father arrived in America. He died in early 1841 in Monroe Co., GA. His will was recorded there on February 10, 1841, and the sale of his personal property was held April- June 1841. He married Deborah Jackson, ca. 1775-1777. This is based on the estimated birth date of their first son, Joseph. We know that they were married before 1777-1778 because Deborah shows in Quaker records with the name McGinty. This marriage took place at the beginning of the Revolutionary War (1775-1783). She shows in the 1830 census of Monroe Co., GA, pg. 225, as age 60-70 (born 1760-1770). She would have been born close to 1760 and married Robert when still in her teens.

Earlier researchers have referred to Robert with the middle name of Earl. I have many documents covering Robert's life. In none of them is he ever referred to as Robert Earl McGinty or even Robert E. McGinty.

Children of Robert McGinty and Deborah Jackson:

Joseph McGinty, b. ca.1775-1780 in GA. The 1820 census of Franklin Co., MS, pg. 41, shows him born between 1775 and 1794 and the 1830 census of Madison Co., MS, pg. 92, shows his birth as being between 1770 and 1780. Based on these censuses, he would have been born between 1775 and 1780. Quaker records show him living in the Wrightsborough, GA settlement with his parents. Based on these Quaker records, he was probably born closer to 1775. In the AR census of 1850 he shows as age eighty meaning that he would have been born in 1770. This 1850 AR census also shows that he was born in GA which is also unconfirmed, but very possible. It is also possible that he was born in NC, depending on when his parents moved to GA from

NC. His name could have been Joseph Jackson McGinty, in which case he would have probably been named for his uncle and mother's brother, Joseph Jackson. He died around 1851 in Conway Co., AR. He married, (1) Elizabeth (last name unproven, but thought to be Hood), (2) Louise (last name unknown but possibly Scroggins), (3) Melissa (last name unknown, but could be Shaw). One source says that he was married four times. In the 1793 muster roll of the GA Militia, Joseph is shown as a corporal in the 2nd Co., 2nd Bat. 2nd Reg. (Capt. John McKenzie). In 1797 he is shown as a tax defaulter in Warren Co., GA, Capt. Hill's District. He is also shown in Warren Co., as a witness to a deed dated 31 August 1797 (Deed Book A, pg. 603). In 1800 he is shown in Hancock Co., Capt. Boothe's District, also as a tax defaulter. He was "received by experience" into the Island Creek Baptist Church, March 1, 1800. Joseph's land records show two draws in Hancock Co. in the land act of May 11, 1803, for a fee of $8.10. This draw was actually made in 1805. He sold this land after moving to MS. In his military record, a report dated April 13, 1804, reads "Joseph McGinty, sergeant to Captain Graybill's Company, Hancock Co., GA, being duly called as a delinquent for not attending the muster of officers on the sixth, is fined three dollars."

He left the Island Creek Baptist Church in December 1805 (no wife is shown) and moved to the area that became Amite Co., MS, ca. 1809. He shows in the tax list of 1809 owning 153 acres in what was then Wilkinson Co., but soon became Amite Co. This land was located on what today is Hwy 48, three miles west of Centerville, MS. He shows in the 1810 and 1816 Territorial census of Amite Co., MS (formed in 1809 from Wilkinson). In 1810 he already had seven children, so he had to be married before he left GA. By 1815 he is found in the minutes of the Zion Hill Baptist Church in Amite Co. (*History of Amite County*, vol. II, by Casey. Unconfirmed records show that he ultimately had thirteen children. Two of his girls were married in this church and some of his sons are mentioned in the church minutes. He fought in the War of 1812 as part of Lt. Col. Neilson's detachment of MS militia. His service is further confirmed by an 1887 letter from his son, Eli Hood McGinty to his brother, Thomas. In 1812 he is said to have signed the petition to Congress, made by inhabitants of the Territory of MS, to make MS a State in the Union. In the Amite Co. tax report of 1816 he or his son, are shown with 154 acres, and paid taxes of $307.00. This land was located in today's Franklin Co., five miles north of Hwy 98 near Little Springs, MS. In the Amite Co. tax report of March 3, 1825, Joseph owned 78.87 acres and paid taxes of $98.00. This land was purchased from the federal government under land patent certificate 534, through the land office in Washington, MS on June 1, 1825. Pres. John Quincy Adams signed the patent. This patent document shows that he was from Franklin Co., MS at the time, and this land is in what is today, Franklin Co., in the southeast corner, north of Hwy 98, near Bude, MS. A land patent was the transfer of land ownership from the federal government to individuals. He is found in the Franklin Co., MS census of 1820 (pg. 41/49), with his wife and a large family of ten (four boys and four girls) and also in the Madison Co., MS census of 1830 (pg. 92) with a wife and large family of eleven. In this census, his name is misspelled as McGinly. The area where he lived was labeled "Indian Country." No township had yet been formed. On July 13, 1835, he purchased land in Holmes Co., MS, granted to him by the government land office (patent #16304) which is now Yazoo Co. In 1836 he sold this land to John Herrod for $1,200, and his wife's name is confirmed on this deed as Elizabeth. Something happened between Joseph and Elizabeth because he then moved to AR and the Holmes Co., MS census of 1840 (pg. 263) shows Elizabeth, age bracket 50-60, as the head-of-household with one male child, age ten to fifteen (possibly Eli Hood McGinty).

We next see Joseph in AR where he is shown as a taxpayer in Van Buren Co. in 1841. He purchased forty-acres of land from the federal government under patent certificate 3651, through the land office in Little Rock, on September 5, 1842. Pres. John Tyler signed this patent. At the time he was listed as being from Conway Co., AR. In 1846 he and second wife, Louise show selling 160 acres to a Samuel Asendell for $200 (Conway Co. courthouse, Morrilton, AR, record book C, pg. 50). He is also shown as homesteading 160 acres in Conway Co., AR, in 1846. He first settled in Union Township in what was known as "The Georgia Community." He is shown in the 1850 Conway Co., AR, census (pg. 268) in Union Township, house 575, at age eighty, occupation farmer. In this census, Malissa, age thirty-two is shown as wife. She was born in AR. In this census, there are four children, age two through eleven living in his house. His son, J. J. McGinty (Joseph Jackson), age thirty-six, born in MS, and his family are living next door in house 576. Joseph died ca. 1851. In the 1860 census, Melissa is now living with Moses House and shown as his cook. Two of the McGinty children, William Thomas and Mary Ellen lived with them, along with a Sarah J. House, age 5 who could be his granddaughter. Mary Ellen went on to marry Levi Wofford and they lived in Faulkner Co., AR. She died there in 1889.

Isaac McGinty, b. 1775-1780 in GA (confirmed by the 1850 Henry Co. GA census, pg. 201, and the Griffin, Spaulding Co., GA census of 1860, pg. 225), d. date unknown, but after 1860. There are War of 1812 service records in the National Archives showing Isaac as a private serving in Newman's command (with brothers, Robert and William) and also in the 2nd Reg., Jenkin's command, GA Vols. and Militia (Wilkes Co.). He married (1) Sarah Samples on July 7, 1814, in Baldwin Co., GA., and (2) Mary Malone on February 2, 1832, in Pike Co. GA. He shows as a creditor in the estate settlement documents of a William Millinden, January 1814 in Baldwin Co. He served as a private in Wimberly's 1st Regiment of the GA Volunteers during the first Seminole War in 1817-18. His brother, Abednego, served in this same unit. He also served as a private in Capt. Cox's Co. in the War of 1812 and by the Act of 1855 received an 80 acre Bounty Land Warrant # 35418 for this service.

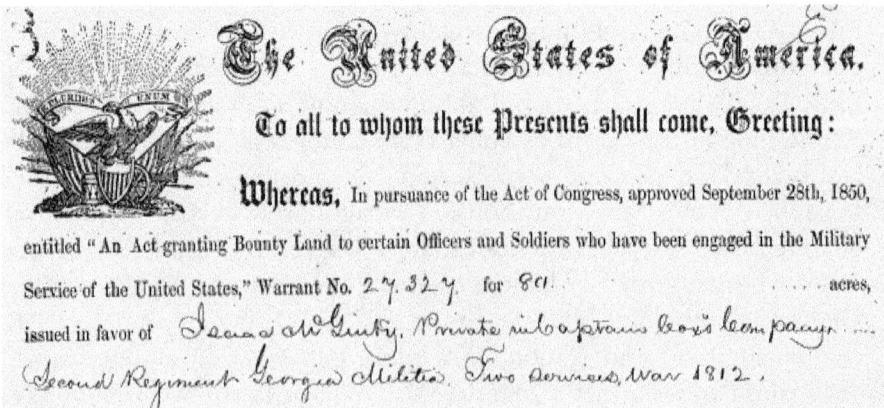

Bounty Land, 1812

Isaac and Sarah Marriage
Baldwin Co. Marriage Book, pg. 336

Georgia, Baldwin County
To any Judge, Justice of the Inferior Court, Justice of the Peace, or Minister
of the Gospel – You are hereby authorized to join together in Matrimony,
Isaac McGinty and Sarah Samples and for so doing this shall be your
sufficient license. Given under my hand and seal this 7th day of July, 1814.

Abner Locke, CCO (seal)

Georgia, Baldwin County – I hereby certify that the above named Isaac
McGinty and Sarah Samples were duly joined in the Bonds of Wedlock by
me this 7th day of July, 1814.

Nathaniel Walker, J.P.

Isaac and Sarah had a son, Shadrach L. McGinty, b. May 7, 1815.
This Shadrach is sometimes confused with Isaac's brother. On
September 15, 1827, Isaac gave his brother, Thomas, legal custody of
his son, Shadrach, who was twelve years old at the time. This document
is in Book E, # 241, Monroe Co. record of deeds. This document
shows that Shadrach was to live with Thomas until he was twenty-one
years old and be an apprentice in the art of farming. The document was
witnessed by Robert McGinty. Shadrach went on to marry (1) Winefred
Mary Davidson, daughter of James and Elizabeth Davidson, November
24, 1836, in Monroe Co., GA and (2) Margaret Johnson, December 12,
1885, in Coffey Co., AL. There are pension records for him in the
National Archives for war service in FL in 1836. He served in the GA
Volunteers. This was during the second Seminole War. He shows in the
1840 census as living in Sumpter Co., GA, with a young family. On July
15, 1854, he purchased forty acres of land from the federal government
under land patent certificate 43229. At this time he was shown as being
from Coffee Co., AL. Pres. Franklin Pierce signed this patent
document. He received land in 1857 for his military service. The land
was in southern AL in Coffee Co. Shadrach is shown in the 1860 AL
census of Coffee Co., living in Henderson Store, as a prosperous
farmer, age forty-five, with his wife Winefred and four children. He
purchased eighty more acres of land from the federal

167

government on April 2, 1860, in Coffee Co., land patent 50670, signed by Pres. James Buchanan. They do not show in the 1870 census, but are there again in the 1880 census of Coffee Co. AL).

Isaac and Sarah are shown in the *History of Upson County, p. 234.* He does show in some of the GA census records from 1820 through 1860. There is an Isaac shown in the 1830 census of Monroe Co. (pg. 190), but his age bracket is 40-50, meaning that he is not the same Isaac, or this age is an error. He would be too young. Isaac McGinty, listed as a soldier, had a successful draw in the Cherokee land lottery of 1832. He is shown as living in Martin's district, Pike Co., GA. In the 1840 census, he was living in Henry Co. with his wife and two grown children. In 1850 he is shown in Henry Co., GA at age seventy-five with Mary, his wife, age sixty and a thirteen-year-old child named E.S.R. McGinty (pg. 201). There is an Isaac McGinty who was granted land warrant #27327, January 22, 1852, in the old Mardisville, Lebanon and Centre land office. This land was in section 15, township 18, and range 10 and is shown as being settled by him. Because of the date, this must not be Isaac, Sr. but could have been his son. I do not have the names of all his children. He and Mary show in the 1860 census of Griffin, Spaulding Co., GA, pg. 225. He is shown as age eighty and she is shown as sixty. He is listed here as a pauper.

John McGinty, b. unknown, but probably ca. 1775-80, in GA, d. date unknown, but possibly after 1841 because he is shown in his father's will. He shows as a member of the Island Creek Baptist Church in Hancock Co., joining by letter on February 1, 1800, a few months after his parents had joined. He was a member here until he lettered out November 30, 1811. He is shown in the 1804 tax records as having 112 acres on Derrisos Creek (now Champions Creek). He also received two draws in the 1806 lottery, in Capt. John Young's district. He is shown in the Baldwin Co. tax list of 1808 in Capt. Gumm's district with 100 acres, on Rocky Creek, of type 2 land and then again in 1809 on Rocky Creek, with 200 acres of type 2 land. In 1810 he has 210 acres on Rocky Creek adjacent to that of his father. In 1811 he shows with 120 acres at the same location. His Rocky Creek land was originally granted to a J. Walker. He served in the War of 1812 in the 1st Reg., Harris's GA Militia. His brother, William, served in this same unit. He appears to have had an extensive military career. On May 30, 1804, "Executive minutes of the State of Georgia," at the State Archives show that he was promoted to ensign and fifteen months later, on August 30, 1805, John resigned his commission. His position was filled by his brother, Robert McGinty. John must have continued with his military service because on April 24, 1810, he was promoted to lieutenant while living in Baldwin Co., Gumm's District #105. Just two months later, on June 18, 1810, he was promoted to Captain of District #105, replacing Gumm. The 1811 Baldwin County tax records show this district as "Capt. McGinty's District."

His father, Robert, shows in the 1820 census of Baldwin Co. with a male, age 26-45, living in his home. This could be John, because he has not been found in the 1820 census as head-of-household and we know that they previously lived close together on Rocky Creek.

He shows as an heir in his father's will, written in Monroe Co., in 1841. However, he is not shown at the estate sale of his father's possessions, meaning that he probably lived somewhere else. He has not been found in the 1840 census.

James C. McGinty, b. ca. 1781, in GA (1860 census shows him age seventy-nine, occupation, farmer), d. date unknown. He married Lister Temperance "Tempy" (last name unknown). She was born in GA, ca. 1790. Nothing is known about his early life. He first shows up in the 1830 census of Monroe Co., GA, pg. 225, at age 40-50, with his wife, age 40-50, and one male child. They moved to AL, first to Chambers Co., where they show joining the Ephesus Church, by letter, December 20, 1850. They show in the 1850 census of Russell Co., AL, pg. 31B, as James, age seventy-two, and Temperance, age sixty-three, living in the home of probable nephew Benjamin F. McGinty, age twenty-eight. James and Temperance returned to Chambers Co. and joined the Ephesus Church. Then, in 1859 they lettered-out again.
James Cooper McGinty (Jr.?) is also thought to be their son, b. ca. 1811-14 (see Nancy B. McGinty).

James did get a lottery land grant draw in 1805 but only one, indicating that he was not yet married. He is shown as living in Hancock Co. at the time.

We do not see James in the records of the Island Creek Church but we know that he belonged to a Baptist church in GA because he joined the Ephesus Primitive Baptist Church in Chambers Co., AL, by letter. He moved from GA to AL prior to 1850 and first lived in Russell Co. He then moved to Chamber Co. They were members at Ephesus until they lettered out in 1859. There is a deed dated September 2, 1848, showing James purchase of land from James M. Spear, *Chambers Co. Deed Book 8, Page 544.* The 1860 census shows him, at age seventy-nine, living in Chambers Co. as a farmer (southern division, Oakbowery P.O., M653, roll 4, pg. 997). Temperance is also listed at age seventy. Late in his life, he and Tempy lived with Mollie McGinty Wyatt, the daughter of Robert A. McGinty and the granddaughter of Washington McGinty. The story told by Mollie is that at some point after Aunt Tempy's death, Uncle Jimmy went for a walk on a very cold day and fell off of a fence that he was climbing over. Apparently, he then froze and died of overexposure. He would have been well over eighty when he died. There are War of 1812 service records in the National Archives showing a James McGinty serving as a private in the 2nd Reg., Jenkin's command, GA Vols. and Militia. He also received an 80 acre Bounty Land Warrant for this service, stating that he served in Capt. Astin's Co., GA Militia, in the War of 1812.

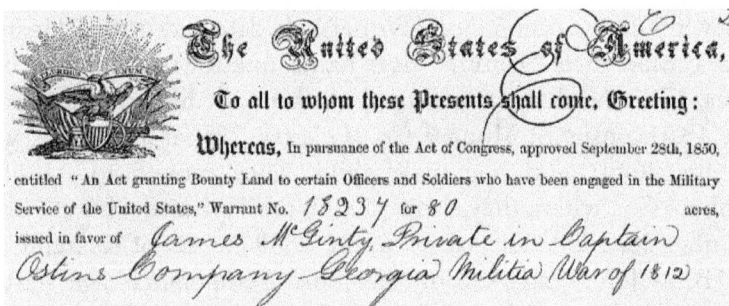

Bounty Land, 1812

There is a **Nancy B. McGinty** showing in Chambers Co. records who is easily confused with Nancy McGinty Means, daughter of George Washington McGinty. Coincidentally, they both have the same middle initial. This Nancy shows in the 1850, 1855 and 1860 census as a head-of-household farmer, born in GA. She is thought to have been married to James Cooper McGinty (Jr.?), the son of James and Temperance McGinty. There is a James McGinty in the 1830 census of

Wilkes Co., GA, pg. 294, age twenty-thirty. This is thought to be him. James was married to (1) Phebe Martin in 1829. They had two children including a son, John B., b. March 1, 1833. Phebe died in 1837. He married (2) Nancy B. Griswold (b. 1814) on July 13, 1837, and they had five children. These included Emily Francis (1838), Rebecca Cannon (1840), James Alexander Cato (1843), Joshua Soule Wilson and Mary Jane (1848). There is a deed showing that James C. purchased fifteen acres from James M. Spears on January 6, 1846. This land was in Township 20, Range 28, Section 2 (Chambers Co. Deed Book 8, pg. 644).

One of their children, Mary Jane, was born in Notasulga, Macon Co., AL (west of Auburn) in 1848 indicating that this is where they lived at the time. James, who was born ca. 1811 died in 1848 and Nancy moved the family to Chambers Co., AL, close to James and Temperance McGinty, parents of her husband. She shows there in the special AL State census of 1855 with one male and three female children under twenty-one. She shows again in the 1860 census, still living next door to them with Emily, age eighteen, Joshua, age seventeen, and James, age twelve (southern division, Oakbowery P.O., M653, roll 4, pg. 997). A family recollection is that James was a Methodist "circuit rider preacher." He does show up in *Methodist Preachers in Georgia, 1783-1900*, by Harold Lawrence, published in 1984, as a "local preacher" and as attending the Georgia Conference in 1844. He is also shown here as a deacon.

One of their children, Joshua Soule Wilson, enlisted as a private in Co. A of the 14th AL volunteer infantry regiment on July 26, 1861. He was eighteen years old. In January of 1862 he was listed in the military records as "sick at Fredericksburg" and he died February 5, 1862, in Richmond, VA, only six months after enlisting. His mother, Nancy B. McGinty, received his back pay consisting of four months and five days pay at $11.00 per month, the balance on his first commutation of $4.00 and his second clothing allowance of $25.00. The total was $74.83 and it was paid to her August 1, 1862. (*His records are in the National Archives, M374, roll 30*). The 1870 census of Harris Co. GA shows her living with daughter Mary Jane and her husband, James H. Sands. The 1880 census shows her living in Harris Co., GA, as a sixty-six year old widow, keeping house. There is a ten-year-old grandson, Charlie Shaw, living with her. He is the son of her oldest daughter, Emily, who married

Joseph Shaw in 1862 and died in 1873. Her youngest daughter, Mary Jane, died in West Point, Harris Co., GA, August 29, 1875, at age twenty-seven. Nancy died in February 1883.

Robert McGinty Jr., b. 1782 in GA (the 1850 census of Hancock Co., GA, pg. 39, gives his age as sixty-eight), d. Grimes Co., TX, after 1850. He married (1) Penelope "Nelley" Moore, daughter of Elijah Moore, Sr., July 5, 1807, in Hancock Co., GA.

Hancock Co. Marriage Book, Page 10

He may have married again before 1851. This wife (2) is shown as Eleanna in the 1850 Hancock Co. census, pg. 39, age fifty-seven, born in MD. The Island Creek church records also show her as Robert's wife, Elan, when they lettered in on September 27, 1851. They both then lettered out September 17, 1853. However, this could be Penelope because one unconfirmed source shows her name as Eleanor Penelope.

He had two draws in the land lottery of 1805 and is shown as living in Hancock Co. at the time. He was not successful, drawing two blanks. He had one draw in the Ocmulgee Lands lottery of 1806. There is a War of 1812 service record in the National Archives for a Robert McGinty. He served as a private in Newman's command, GA Volunteers. His brothers, William and Isaac also served in this unit. Robert did receive two land draws in Baldwin Co., GA, under the Act of 1820.

Robert shows in the 1820 census of Hancock Co., GA. Robert and Penelope were baptized at the Island Creek Baptist Church on December 1, 1827, and they departed the church by letter on October 24, 1835. Church minutes show that he was an active member. He was already forty-five years old when he was baptized, indicating that he could have been of a different religion prior to this. He shows in the 1830 census of Hancock Co., GA, with his wife and two children. He has not yet been found in the 1840 census. He shows in the 1850 census of Hancock Co., pg 39, age sixty-eight, with the occupation of house carpenter. His son, John, age twenty-six, lived next door with his wife, Mary L. age twenty-seven.

There are references to him in the Milledgeville, GA newspapers, such as *The Southern Recorder*, as an executor of estates. He also shows in numerous records in the Hancock Co. Court of Ordinary, thru 1825. The August 8, 1807, issue of the *Farmers Gazette*, shows that he ran for the Georgia House of Representatives. He was a county commissioner and also a justice of the peace (in Hancock Co.) in 1835. There were several marriages performed by Robert McGinty in Hancock Co., from 1812 thru 1816. Some of them may have been performed by his father. Two of his sons, John Moore McGinty and William Augustus McGinty, moved to TX, after taking their letters out of Island Creek church between 1852 and 1853. Robert and wife, Eleanna, who had re-joined the church, September 27, 1851, are also shown as departing the Island Creek church by letter in 1853. John Moore McGinty and his wife, Mary L. Brown McGinty are later found in central TX on the Brazos River (1860 census of Grimes Co., TX, pg. 244/245 and also the 1870 census of the same area). They have a child, age three who was born in TX, so they were there by 1857. In 1857 John organized the Harmony Baptist Church at Navasota on the Navasota River. He was pastor there until his death. William A., who had been a justice of the peace in Hancock Co., and his wife, Lucretia, came to Goliad Co., TX after 1851 and show there in the 1860 census. They then moved to Grimes Co., TX and show there in the 1870 census, pg. 265. Robert, Jr., and Eleanna have not been found in any TX census records, but I discovered his death and probate records in the Grimes Co., TX probate index. His son, John Moore was named administrator of his estate. I have not seen the original probate records, so the exact date of their death is, as yet, unknown.

The following unconfirmed information is from one of Robert's descendants: "Robert McGinty is buried in Harmony cemetery. His grave was marked with a large rock between John Moore McGinty's grave and the fence that marks the cemetery boundary. This is oral information that was given from my grandfather Andrew Maurice McGinty to several people. The rock has long been moved or stolen. I definitely remember that there were many rocks with names and dates scratched on them in that cemetery when we were growing up in the 50's." There are also said to be church records showing a Mr. and Mrs. R. McGinty among the original founders.

Thomas McGinty, b. September 29, 1784 (date shown in family bible and confirmed in the Muscogee Co., GA census of 1850, where he shows as age sixty-six). He is said to have died in 1868 in Morehouse Parish, LA. He was raised in Hancock Co., GA, and married Sarah Castleberry (b. December 16, 1780), the daughter of John and Mary Ann Castleberry, in 1804. They produced a large family of eight girls and three boys. The Island Creek Baptist Church records show that both of them were baptized into that church on September 1, 1804. He shows as living in Baldwin Co. in 1806 getting 60¾ acres of fractional lots in the "Commissioner's Sales." He had two land lottery draws in the Ocmulgee Lands lottery in 1806. On July 2, 1808, they took out their letters from the church and moved to Wilkinson Co., GA.

The story of Thomas in Wilkinson Co. has been told partly in *The History of Wilkinson County* by Victor Davidson and partly by other sources. Thomas McGinty was one of the first settlers in that part of Wilkinson Co., on the west side of the old Indian boundary line when the limits of the county were extended by the legislature following the Treaty of Washington in 1805. He made his home on the "Ridge" separating Commissioner and Big Sandy Creeks, where the old Hartford Road crosses the Irwinton and Macon Highway (Hwy 57 today). With him were families connected by blood and marriage including the Gays and the Castleberrys. Together these Baptists from Wilkes Co. early settlements, and then from Hancock Co. and Baldwin Counties, organized the Ramah Baptist Church, and Thomas was one of the charter members (having at his own expense built the church on his land).

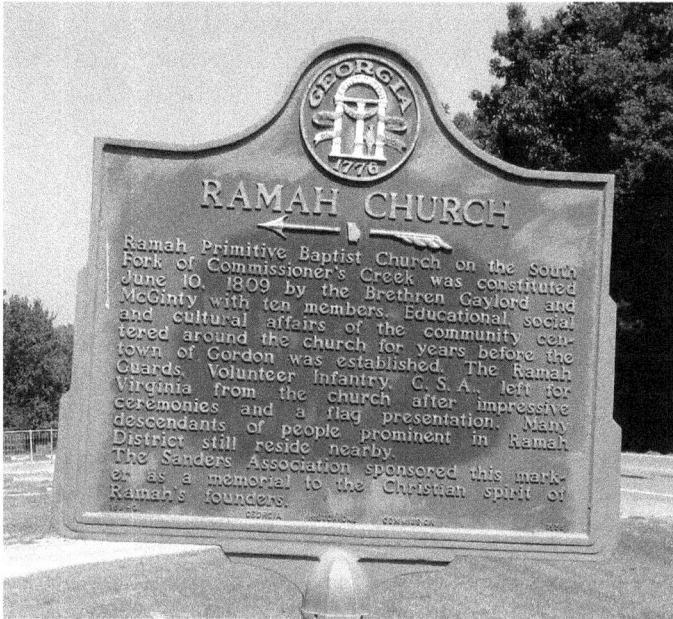

In 1810 he was selected by the Georgia Legislature as one of the commissioners from Wilkinson Co. to construct the Hartford Road from Hartford (now Hawkinsville) in Pulaski Co. to Milledgeville, the state capital. There was an urgent necessity of building this road with the least possible delay in order to avert the great crisis about to confront GA. Hartford at the time was a frontier town situated at the head of navigation on the Ocmulgee River. British agents, stationed beyond the Ocmulgee were constantly stirring up trouble with the Creek Indians. This road became necessary so that troops, artillery and ammunition could be rushed to Hartford as well as other points. The assignment of this task shows the confidence of the Legislature in his ability and his patriotism. It was necessary to draft able bodied men subject to such duties, assign them into squads, direct clearing of the underbrush, the cutting of the big trees to a level with the ground, the leveling of the rough places, the making passable of boggy places and streams, and all the other things essential to the construction of a road through "forest primeval." In 1927 when the John Ball chapter of the DAR erected the marker on the Old Hartford Road (Hwy. 57), the site of his tavern and home was selected. I visited this site in January 2002 (photo below). The gully of the old stagecoach road, where they crossed Hwy 57 still appears to be partially visible on the site.

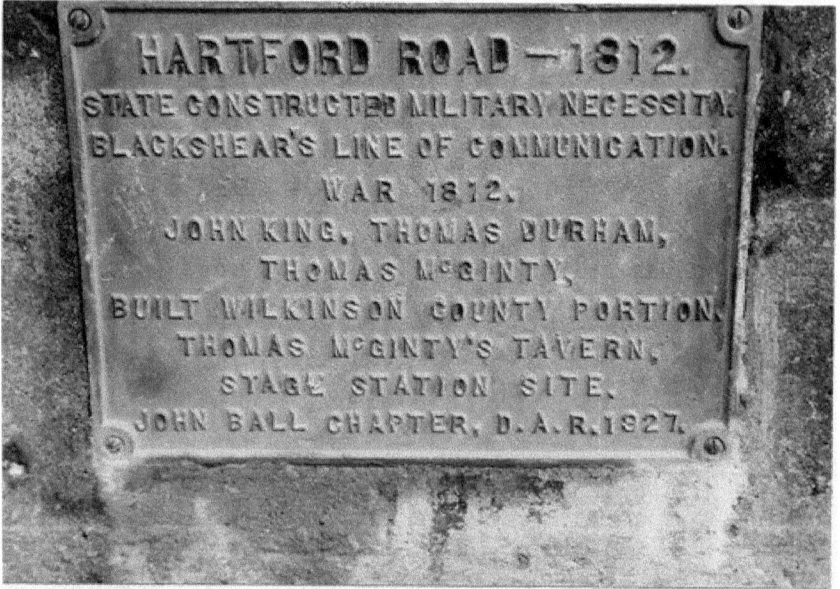

**DAR monument marking the site of the old
Hartford Road and home of Thomas McGinty
Located on Hwy. 57 in Wilkinson Co., GA.
(photo taken January 2002 by author)**

The growing travel between Milledgeville, Marion and Hartford and the establishment of a line of stage coaches made it necessary for stations to be established every ten miles where the tired horses having been driven at a gallop the greater part of the way were exchanged for fresh ones, which had been hastily harnessed and gotten ready when the stage driver's bugle was heard in the distance announcing his approach. Quick to grasp the opportunity, McGinty built a tavern which tradition says was well equipped to satisfy the hunger as well as the thirst of the wayfarer. He also received an appointment to supervise and build a stage road on the ridge called the Ridge Road between the east coast of GA and Macon, which was the western frontier at the time.

He is shown in the 1811 minutes of the Ocmulgee Baptist Assn., as a delegate to the annual meeting, representing the Ramah Baptist Church in Wilkinson Co. The church is shown as having twenty members. He shows again in their 1813 minutes, representing Ramah and the membership is shown as fifty-four. These minutes show that the Ramah church dropped out of the Ocmulgee Assn. in 1814. They became a Primitive Baptist church (Tarver Library, Mercer University, reel #1180).

He served on the grand jury in Wilkinson Co. in 1812. He is listed as a tax collector in Wilkinson Co. in 1817 and again in 1821 for a four-year term. He was also a justice of the inferior court. He is shown in the 1820 census of Wilkinson Co. with three males under ten and himself under age forty-five. There are three females under ten, three under sixteen and his wife, under age forty-five. He was living in Brooks military district (same as brother, Washington) in 1821. He drew in the GA land lottery and received land in both Monroe and Houston counties.

He lived in Baldwin Co., GA, until the late 1820's when he moved the family to Monroe Co., GA, near Montpelier Springs, south of Forsyth, GA. There are deeds on record showing his purchases of land in Monroe Co. as early as 1824 (Deed book C, pg. 41). He sold a parcel of land there in 1827 and his father Robert witnessed both of these deeds. There are other land sales recorded in the late 1820's and 1830. This land was very near his brother William in the twelfth district of Monroe Co. He shows in the 1830 census of Monroe Co., pg. 189, with seven white people and six slaves in his home, including a female, age 60-70 that could be his mother-in-law. Thomas is then found in the 1840 and 1850 Muskogee Co., GA census. There is a deed (book H, pg. 84-85) recorded in Talbot Co., GA, showing Thomas McGinty of Muskogee Co., selling 202½ acres of land to James Barnes, January 24, 1844. In the 1850 Muscogee census, pg. 311, he is head-of-house, age 66. No wife is shown. He also shows twenty slaves in 1850 Muskogee. Family lore says that in 1859 after the death of Sarah, when he was then living in Muscogee Co., he is said to have gone with his son William Jones McGinty (1814-1896) and his family to Ashley Co., AR. William Jones shows in the Ashley Co., 1860 census, but Thomas is not living with him. The trip was said to have been made from GA in covered wagons. Ashley Co. is on the LA line and adjacent to Morehouse Parish, LA. William Jones had a grandson, Joseph Eugene McGinty, b. 1876, who was a member of Roosevelt's Rough Riders.

Historical Collections of the Georgia Chapters of the DAR, Vol. IV shows that a family bible belonging to Sarah Castleberry McGinty of Conyers, GA contained the marriage of Thomas to Sarah Castleberry and the following birth dates for their children. They are not all correct. Note that this was written in Bienville Parish, LA. Two of their children, Mary Anne and William Jones, died in this Parish. One of them must have copied this from the family bible.

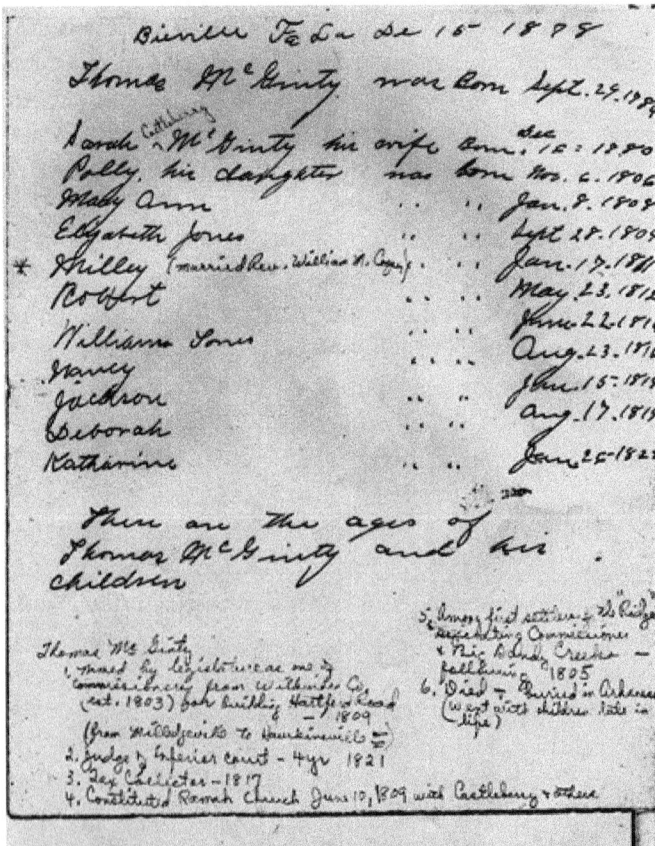

Castleberry Bible

George Washington McGinty, b. 1786 in Wilkes Co., GA, d. March 14, 1874, in Randolph Co., AL. See extensive research on Washington starting on p. 117 of this book.

William A. McGinty, b. 1792 (confirmed by the census of 1850) in what was Washington Co., now Baldwin Co., GA., d. April 7, 1858 (*The Christian Index*, page 3, col. 7), in Monroe Co. GA. His will was prepared February 1, 1858. He married Martha Grant (b. ca. 1800) at the house of Levi Speights, March 14, 1824, by Sterling Bass; Esq. He may have married again. He is shown in the 1820 census living in Baldwin Co. (pg. 36-37), age bracket twenty-six to forty-five, with two male children under ten and one slave. He is living next door to his father, Robert. He also shows in the Baldwin Co. land lottery of 1821 with his father, living in Maj. Ellis's district. He was a justice of the peace in the 305th district from 1813-1817.

He produced a very large family of at least eleven children and one of his sons, John Thomas, was editor of the *Monroe Advertiser*, a schoolteacher and was Ordinary of Monroe Co., GA for many years. William's grandson, George Banks McGinty was Secretary of the Interstate Commerce Commission in Washington, D.C. He was the son of John T. It is interesting to note that in William's will, he specifically mentions John T. as follows: "It is my will that my son, John shall not come in for any part of my estate as I have provided him with a liberal education which I consider equal to what the balance of my children will get." As it turned out, John T. was very successful in his life. Four of his sons, Cornelius, John T., Richard W., and Sidney F. enlisted in the Confederate Army; all in Monroe Co. Records show that they all survived. Sidney moved to TX and shows in the 1880 and 1900 census in Smith Co., TX.

There are War of 1812 and other war service records in the National Archives showing William serving as a private in Newman's command, GA Vols. His brothers, Isaac and Robert also served in this unit. He is also shown as serving, with his brother, John, as a private in the 1st Reg., Harris's command, GA Militia and later as a corporal in the 2nd Reg., Thomas' command, GA Militia. There is an article in the *Georgia Journal*, December 16, 1817, saying that William and Levin Moore (father of Ann Moore who was wife of William Pitts McGinty) were drafted into the 1st Reg. of the GA Militia but had not joined the company by the required date. A reward of five dollars was being offered for their delivery to Ft. Hawkins. He shows in the 1820 census of Baldwin Co., living next door to his father, Robert. Records show that he was living in Russell's district, Baldwin Co., in 1821. He drew in the GA land lottery that year and received land in Henry Co. William and his first wife Martha both joined the Island Creek Baptist Church in Hancock Co., GA, by experience in 1827. William was elected clerk of the church, February 29, 1828, and served in this position until he departed by letter in 1836. He shows in Baldwin Co. census of 1830, pg. 37, with seven children and two slaves. He shows as a Baldwin Co., JP in 1832 administrating the estate of Nubal (Nubold) Moore. There are records showing that he had two successful draws in the land lottery of 1827. In one draw he is shown as a soldier. The land that he drew was in Muscogee Co. He shows as the owner of 202½ acres here in the tax list of 1828 but he never lived on this land. It does not show up in later tax years, so he probably disposed of it, possibly to his brother, Thomas, who lived in Muscogee.

He left Baldwin Co. in 1836 and moved to Monroe Co., GA. This is proven in the death notice of his son, Cornelius in 1907 which says that he came to Monroe with his parents in 1836. Deeds on record at the Monroe Co. courthouse in Forsyth, GA show many of his land transactions. He shows in the 1840 census of Monroe Co., District 634, pg. 158, listed as W. McGinty with six male and three female children. His father, Robert, is also living with him, age 80-90.

Note: There was another William McGinty in Monroe Co., shown purchasing land as early as 1824 and he also shows in the 1830 Monroe Co. census, pg. 177, in the age bracket twenty to thirty. He shows a wife and two female children under five years old. He then shows in the 1840 census of Talbot Co., GA, age 40-50. An 1823 document in the GA Archives shows his promotion to Captain of the 296th District (Jasper). *The State of GA Military Records*, roll 40, box 16, pg. 109, shows (I think) William as a Captain, August 5, 1824, in Jasper Co. (GA Archives). There is also a marriage to Anne Morris on August 21, 1823, in Jasper Co. (marriage book, pg. 46). I think that he is the son of John McGinty II.

In 1842 the minutes of the Flint River Baptist Assn. show that William A. was the delegate from New Providence Baptist church to the annual meeting of the association. By this time, New Providence had seventy-six members. His father, Robert had been pastor of this church until 1829.

He is shown in the 1850 census of Monroe Co. with wife, Martha and six children. He was still living in Monroe Co. in early 1858 on the land that is mentioned in his will as "the land I currently live on." He owned several slaves, and they were given to his wife and children in his will. His will listed the following fifteen people: Elijah, Robert, William, Lewis, Maranda, Francis, Cornelius (executor), Elisha, Manerva Ann, Clayton, Martha Marietta, Richard, Sidney and John. He also listed nine slaves by name and to whom they were left; seven to his wife Martha, one each to daughters Manerva Ann and Martha. His obituary published in the April 7, 1858, issue of the *Christian Index*, says that eleven children survived him. His son, Cornelius was named the executor of his father's estate. There were several land sales from his estate beginning in 1858. Wife, Martha, is shown as the head-of-household in the 1860 Monroe Co., GA census, pg.749, with several of her children, and again in the 1870 census, pg. 394, with daughters Manerva and Mary. She died April 4, 1876, at her residence in Monroe Co. Her obituary, published in *The Advertiser* on April 11, 1876, reads as follows: "She was a native of Baldwin Co. and united with the Island Creek Baptist Church more than forty years ago. The profession, which she then made, she continued to adorn to the close of life, having attained a ripe age of seventy-seven years. She was highly appreciated in the community for her many sterling qualities, and for the worth of the large and interesting family she raised. Like a shock of corn fully ripe, she seemed only to await her Master's pleasure when she should be gathered into his garner." She was buried at the Cleaveland Scott Cemetery near Brent, GA. The final 202½ acres of land of William's estate was sold by son, Cornelius at public auction in Forsyth, GA, December 11, 1877, for $800. This may have been the land with the home Martha was living in and was sold after her death.

Mary (Polly) McGinty, b. ca. 1794 in GA, d. unknown, but possibly after 1841 because she is shown in her father's will. She went to MS with her brother, Joseph. She was a member of the Zion Baptist Church in Amite Co. and shows in the church minutes. A marriage license was issued on March 4, 1811, in Amite Co., MS for her marriage to John Russell. The 1820 census of Franklin Co. MS (next to Amite

Co.) shows a John Russell with several children. It also shows a female between the age of sixteen and twenty-six, which should be Polly. There is a Mary McGinty shown in the 1840 census of Warren Co., MS, pg. 260. Two females are shown in age bracket 40-50. She also shows in the 1850 Warren Co. census as Polly McGinty.

Shadrach McGinty, b. ca. 1800 based on the 1850 census of LA, but the 1820 thru 1840 census records put his birth date between 1794 and 1800. Since he has War of 1812 records, his birth date is probably closer to 1795. He died after 1859 probably in AR. He married Mary "Polly" Lamar August 5, 1818, in Putnam Co., GA. Mary was born, ca. 1805 according to the 1850 LA census records, but had to be born earlier than this because of her marriage date (assuming that it is correct). Her father, James Lamar, is said to have been the cousin of Mirabeau Lamar, second president of the Republic of Texas (after Sam Houston). Her mother was Catherine "Caty" Richardson. Mary's nickname, "Polly," is confirmed in her mother's will, written in Autauga Co., AL, February 22, 1827, RB-1. Previous research shows that prior to their marriage, Shadrach had been appointed guardian of Mary's brother and sister. There are War of 1812 service records in the National Archives showing Shadrach serving as a corporal in the 2nd Reg., Thomas' command, GA Militia. There is a record in *Index to Volunteer Soldiers in Indian Wars and Disturbances, 1815-1858*, vol. II by Virgil D. White, showing a "Thadiac" McGinty, Pvt., serving in Russel's Co., 1st GA militia as having been drafted for the Creek War. By the Act of 1850 he received Bounty Land Warrant # 65963 for 40 acres of land for this service in the Creek War.

He shows in the 1820 census in Putnam Co., GA (pg. 173), age 16-26, with one male child (James) and seven slaves. He shows in the 1830 census in Bibb Co., GA (pg. 65) with two male children, five to ten (James and Robert), and a total of twenty-nine slaves. This indicates a large farming operation. He moved to Jones Co., and is shown as an executor of the will of Robert Carey in 1823. He is also shown in the *State of GA Military Records*, roll 40, box 16, pg. 43 as a 2nd lieutenant, from September 15, 1819 to May 16, 1820, in Jones Co. He shows again on pg. 201 as a Captain, from July 18, 1828, until 1830. He was promoted to Captain of the 305th District of Jones Co. in 1828.

The United States of America,

To all to whom these Presents shall come, Greeting:

Whereas, In pursuance of the Act of Congress, approved September 28th, 1850, entitled "An Act granting Bounty Land to certain Officers and Soldiers who have been engaged in the Military Service of the United States," Warrant No. 65963 for 40 acres, issued in favor of *Shadrac McGinty Private in Captain Russell's Company, Georgia Militia Creek War*

Bounty Land, 1850

State of Georgia.

BY HIS EXCELLENCY *John Forsyth* Governor and Commander

in Chief of the Army and Navy of this State, and of the Militia thereof.

To *Shadrach McGinty* GREETING:

WE, reposing especial trust and confidence in your patriotism, valor, conduct and fidelity, do by these presents constitute and appoint you *Captain of the 365 Company, District of militia* Formed for the defence of the State, and for repelling every hostile invasion thereof—You are therefore carefully and diligently to discharge the duty of *Captain* by doing and performing all manner of things thereunto belonging. And we do strictly charge and require all Officers and Privates under your command, to be obedient to your orders as *Captain*

And you are to observe and follow such orders and directions, from time to time, as you shall receive from me, or a future Governor and Commander in Chief of this State, for the time being, or any other your superior Officers, in pursuance of the trust reposed in you. This Commission to continue in force during your usual residence within the *Company, district* to which you belong, unless removed by sentence of a Court-Martial, or by the Governor, on the address of two-thirds of each branch of the General Assembly. Given under my hand, and the seal of the Executive, at the State-House in Milledgeville, this *25th* day of *June* in the year of our Lord, one thousand eight hundred and *twenty eight* and of the Independence of the United States of America the *fifty second*

BY THE GOVERNOR:

A Hamilton Sec.

Promotion to Captain, June 25, 1828

Shadrach and brother, Meshach both show in the Jones Co. land lottery of 1826. In 1828 he sold 101 acres in Jones Co., GA, to Alfred Iverson (Deed Book "O" page 158, Jones Co. courthouse, Grey, GA). He was in Jones Co. after 1830 and is listed in a sheriff's sale of 101 acres of his land. He was in Milledgeville, GA in 1834 as part of the city's "Board of Visitors," which must have been similar to the chamber of commerce. Family legend says that he was a Baptist minister, but I have found no church records to confirm this. He moved to Monroe Co., and records show that he had a successful draw in the Cherokee land lottery of 1832. At this time, he was living in Brewer's Military District in Monroe Co. He is listed as a soldier. Records show a land sale of 362 acres that he made in Monroe Co., GA in 1838. The deed shows that it included land that he was living on. The buyer was Chosen Boynton. He is shown in the Monroe Co., GA census of 1840 with three males (himself, James and Robert), two females (his wife and a probable, but as yet unidentified, daughter) and no slaves in his household (district 554, pg. 184). His name is grossly misspelled in the census index as Shederick Mcyinty.

Shortly after 1840 the family relocated to Dallas Co., AL. Mary Lamar's family was already established in this area of AL. Earlier researchers erroneously thought that Shadrach died in Jones Co., GA in 1843. A recent discovery in the 1850 census, shows him listed as "Shadrick," age fifty, wife Mary, age forty-five, and son James L., age thirty, living in Catahoula Parish, LA (pg. 73A). His occupation was planter. His son, Robert H (Henry), age twenty-five, is living next door. Sadie Burt McGinty, the great-great-granddaughter of Shadrach, says that they were all living on the Dubois Plantation when this census was taken. Sometime after 1850 the family moved to AR and there is a federal land patent showing Shadrach with forty acres in sec. 40, twsp. 16S, range 15W, dated September 1, 1856. There is also a Union Co. deed showing his sale of two quarter sections of land to Mirick Harrell, dated February 17, 1855. This land was located just west of downtown El Dorado, AR on highway 335. Shadrach has not yet been found in the 1860 census so it is assumed that he died before then because Mary, his wife, age fifty-eight, is shown in the 1860 census of Union Co., AR living in El Dorado with her son. R.H. (Robert Henry) McGinty (pg. 322B). Robert served in the Civil War. His service record is as follows: "McGINTY, ROBERT H., Second Sergeant. Enlisted in Co. I, 6th

Arkansas Infantry, June 1861; discharged, 1861; enlisted in Co. C, 2nd Arkansas Battalion, at El Dorado, Arkansas, September 23, 1861; appointed second sergeant, September 23, 1861; absent sick in hospital at Dumfries, Virginia, October 31, 1861, 'wounded by a shell from enemies battery;' absent wounded in hospital at Dumfries, Virginia, December 31, 1861; absent sick in hospital at Dumfries, Virginia, February 28, 1862; discharged for wounds at Fredericksburg, Virginia, March 18, 1862; born in Georgia, c1824; listed in Union county 1860 census, with wife E.J.; occupation farmer; bought land in Union county in 1860 and 1869." The other son, James L. McGinty stayed in LA and shows there in the 1860-1880 censuses. He is shown as a Primitive Baptist preacher in the 1860 census of Winn Parish, LA (pg. 963/121, house 829). Robert Henry moved on to TX and shows in Lavaca Co. in the 1880 census (pg. 10/469B). It is said that his mother, Mary, died in some kind of an accident while traveling through LA. Robert died in Lavaca Co., December 19, 1896, and is buried in the Old Moulton cemetery.

Meshach McGinty, b.1800 (confirmed by the Autauga Co., AL census of 1860), d. unknown, but after 1869. He could have been married twice or even three times. He received a lottery land grant in 1819 drawing in Watson's Battalion District, Baldwin Co., GA, along with his brother, Abednego and father, Robert. He drew again in 1826. He was then allowed two draws indicating that he was married. He is shown in the 1820 census in Baldwin Co., GA, pg. 26, as "Meshac," with a wife and no children. He also drew in the 1821 Baldwin Co. lottery. He is shown in the 1830 census of Jones Co., GA. with four girls and no boys in his household. He and his wife's age brackets are 30-40. In 1832 he shows in the Jones Co. land lottery draws. He was an ordained minister at Pope's Meeting House, which was a Baptist church in the Ocmulgee Assn. in 1833. In 1836-37 he was a member of the Union Baptist church in Jones Co., GA, and was a licensed Baptist minister. In 1838-42 he was minister of the Eanon Baptist church in Putnam Co., GA, showing that he had relocated his family here. This is confirmed in the 1840-1841 minutes of the Ocmulgee Baptist Assn., showing that he was the messenger to the annual meeting from the Eanon church in Putnam Co. He was an ordained minister by then. He shows again as a messenger in the 1842 assn. minutes (Tarver Library,

Mercer Univ., reel 1180). He was a justice of the peace in Milledgeville, GA in 1835. He shows in the 1840 census of Putnam Co., GA. with five girls and one boy in his household. In 1842 the local newspaper, *Southern Recorder* in Milledgeville shows him involved in the settlement of the estate of Benjamin Talbot. In 1843 he is shown as a member of the Upatoie Baptist Assn. He lived for a few years in Upson Co., GA (589th military district of Hootenville) and is shown performing two marriages there in Aug., 1846 and Apr., 1847. He shows in the Upson Co. tax list in both 1847 and 1848 (GA Archives). He also shown in the 1848 list, still living in Hootenville, but also paying tax in on 202½ acres, lot seventy-seven, district 5, in Houston Co., GA. The 1846 poor school records of Upson Co. show his children, Martha, Sarah and William. Based on the age and place of birth of his son, Robert (1848 in GA), as shown in the 1860 Autauga Co., AL census, he relocated to AL sometime after 1848. He then shows in the 1855 AL census, living in Autaugaville, AL and is the pastor of the Mt. Zion Primitive Baptist Church.

On September 15, 1855, he was deeded property adjacent to this church. The deed shows him as an elder. He was the pastor at this time. Then, in an Autauga Co. deed dated September 21, 1860 (pg. 233), he sold this land to Charles P. Shilley, acting agent for the church, indicating that he was no longer pastor and had moved or was moving to another location. He is shown in the 1860 census of Autaugaville, Autauga Co., AL (pg. 140, house 979) age sixty with his wife, Frances, whose age appears to be fifty. If correct, she is not his first wife because her age does not match earlier census records. In 1860 they show four children, Sarah, William, Rebecca and Robert, all born in GA. His occupation is "Primitive Baptist Minister." Census records show that he had a total of two boys and six or seven girls. One of his daughters, Nancy, married Jeremiah Stewart in 1836. Meshach is shown as her father in the Stewart family bible. Nancy is shown in this bible as being born October 1, 1820, so she would have been one of his first children. The bible shows her death date as January 16, 1899. Nancy and "Jerry" Stewart show in the 1870 census of Bibb Co., AL, pg. 227. She is age forty-nine, meaning that she was born in 1821. They had a very large family. Nancy also shows in the 1829-30 poor school records in Jones Co., GA, age 10. Meshach's wife, Frances, shows in the 1860 census as possibly being age fifty. If correct, she would have been born in 1810 and could not be the mother of Nancy. This would confirm that Meshach had another wife before Frances. Her name could have been Tabitha (*Heritage of Bibb Co. Alabama*, pg 246). Another Tabitha, possibly Meshach's daughter, married William H. Clayton on April 25, 1858, and shows as his wife in the 1860 census of Tuscaloosa Co., AL, pg. 459. She is then age twenty-two, showing that she was born in GA in 1838. Clayton is shown as a member of Co. D, 43rd Reg., AL Inf., which was organized in May, 1862. He may not have survived the war, because he has not been found in the 1870 census. I have the marriage license from Bibb Co., AL, dated December 5, 1863, showing Meshach McGinty marrying Telitha Townsend. She would have been his third wife. In December 1869 a new primitive Baptist church was founded near Pondville, Bibb Co., AL. Meshach was asked to be the moderator of the first meeting. Tabitha McGinty, probably his daughter, was also shown as one of the charter members of this church. The fact that he was moderator does not mean that he had relocated to Bibb Co., and he does not show up on the 1870 census. The date of his death is unknown at this time. His two sons have not been found after the 1860 census.

Abednego McGinty, b. 1800 in GA (confirmed by the 1850 and 1860 census), d. June 28, 1862 in Union Springs, Bullock Co., AL. He relocated to Decatur Co. (Bainbridge, GA) before 1824. In 1824/25, he was the "receiver of taxes" in Decatur Co. He actually paid taxes in Capt. Carson's district. The January 20, 1825 court records show that he was a member of the jury in a murder trial. In January 1831 he was the successful bidder to construct a new brick courthouse for $4,120. The building was not completed, possibly because of his military transfer to FL. In February, 1832, the court canceled his contract and awarded it to another man who completed it (*History of Decatur County Georgia*, Frank S. Jones, 1980). Two hundred thirty two acres of his land in Decatur Co. was later sold in a sheriff's sale. There is a general index card in the National Archives showing that he was a corporal in Wimberly's 1st Reg. of the GA Militia, in the Seminole War, 1817-1818. His brother, Isaac, served in this same unit. He was promoted to 2nd Lieutenant, 15 August 1822. *The State of GA Military Records*, roll 40, box 16, pg. 134, show him as an ensign in Decatur Co. from 29 October 1824 until 22 June 1825. Page 134 shows him as a 2nd lieutenant in

Putnam Co., July 1825 (GA Archives).

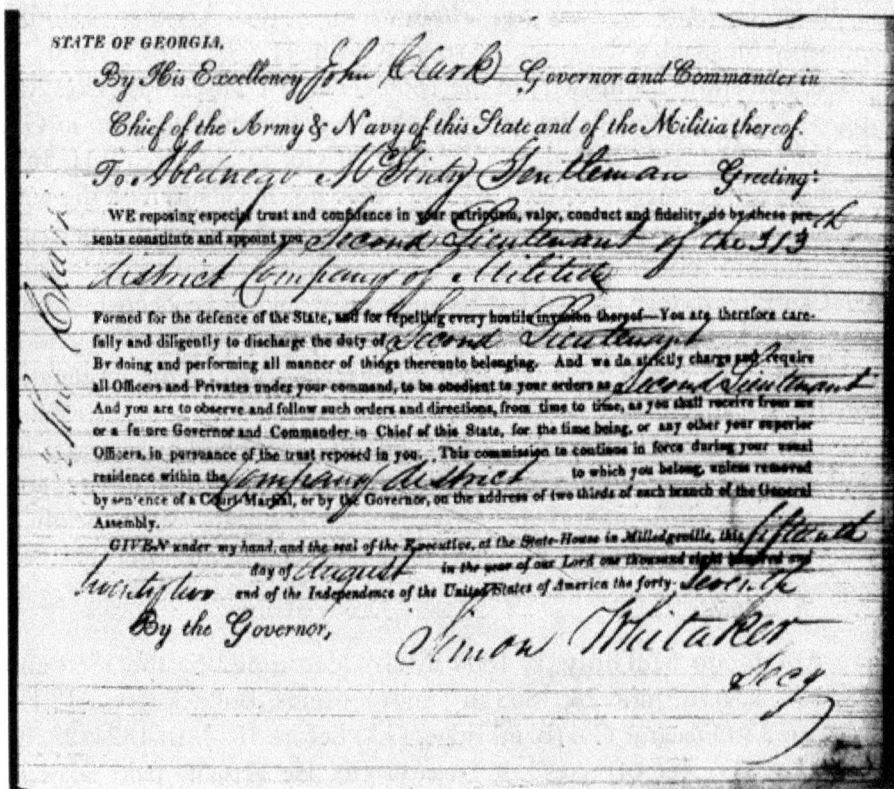

Promotion to 2nd Lieutenant, 15 Aug 1822

He was stationed in FL, and shows in the 1830 census of Quincy, Gadsden Co., FL. His son, George Washington, and daughter, Ann, are shown. The *Military Record Book of 1829-1841, p.83,* located in the Georgia Department of Archives, shows him listed as a colonel in the 88th Reg., GA Militia (Early Co. GA), and as being commissioned on August 27, 1835. To attain the rank of colonel indicates that he spent a great deal of his life serving in the Georgia Militia. He was a colonel in the 88th Georgia Militia and the commanding officer at Ft. Gaines (est. in 1816) in Early Co., GA. This fort was named for Edmund P. Gaines who was second in command to then General Andrew Jackson during the Seminole wars. This part of Early Co. is now Clay Co. (formed in

1854). This was on the extreme frontier at the time and there were many problems with hostile Indians. There are several letters in the archives that he wrote to the Gov. of Georgia asking for workable muskets and other desperate needs for his men. There are also interesting documents in the Hargrett Rare Book and Manuscript Library at the University of Georgia, showing some of his actions while at Ft. Gaines. These include the forming of military units to defend against the Creek Indian uprisings. Early Co. is in extreme southwest GA, next to Seminole Co., and near the FL border. It is interesting to note that the second Seminole War started in 1835 and lasted for seven years. Also of note is that his older brother, Washington, served in the first Seminole War in 1818.

He is shown in the 1840 census of Early Co., GA under the name A. McGinty, in a section of the census record covering the personnel stationed at Ft. Gaines (pg. 202). He was in Capt. Wilson's district. There are two children shown, a son under five years old (Robert Tamerlin) and a daughter (Anne) between ten and fifteen years old. His son, George W. had left home by then. He is listed at age 40-50, with his wife age 30-40 (pg. 113). On July 13, 1844, he was given military land warrant 8778 in Barbour Co., AL. for 80.22 acres, however it is unclear as to whether he actually lived on this land because by 1850 he was living in Macon Co. However, the land warrant shows that he was then from Barbour Co., AL which is directly across the river from Ft. Gaines, GA. He is then listed in the 1850 census in Macon Co., AL, pg. 199, at age fifty, living in the home of John A. Boling with wife, Elizabeth, age forty-five and son, Robert T., age ten. His occupation is shown as carriage maker. We see him as an MG performing marriages in 1853. He then shows in the special census of 1855 with three slaves. We then see him listed in the 1860 census of Macon Co., along with a wife, which, on the census sheet, looks like either Mrs. Ellia or Ellisa (short for Elizabeth), and son Robert T., age twenty. His occupation is then postmaster of Union Springs and the U.S. postal records show his appointment to this position in 1857. Based on the obituary of son, Robert T., who died at age eighty-five, the family moved to Union Springs around 1850 but they actually arrived before 1846 when his daughter, Anne, was married there. No further records have been discovered on Abednego, but Elizabeth is shown living with her daughter, Anne McGinty Rutherford in the 1870 Union Springs,

Bullock Co., AL census (Bullock Co. was formed from Macon Co. in 1866). After Anne died in 1880 she moved to AR and lived with her grandson Franklin Abednego Rutherford. Son, Robert T., is also shown in Union Springs, Bullock Co., AL in the 1870 census (pg. 41/219) as a farmer, age thirty, with wife, Martha and three children, Walter, George and David. Robert and family show again in the 1880 census in Bullock Co. In 1900 Robert is married to a second wife, Tommie Jett Jones, (Mrs.). He then shows as a widower in the 1920 census, and Sexton at Oak Hill Cemetery in Union Springs. Robert died in April 1920 and is buried at the Oak Hill cemetery in Union Springs with second wife, Tommie. He had been the city sexton for over thirty years. I visited his gravesite in February 2004. Abednego's daughter, Anne Louisa, married Patrick Henry Rutherford in Macon Co., AL, November 10, 1846. They show in the 1850 census of Barbour Co., and the 1860 census of Macon Co., AL. Robert T. and Patrick Rutherford both served in the Civil War. Rutherford could have died in the war because his wife, Anne, is a widow in the 1870 census.

Note: It is possible that Shadrach, Meshach and Abednego were triplets or S, M as twins and then A? Separate census records show that all were born around 1800 and speculation as to how and why their parents chose these biblical trio names is most interesting.

Josiah McGinty, b.1801-1802, in GA (confirmed by the 1850 and 1860 census of Bibb Co., GA.), d. unknown. He married Marion Penelope Russ on March 17, 1825, in Monroe Co., GA, W.F. Bayne, JP, and they had a family of three sons and two daughters, Benjamin R., Jeremiah, Perry, Marion Elvena, and Mariah Penelope. He is shown living in Huson's district, Baldwin Co. in 1821. He drew in the 1821 land lottery and was awarded land in Dooly Co., GA. He then shows in the 1827 tax list of Pike Co. with 202½ acres in the 2nd district, lot 220. Pike was formed from Monroe in 1822. He paid taxes in 1834 Monroe Co., 50 acres, Dist. 12, plot 55. In 1830 and 1840 he is listed in the Pike Co., GA census and later in the 1850 and 1860 census in Bibb Co., GA. In the 1850 census of Bibb Co. he is shown at age forty-nine, occupation, wagon-maker. Also shown are his wife, M.P, and children, Jeremiah Q., Mariah P. and Perry A. Jeremiah Q. is shown at age twenty-two as a carpenter. The last record we have is the 1860 census of Macon, Bibb Co., GA, pg. 474, which shows him at age fifty-eight, occupation, wheelwright (wagon maker). Also shown is his wife, age fifty-three and son, Perry, age sixteen.

Josiah and Penelope, Marriage Book A, pg. 19

Georgia, Monroe County

To any Judge, Justice of the Inferior Court, Justice of the Peace or Minister of the Gospel. You are hereby authorized to join Josiah McGinty and Penelope Russ in the holy state of Matrimony, according to the constitution and laws of the state and for so doing, this shall be your sufficient license. Given under my hand and seal this 7th day of March, 1825.

John M. Gray C.C.O. (seal)

Note: Census records before 1850 do not list family members by name, only by number within age brackets.

The Life of Robert McGinty

Robert was born in either Ireland or PA depending on when his father, John arrived in America from Ireland. He married Deborah Jackson, ca. 1770. Quaker records show that in 1778 she was in the process of transferring her membership from the Cane Creek Meeting in Orange Co., NC, to the Wrightsborough Quaker settlement in St. Paul's Parish, GA. It is not known how they met or exactly where and when Robert and Deborah were married, but this could have occurred in PA. According to the 1850 census of Conway Co., AR, pg. 268, their first son, Joseph, was born in 1770 in GA, so we can assume that they were married before this time. It is also possible that our McGinty family was acquainted with this Jackson family back in PA.

Deborah's father, Thomas, was killed by Indians in August 1770 leaving wife, Mary a widow. I think that Robert and Deborah arrived shortly after this and lived with Mary in her home for a time. This is why we do not see Robert buying land at this early date.

Recent information from a website that includes *Quaker Wrightsborough Township Records of Landholders, Residents, and Associated Families 1768-1810*, shows Deborah Jackson married to Robert McGinty. It also shows that her parents were Thomas and Mary Jackson and that her brother was Joseph. Earlier researchers thought that Deborah was the daughter of a Baptist minister named John Wright but this is an error. *The Encyclopedia of American Quaker Genealogy, Vol. 1*, by William W. Hinshaw shows an entry on pg. 405 of the Cane Creek Monthly Meeting minutes that says, "1778, 12 (day), 6 (month)., Joseph Jackson and Deborah, now McGinty, children (of) Thomas (Jackson), deceased, were granted a certificate (from), Cane Creek Monthly Meeting." This confirms that she was in good standing and had permission to transfer to the Wrightsborough Monthly Meeting in GA.

There is a later entry from the Wrightsborough Monthly Meeting minutes, pg. 1049, dated September 4, 1779, showing Deborah Jackson, now McGinty, being received into the monthly meeting in Georgia. This entry also shows that her father was Thomas Jackson, and that he was deceased (ca. 1770). The Cane Creek Meeting was established in Orange Co., NC in 1751. These Quaker records prove that they had moved to the Wrightsborough, GA area which, at this time, was in newly formed Richmond Co. (est. February 5, 1777). This area was previously part of St. Paul's Parish. It is also interesting to note that Robert is not shown in these Quaker records with Deborah, but he could have also been a Quaker at this time. He married a Quaker girl who was not excommunicated and moved to the Quaker settlement of Wrightsborough. He also has no known Revolutionary War record.

Wrightsborough was named for Sir James Wright, Governor of the Colony of GA in 1760. At this time, the government of the GA Colony was located in Savannah. Most of the original settlers were from the Orange Co. area of NC. Thomas Jackson, who was from the Cane Creek meeting in NC and one of the first settlers, received warrant #252 for 250 acres. This warrant is dated February 7, 1769. On July 3, 1770, he also received a town lot, number thirty-one. A reconstructed 1807 map of Wrightsborough town, published in *The Story of Wrightsboro, 1768-1964*, by Mrs. Pearl Baker, shows that this lot was located between Tower Ln. and Habersham St. Settlers like Thomas were given both acreage to farm, and a lot in the newly surveyed town.

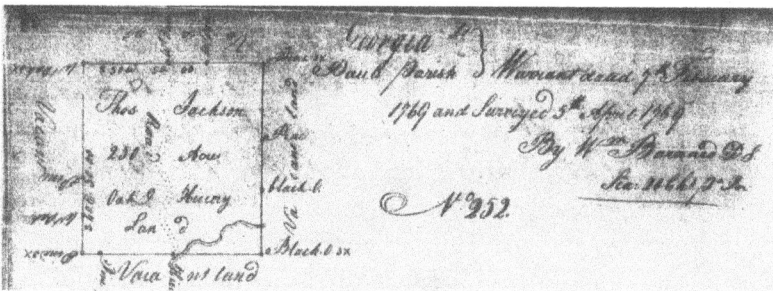

Thomas Jackson Land Warrant
Wrightsborough, 1769

The Wrightsborough settlement, founded in 1769 was originally in St. Paul's Parish. After the war, on February 5, 1777, this area became Richmond Co. Later, in 1790 it became part of Columbia Co., and is now in McDuffie Co. (est. 1870). It is in an area near present day Thomson, GA, about thirty miles west of Augusta, GA. The general assembly of GA granted 40,000 acres of land to the Quakers for this settlement. At this time, the provincial government of the GA colony was located in Savannah and Gov. Wright personally owned substantial acreage adjacent to the granted tract. Beginning in 1768 forty Quaker families moved from the Hillsborough, Orange Co., NC area with their leader, Joseph Maddock, and settled in the area. They left NC mainly because Gov. Tryon did not like the Quakers and was making life miserable for them. Gov. Wright in GA was supportive of the Quakers and agreed to let them settle the land.

An interesting account of the Wrightsborough settlement is found in the book, *Bartram, Travels and Other Writings,* edited by Thomas P. Slaughter. William Bartram (1739-1823) was a noted naturalist, writer, botanist and explorer that visited the settlement during a 1773 journey through the Carolinas, Georgia and Florida. He described the settlement as follows: "We arrived at a small village on Little River, a branch of the Savanna: this village called Wrightsborough, was founded by Jos. Mattock, Esq., of the sect called Quakers. This public spirited man having obtained for himself and his followers a district, comprehending upwards of forty thousand acres of land, gave the new town this name, in honor of Sir James Wright, then governor of Georgia, who greatly promoted the establishment of the settlement. Mr. Mattock, who is now about seventy years of age, healthy and active, and presides as chief magistrate of the settlement, received us with great hospitality. Wrightsborough is a late but thriving settlement…the inhabitants are for the most part emigrants from the North Colonies. The town is already laid out and about twenty houses built. Several traders are in it and goods are sold as cheap here as Augusta, sugar, rum, salt, dry goods, etc. The settlement being upon the head of Little River, a very considerable branch of the Savannah River. The soil is very fruitful, hills and vales watered and beautified by numbers of salubrious waters…mills are erected on the swift flowing streams…The inhabitants plant wheat, barley, flax, hemp, oats, corn, cotton, indigo, breed cattle, sheep and make very good butter and cheese. Fruit trees thrive very well here.

"I saw in Mr. Mattox (Mattock) garden, very fine large apples two years from the seed and grapes two years from cuttings…The distance from Augusta to this place is about thirty miles; the face of the country was chiefly a plain of high forests, savannas and cane swamps, until we approached Little River, when the landscape varies, presenting to view high hills and rich vales. The soil is a deep, rich, dark mould, on a deep stratum of reddish brown tenacious clay…The forest trees are chiefly of the deciduous order…Leaving the pleasant town of Wrightsborough we continued eight or nine miles through a fertile plain.…"

The settlement thrived for a number of years, but between 1805 and 1809 for a variety of reasons, the inhabitants moved on and the Quaker town of Wrightsborough ceased to exist.

I visited Wrightsborough on March 23, 2012, with my brother, Phil, his daughter Andrea and our cousin Tom Wood. We saw the Quaker burial ground, a dam on Maddox Creek and other interesting sites. The dam was of particular interest, because Thomas Jackson's 250 acre grant joined the Maddock land at the location where the dam is built.

Another excellent account of the families that lived in the Wrightsborough settlement and their involvement in the Revolutionary War is the novel by President Jimmy Carter, *The Hornet's Nest,* published in 2003. Although fictional, it is based on historical facts and tracks the movements of our own McGinty family.

As mentioned above, Deborah's father, Thomas Jackson, was one of the founders of the Wrightsborough colony of the Society of Friends (Quakers) in 1769. The records show that he was born April 22, 1731, in East Marlborough, Chester Co., PA. His wife was named Mary (maiden name unknown), and they had at least two children, Deborah and Joseph. This is speculation, but Mary may have been the daughter of Joseph Maddock who led the Quakers from NC to Wrightsborough. More research is needed here. It is also interesting to note that Thomas was the son of Isaac Jackson who was born ca. 1705 in Ireland and came to America as a small boy, growing up in PA. In 1730 Isaac married Mary Miller in Chester Co., PA. Around 1751 Isaac moved the family to NC, and was a charter member of the Cane Creek Monthly Meeting in Orange Co. He shows in these minutes as one of about thirty original families. Son, Thomas shows in a 1755 Orange Co., NC deed, purchasing 350 acres of land from his father, Isaac (deed book 1, pg. 120). Thomas and family then moved with father, Isaac, mother, Mary, his brother, Nathaniel and sister, Ruth, to the Wrightsborough settlement in GA, ca. 1769 when he was about thirty-eight years old. According to colonial records of Gov. James Wright, he was murdered by Creek Indians in August 1770. Court records dated May 24, 1772 show wife, Mary appointed to inventory and settle his estate.

That notwithstanding the said treaties and solemn engagements entered into as aforesaid, yet the Creek Indians have frequently stolen great numbers of horses and cattle from many of His Majesty's subjects and have also committed several murders since that time, the last of which was in August 1770 when some of the said Indians in cool blood and without any cause or reason whatever barbarously murdered Thomas Jackson and George Beeck, two of the inhabitants of Wrightsborough Township, and that notwithstanding a complaint was made and satisfaction regularly demanded by your memorialist agreeable to the treaty aforesaid, yet no satisfaction has been given by the said Indians, and although not positively denied yet the same is evaded by them and none intended to be made or given on account of the said murders.

A letter from Gov. James Wright to the Earl of Hillsborough
December 12, 1771
"Documents of the American Revolution, 1770-1783"
Vol. III, pg. 269-270

**Mary Jackson Administrix Bond, Thomas Jackson Estate
27 May 1772**

The records of the Jackson family are somewhat sketchy but show at least nine generations up to Deborah. The family was living in England as early as 1505. From there, they went to Cavan, Ireland, probably around 1650 and then came to America and Chester Co., PA, sometime before 1727. Quaker minutes from Wrightsborough show Thomas's son, Joseph, was "disowned" on April 1, 1780, for "bearing arms in a warlike manner, and of partaking of plundered goods, and also of accomplishing his marriage disorderly or out of the unity of

197

Friends." Joseph moved to Wilkes Co., receiving a 400 acre grant, which we have located. Later, Robert acquired Joseph's land (no deed has been located) on Harden's Creek, and lived there for several years. There are records of several land transactions and the mention of their slaves. Columbia Co. early deeds show this transaction on Pages 50-56: "Nov. 13, 1786, recorded, Aug. 23, 1799. Joseph Jackson of Wilkes County and Mary, his wife, to John Embree for 150 pounds, sells 250 acres in Wrightsborough Township on Upton Creek. Originally granted to Thomas Jackson by Sir James Wright, July 3, 1770, said Joseph being the only son and heir of Thomas. Mary relinquishes dower." Joseph and Mary were divorced in 1801 and their property split between them. He moved to Clarke Co., AL, and married Jincy Smith in 1814. He died here ca. 1835.

The first record written of Robert was a deed that he witnessed in Wrightsborough Township, St. Paul's Parish on August 6, 1777. This deed was a sale by Absalom Bedell to David Robertson for 250 acres. The deed references an original grant dated January 7, 1772. On the back of this deed is written, "Be it remembered that on the twenty-third day of November in the year of our Lord, one thousand seven hundred and eighty-eight, personally appeared before me Robert McGinty and made oath that he saw the within named Absolom Bedell duly sign, seal and deliver the within deed for the purposes therein mentioned and that he also saw the within named Jonathan Robertson, one of the witnesses to said deed sign his name thereto." This statement is signed by Jonathan Lindsay, J.P., and Robert. Since this deed was issued before the war by the British Crown, perhaps after the war it needed to be reaffirmed, and Robert was called to do this. Absalom Bedell had married Ruth Jackson back in North Carolina, before the move. She was the aunt of Deborah. Absalom was not a Quaker, and Ruth was dismissed at the Cane Creek Meeting in 1768 for marrying outside the church. Absalom became one of GA's first justices, showing as a county judge in August 1779 and he also served as a major in the Rev. War, and signed the GA Declaration of Independence.

After the war, Robert and Absalom were neighbors on Little River in Wilkes Co. Wilkes Co. land grant books at the GA Archives in Atlanta, show that Robert had land here by 1783 that was later granted to him in 1785. An entry dated August 12, 1783, shows Absalom Bedell with 450 acres of land joining Robert McGinty (pg. 85, #207). Two other entries show Robert's land in 1784 (pg. 97, #274 and pg. 196, #580). There are also several "headright caveats," involving Robert, on file at the GA Archives. These are in Wilkes Co. and all dated 1784.

After moving to Wilkes, Robert purchased for 30 pounds 270 acres of land from Peter and Sarah Buffington, who were from the Old 96 District of SC, on August 4, 1785 (Richmond Co. Deed Book B-1, page 221-222). It is possible that Robert had been leasing this land from Buffington prior to the purchase. This land was an original Crown grant that had been made to William Fanner in 1770 and was located on the waters of Germany's Creek in Richmond Co. Robert sold this land October 15, 1785, to Thomas Napier (Richmond Co., Deed Book F-1, page 26-27) for 100 pounds. The deed date shows that, by this time, Robert had already relocated to Wilkes Co. A later "gift deed," dated February 26, 1792, from Thomas Napier to his daughter and son-in-law, described the land location as being on the north side of Malone's Branch. This land was at the junction of Malone's Branch and Germany's Creek.

Robert shows as "McGintee" in the 1785 "remnant" tax digest, living in Wilkes Co., Capt. Karr's district with 1½ polls, one slave and 300 acres. Absolom Bedell was the tax collector. This tax list was published in *Early Records of Georgia*, vol. II, pg. 24, by Grace Gillam Davidson, Macon, GA, 1933. Land plats show that Karr and Bedell were Robert's neighbors on Little River. There is no further record of Robert during the war years. Earlier researchers speculated that he might have gone with families that were taken to safety in the NC mountains by Elijah Clarke and his men during this part of the war but as yet, there is no proof.

The Revolutionary War (1775-1783) reached these settlements in late 1779. Robert's actual involvement, if any, in the war is unknown. Conditions in this area during the war were very bad, and several families fled the area and lived in the NC mountains, returning after the war. He did receive a land bounty cert. after the war for 250 acres (tax-free). This was later increased to 287.5 acres (taxable) and the land was located in Washington Co. However, according to the office of the Surveyor General of GA, he never exercised the warrant nor took possession of the land. The land cert. was granted to him under a proclamation from Col. Elijah Clarke on February 2, 1784. However, it was common for citizens that did not actually bear arms to receive land. In his cert. there is no mention of him actually serving in the war.

An interesting paragraph in *Sketches of Some of the First Settlers of Upper Georgia, by George R. Gilmer, pg. 155* describes some of the actions by Elijah Clark immediately after the war. "King George had granted land in the GA Colony very stingingly to his subjects. Everyone was especially hungry for more land. After the war, Elijah Clark and other N.C. settlers in Wilkes Co. took possession of the fertile territory between the Oconee and Ocmulgee rivers, without regard to the occupant rights of the Indians, established a republic, made Clark their chief ruler and were prepared to parcel out the lands when the GA militia, ordered into service by Gov. Matthews and the regular troops by Pres. Washington, drove them off." Our Robert McGinty could have been involved here (speculation by me).

A search was also done at the National Archives, and there is no record of military service for Robert McGinty. *Georgia's Roster of the Revolution*, by Lucian Lamar Knight, shows no record of Robert McGinty serving in GA. This book contains many official documents from the war. However, the DAR lists him as a patriot (reference code RXYJBAXK) but this certification is based on earlier, incorrect McGinty research.

There is a record in the National Archives of his brother, James McGinty, serving in the NC militia as a foot soldier with the rank of private. The records show that he served in Capt. Charles Polk's company from July 1776 until after January 1779 when he was at Cross Creek. His brother, John II also served in this unit and was the company's sergeant.

On September 16, 1785, Robert was given a 200 acre "headright grant" in Wilkes Co. (*Grant Book HHH, page 448*). The grant was bounded on all sides by vacant land and shows that it was on the waters of Little River. I have a copy of this land plat. The plats show that it was located next to the land of Samuel Hoof, somewhere along Beaverdam Creek, and north of Little River. On October 12, 1785, he was given an additional "headright" for 300 acres in Wilkes Co. (*Grant Book III, page 90*). The grant shows the location of the land with the north side bordered by Little River. Absalom Bedell shows, owning the property on the other side of the river. Bedell is shown on the grant as the justice presiding over the land court that gave Robert the grant.

This is where Robert lived. This property was located just west of today's Little River, GA. The then Governor of Georgia, Samuel Elbert name appears on both of these original headright grants. Both of these headright grants are confirmed by the office of the surveyor-general in Atlanta where all land grants since 1752 were recorded. The grant books are now in the Georgia Archives in Morrow, GA. A "headright" was land that had not been surveyed and divided into land districts and land lots. It was only surveyed in response to an application for a headright grant and could be any shape the grantee desired so long as it conformed to the amount of his grant.

In February 1785 Robert signed the deed, selling 122 acres of land that was part of his father, John McGinty's estate (Mecklenburg Co. deed book 12, pg. 491). This land was located on McAlpin's Creek and was a tract originally granted to Thomas Polk, March 4, 1775, and sold to John McGinty, April 10, 1779. Robert sold the land to William Kenady for 60 pounds (note: Kenady later married Mary Ann McGinty, the granddaughter of Alexander McGinty Sr.). After this sale, Robert's mother Rebecka and brother James moved to Wilkes Co., GA. This deed also names Robert as the son of John.

As I said earlier, on October 25, 1785, Robert sold the 270 acre tract on Germany's Creek to Thomas Napier (Deed Book F, St. Paul's-Richmond Co.) for 100 pounds. Several years later, in 1797, Napier's land on Germany's Creek, which was then 600 acres, was sold at a sheriff's sale in Columbia Co. at the instance of Robert McGinty *(Augusta Chronicle, June 3, 1797, pg. 3, col. 4).* I am not sure what this was all about, but it indicates some problem arose with the property.

After settling in Wilkes Co., Robert and Deborah sold part of their land grants in several parcels. One hundred acres on the waters of Kettle Creek (HHH, 448) were sold to Thomas Daniel (deed book AA, pg. 248). Three hundred acres were sold to Edward Butler, November 24, 1786 (deed book CC, pg. 257). This is the land on the south side of Little River and is described as land "whereon said McGinty now lives." This was the 1785 grant. There is an additional record of some land "granted by the government to said McGinty" that was sold to Charles Smith on August 4, 1787 (deed book CC, pg. 97). This is thought to be the other 100 acres from the original 200 acre grant (HHH, 448). All of these sales are shown in *Early Records of Georgia, Vol. 1, Wilkes County* compiled by Grace Gilliam Davidson in 1932. The book is located in the Jack Tarver Library at Mercer University in Macon, GA.

It is interesting to note that some of Robert's neighbors on Little River were distinguished individuals, such as Silas Mercer, pioneer Baptist minister, Judge Absalom Bedell and Lt. Col. Micajah Williamson, Revolutionary War hero.

Robert converted from either Presbyterian or Quaker, to the Baptist faith and the church records show that he joined the Phillips Mill Baptist Church by "experience" on April 7, 1787. Deborah joined "by experience" on May 11, 1787. Records show that they were attending this church as early as 1785 along with Robert's mother, Rebecka and his brother, James McGinty. These records are on microfilm, *Philips Mill Baptist Church, Wilkes Co. GA, pub. 1111, Historical Commission, Southern Baptist Convention, Nashville, TN. (Abstracted in 1989 by Charlotte G. Tucker).*

Why did his family convert? Probably the main reason was that Silas Mercer, pastor of the Phillips Mill church, and his son Jesse, were neighbors and friends of Robert after he moved to this area from Wrightsborough. I have land plats showing Silas Mercer's property, very close to Robert, on Harden's Creek. Although reared an Episcopalian, Silas Mercer had also became a Baptist from conviction. He baptized his 17-year-old son Jesse and Robert, at the same time, into the Phillips' Mill church. Also, Deborah's father and brother had been excommunicated by the Quakers, as well as her aunt, Ruth Jackson. This might have caused ill feelings. There could be other contributing reasons. At this time in history, there was a severe shortage of ministers in the Presbyterian Church, particularly in these new southern territories. The Presbyterian Church had a rule that only well educated men could become ministers. Because of demand, there were not enough that met this requirement. The Baptist religion did not require any education for becoming a minister. What the Presbyterians could not do, the Baptists accomplished. To them, the gospel was simple, uncomplicated and within the reach of all. It required no complex organization to form a Baptist church. A group of like-minded Christians could form a congregation and select as their minister a dedicated Baptist who felt the "call." The Phillips Mill church certainly had an experienced minister in Robert's neighbor, Silas Mercer. The success of the Baptists in attracting new members was phenomenal among the Scotch-Irish during this period. This conversion of Robert

McGinty to the Baptist faith was a significant event in McGinty history. Future generations in GA, AL and other states, remained devout Baptists with several becoming well-known ministers and pastors.

When we examine the early Phillips Mill Church history, we see some of the hardships experienced by the congregation, which included Robert and his family. Since the original building where Robert was baptized in 1787 only had a floor, shutters and doors for a short time, if at all, it was probably a log structure. Pews were benches without backs. The site was known as "meetinghouse hill" due to the ridge on which the building was located. The building was on a hillside with a spring below running into Little River. It was also known as "meetinghouse spring." In 1801 a new church was built on a different site, "on top of the hill above the old one." The old meetinghouse building was moved to Raytown where a new church was formed.

The Phillips Mill Baptist Church was founded June 10, 1785, by sixteen members who met at the home of George Lea. The first meetings were held at the grist mill owned by Joel Phillips. On August 5, 1786, church member, Joel Phillips (Sr.), conveyed land to pastor, Silas Mercer for a new church site (Wilkes Co. deed book SS, pg. 54). The church was later moved to its current location, about four miles from this original site. Silas Mercer, one of the great Baptist preachers in early GA, was the first pastor. Silas came from the church at Kiokee, which was the first Baptist church in GA, established in 1772. It was located about twenty miles northwest of Augusta GA. His son, Jesse Mercer and Robert McGinty were both received into the Phillips Mill church by profession of faith and baptized by Silas in 1787. Jesse was fifteen years old and Robert, about thirty-seven. They remained close associates in the Baptist church for the rest of their lives.

It is very possible that Robert met Silas Mercer and his son Jesse when they were at the Kiokee Baptist Church. Silas's father, James Mercer, had some years before, moved the family from NC to land in Wrightsborough. Kiokee was about ten miles from Germany's Creek where Robert and Deborah had lived prior to moving to Wilkes Co. Land plats in Wilkes Co., dating from 1784 also show that Robert and Silas Mercer were neighbors (Thomas Wingfield warrant #530). However, Robert and Deborah did not officially join this Baptist church until 1787.

In 1787 Robert was appointed by the congregation at Phillips Mill, "trustee to get the meetinghouse floored and seated." By 1791 this had not been fully resolved according to the church minutes and Robert and two other members were ordered to "see how cheap they could get a workman to joint and lay the meetinghouse floor, make seats with backs and a pulpit, and to make doors and window shutters to the same." In 1787 Silas Mercer, pastor, referred to Robert as "one of our beloved brethren at Phillips Mill."

He shows in the 1787 tax records of Wilkes Co., living in Capt. Heard's District, with 374 acres of #2 grade land (pg. 38 & 39, Georgia's Virtual Vault). Also listed here is his brother, John McGinty II.

During the 1789 Spring Term of the Superior Court of Wilkes County (March 31, 1789), Robert was selected to serve on a "special jury." The hearing was an appeal by David Hillhouse and William Terrell against a decision previously rendered for Nathaniel Bullock. Robert, and the jury, denied the appeal and found in favor of Bulloch for the amount of "three hundred and fifty pounds, or the Negroes agreeable to contract, and thirty pounds, by the first of June next and the cost of suit."

In 1790 Robert became a licensed minister at Phillips Mill Church and began a long career of service in the Baptist Church. He remained at Phillips Mill Baptist until January 7, 1791, or about four years.

By 1787 Robert and family had moved to property formerly owned by Deborah's brother, Joseph Jackson, located on Harden's Creek, about two miles south of their previous home on the 300 acre grant. They show in this deed as a neighbor to Henry Karr. "On November 27, 1787, Henry Karr sold 380 acres to Archibald Simpson and lists his property as adjoining Robert McGinty on the SE and John Querns on the SW, Samuel Whatley and George Lea on the NE, and all other side by Jones Spring Branch and Robert Day."

We have located this Jackson plat and placed it on a current map. This land is in what is now Hillman, Taliaferro Co., GA, and includes the "electric mountain" where The Electric Health Resort was located from the 1880's until the early 1900's. This mountain had electrical properties and people came for the curative powers of the electrical shock.

He is shown on the 1790 tax returns of Wilkes Co., GA, in Capt. McCormick's District, owning 250 acres. He is shown in the 1790 census of Wilkes Co. as living in what is now Taliaferro Co., north of Sharon, GA. This was very close to or in the Wrightsborough Quaker settlement. He sold the final two hundred fifty acres in Wilkes Co. to Nathaniel Dean on March 26, 1791, but the sale was not registered until August 21, 1794. Wilkes Co. tax records of 1791 show him owning 150 acres, type #3 land, in Capt. Collier's Dist. The Philips Mill Church records show that on January 7, 1792, Robert and Deborah were "dismissed by letter."

They then relocated the family to Washington Co. and moved their membership to the Mount Pelia Baptist Church. In 1793 this area of Washington Co. became part of Hancock Co., and in 1807 part of Baldwin Co. In 1797 Robert attended a conference back at Phillips Mill and the minutes show that he was from the Mount Pelia church. There is a very good possibility that Mt. Pelia was Robert's first church as a pastor. Records at Mercer University indicate that this church was also named Montpelier and that it later united with the Hephzibah Baptist Church (1804) and that the name was changed to Mt. Olives Baptist Church in 1812. I visited this area in April 2006 and found a historical marker showing the general location of Montpelier. It is east of the Oconee River, off Hwy. 22/24 near Milledgeville, GA.

The Washington/Hancock Co. records show that on November 10, 1792, Robert purchased 116 acres on Town Creek from Isaac Williams. This deed shows Robert McGinty, "of the same place," confirming that he was in Washington Co. by this time. I have a copy of this land plat. At this time in GA history, this area was the western frontier. Indian lands lay beyond. He lived on this land until ca. 1799 and then moved a few miles north to land on Rocky Creek, then located in Hancock Co. (became Baldwin Co. in 1807). He sold the 116 acres back on Town Creek to William Bivins, October 1, 1800, for $1,200.

The tax lists of Hancock and Baldwin Co. show Robert as a property owner on Rocky Creek from 1804-1821. Part of this time, he lived in Capt. Jacob Gumm's district. Jacob Gumm is buried in the small Gumm cemetery nearby (GPS 33 08' 32" N 83 09' 07" W). In the 1808-1809 Baldwin Co. tax list, he is also shown as executor for the estate of Levi Daniel. He is shown in Daniell's will as a "trusted friend."

In October 2004 my brother Phil located the exact position of Robert's land. Today, the southern border of his lot is the shore of the man-made reservoir, Lake Sinclair. These 287½ acres of land was originally in Washington Co., and owned by Peter Perkins. It was surveyed November 11, 1784, when Washington Co. was originally formed. Later, in 1793 this area became Hancock Co. and in 1807, it became part of Baldwin Co. We have the original Washington Co. survey map of the Perkins land. Perkins sold the land to Stephen Horton in 1797. Horton then sold the land to Robert on April 6, 1799 for $460. This land is 2.8 miles south of the Island Creek Baptist church where Robert was so active for many years. The 1811 tax list of Baldwin Co. shows that the District was now Captain McGinty's. After Robert moved to Jones Co., in 1821 this land is shown as being owned by his son, William McGinty.

The Baldwin Co. tax lists for both 1808 and 1809 show Robert with 287½ acres of land and six slaves. Slave ownership was apparently not in conflict with his Baptist ministry.

Note: Washington Co. was formed in 1784. Hancock Co. was formed in 1793 from parts of Greene and Washington. Baldwin Co. was formed in 1803 from parts of Wilkinson, Washington and Hancock, with additions from Washington in 1807, 1812 and 1826.

There is mention in earlier research about his having a bounty warrant, number 1446, for the land in this county, but there is no record in the GA surveyor-general office showing that he was ever actually granted the property (there is also some research showing that warrant 1446, which he was said to receive, was only shown as an example in the records and was not actually given to Robert). Records at the GA Archives show that he served as Justice of the Inferior Court in Hancock Co. from December 17, 1793, through June 16, 1796. He was a member of the Hancock Co. Grand Jury in September 1797. He served a second term as Justice from 1801-1807. He was also a justice of the peace in Hancock Co. from 1799 until 1812. We do know that their family was large by then with twelve sons and one daughter all born by around 1800.

There is an interesting article that was published in the *Augusta Chronicle*, September 17, 1796. It reads as follows: "State of Georgia, Hancock Co., Whereas I the subscriber, did on the twenty-first day of April last, speak slanderous words against the character of Robert

McGinty of Town Creek, in said county, in the hearing of Joseph McGinty, and perhaps some others; saying that the said Robert McGinty was an old dammed thieving son of a bitch; That he had stole my corn. Which words, I do hear by certify to have been spoke through heat of passion; and without any foundation: But on the contrary. From the best information that I have received, and as far as I know of my own knowledge, I do believe the said Robert McGinty to be an honest man. Given under my hand this 10th day of August 1796. William Minor." Land records show that William Minor was a neighbor of Robert and a major land owner. This dispute was probably centered on Minor's corn and the grist mill that Robert owned. Today there is a Minor Road in this area of Baldwin Co.

On June 1, 1799, he and Deborah joined the Island Creek Baptist Church, (est. 14 Mar 1794) in the newly formed Hancock Co., "by letter." This church is still located west of Sparta, GA. He was listed as an ordained minister. Five of their sons were baptized there, Joseph on March 11, 1800, Thomas on September 1, 1804, Washington on August 31, 1805, William on November 11, 1827 and Robert Jr., December 1, 1827.

On April 26, 1800, a petition was published in the *Augusta Chronicle, pg. 3, col. 1*, concerning Robert and the title to 116 acres of land that was formerly owned by Isaac Williams. Apparently, the deed had been destroyed or lost and the Hancock Co. superior court ordered that the deed be either produced by their next session or that a new deed would be created after publishing the issue in one of the local "Gazettes" for three months. He is also shown as a justice of the peace in Hancock Co., beginning January 29, 1801.

In 1801/02 he served as pastor of the Horeb Baptist Church in Hancock Co. According to the church records, the current pastor became ill and Robert was asked to serve for one year. Church records show that "In February, 1802 Bro. McGinty made known to the church that he could not attend them any longer. On leaving, the treasurer was ordered to procure a suit of clothes for Bro. McGinty."

In 1803 he served as pastor of the Island Creek Church and in 1808-1809; he was the substitute pastor or, as they were called, "supply." He was also clerk of this church from 1815-1821. I visited this church on January 24, 2002, with my cousin Tom Wood who lives in Milledgeville, GA. The church is located N.E. of Milledgeville, GA, off of Hwy 22, on Carr's Station Rd. It is a neat, well-maintained small white wood building out in the open country. According to church history, this is the third building. The first and second church buildings were both nearby. There are two entrances in the front of the church. In the primitive Baptist churches, it was customary for the women and men to be segregated with the men sitting on one side of the church and the women on the other side. One front door was for the men and the other for the women. Another primitive church that appears to be the identical building plan is the Camp Creek Primitive Baptist Church (est. 1817) in Baldwin Co., GA. The small cemetery at Island Creek church is full of graves, but there are only a few stones with inscriptions. There are no known McGintys thought to be buried there because none died during their years of membership.

The original minutes of the Island Creek Church are located in the Jack Tarver Library at Mercer University in Macon, GA. Robert wrote some of these minutes when he was clerk of this church from 1815-1821 and they are there in the original book. It is interesting to note that the church was called "The Church of Christ at Island Creek" at this time. I reviewed this material at the library on January 25, 2001, and have since studied the microfilmed minutes.

On May 1, 1803, a committee of twelve Baptist leaders including Robert McGinty, met at the Baptist church in Powelton, Hancock Co., GA, and formed The General Committee of Georgia Baptists. This was actually their third yearly Baptist conference. Abraham Marshall was named chairman. He was a legendary Baptist minister in GA. Jesse Mercer, son of Silas, was also there. They adopted the following resolution: "Resolved, that the encouragement of itinerant preaching, the religious instruction of our savage neighbors, and the increase of union among all real Christians, which were the leading objects of the late conference, shall be zealously prosecuted by this committee." This "conference" might be called the first regularly appointed Baptist convention ever held in GA. The group agreed to meet annually and the Georgia Association was born.

On October 4, 1804, Robert preached the sermon at the Georgia Association meeting. The title of the sermon was "And there was given to me a reed, like unto a rod, Revelations 11:1." This meeting was held at the New Ford Baptist Church in Wilkes Co. Jesse Mercer was also present and was the clerk.

He participated in the Ocmulgee land lottery drawings of 1806 in Hancock Co. These draws were in Capt. Jacob Gumm's district. He drew twice but was not successful. His brothers, James and John, also drew and were unsuccessful. His son, Joseph McGinty was successful in his draw. His son, Robert McGinty Jr. also had one draw along with son, Thomas McGinty, with two draws.

As the Indians were being pushed steadily westward, it usually took up to five years for their vacated land to be surveyed and divided up into lots of two hundred and two acres each. In typical land lotteries, plats of each lot were traced on small cards, about the size of those now used in the game of Monopoly™, which were deposited in wire cages, along with a number of blank cards. At highly publicized events, the cards were drawn one by one, in full view of the assembled crowds. Every white adult male was entitled to one free draw, married men or widows with children had two draws, and extra chances went to Revolutionary War veterans, those who had served honorably in certain public offices, or had some other distinction. After arriving in Hancock Co., Robert became involved in the local government. An article in *The Land Between - A History of Hancock County Georgia to 1940*, chapter IV, by Forrest Shivers, explains how the county was organized. "Before it became a separate county, the area of Hancock had been organized into militia districts and these units played an essential part in local government. The boundaries of the districts also defined the territorial jurisdiction of the justice of the peace courts, the election districts, the return of property for taxation, stock and fence laws, the conveyance of land, and all other matters specifically referred to the districts in the law of the state.

"The new county had nine militia districts, each designated by the name of the captain commanding. (The districts were not numbered until the early years of the next century.) The captains were elected by all the able-bodied men between the ages of 16 and 50 in their districts and hence eligible for military duty. No district was supposed to have more than sixty-three militiamen.

"The nine-militia districts in the county in turn formed two battalion areas, one commanded by Lieutenant Colonel Thomas Lamar and the other by Lieutenant Colonel Harmon Runnels. The governor and legislature appointed David Adams and Richard Bonner tax receivers for their respective battalion areas. They also appointed five justices of the Inferior Court: David Dickson, Matthew Rabun, Peter Boyle, **Robert McGinty** and John Hamilton. The position of justice of the Inferior Court was an important one. Though the court originally had quite limited jurisdiction, it was granted increased powers in the Constitution of 1798 and subsequent legislation so that it would eventually exercise most of the administrative power of the county government. At the same time, six justices of peace were named: John Harbert, Davis Long, James Thweatt, Jesse Veazey, Daniel McDowell and Joel McLendon." Robert held an important position here in addition to his church work.

There is also evidence that Robert was a candidate for the State Legislature around this time. This same article, word for word, appeared in the June 6, 1807, and August 8, 1807, editions of the *Farmer's Gazette*. It reads: "From good authority, we learn that Col. Epps Brown, **Robert M'Ginty**, esq., William Chandler, esq., Richard A. Blount, esq., are candidates to represent this county in the House of Representatives of the next General Assembly."

On April 16, 1810, he was issued a passport by the Governor of GA to travel through Creek Indian lands. On October 15, 1810, he was issued another passport for the same purpose (*Passports Issued by the Governors of Georgia, 1785-1809,* by Mary G. Bryan). These passports were, no doubt, for the purpose of investigating the proposed Creek Indian missionary movement that was well underway. Later, the Ocmulgee Baptist Association agreed to engage in the works of "Indian Reform" among the Creeks and at their annual meeting in 1820, and approved a formal plan to establish a school in the Creek Nation in the area that "lies between the Euchee Creek and the Tallapoosy River." The school was known as the Withington Station, and was located about thirty miles south of today's Montgomery, AL, which at that time was in the midst of the Creek nation. The plan was titled as follows: "A plan of a school to be the germ of a religious establishment among the Creek Indians." By 1823 the school had opened and was flourishing with an initial enrollment of thirty-seven male and female Creek Indian children.

On November 10, 1810, the Ocmulgee Baptist Association (named for the Ocmulgee River, which was the western boundary of white settlements in GA) was formed at Rooty Creek Baptist Church in Putnam Co. It was the fifth association formed in GA and had about

1,200 members. Robert McGinty was part of the committee that formed this association of twenty-four churches. He was then the moderator (chairman) from 1817-1822. At the 1817 meeting, which was held at Elim Baptist Church in Jones Co., GA, Robert preached the introductory sermon from 1st Corin., 2:12, "Now we have received not the spirit of the world, but the Spirit which is from God, that we might understand the gifts bestowed on us by God." He was also elected moderator of the association at this meeting. The Island Creek church became a member of the Ocmulgee Assn. in 1816. It was formerly part of the Georgia Assn. While serving as moderator of the Ocmulgee association, he continued as the delegate or messenger from the Island Creek church in Hancock Co., from 1816-1821. He was also president of the Ocmulgee Missionary Society around 1819 and for some years after.

By 1811 many new churches had been formed in GA by the original twelve preachers who were part of the Association in 1803. Robert was one of these men, "who engaged themselves devotedly in itinerant labors, and constituted churches all over the eastern half of GA, and the general spirit of earnestness, piety and zeal prevailed."

In 1811 Robert helped found the First Baptist Church of Milledgeville in Baldwin Co., GA. Church records say that he drafted the original constitution for the church. Jesse Mercer was also one of the advisors that helped start this church.

The 1811 tax list of Baldwin Co., shows Robert now living on the same 290 acres from Perkins in Capt. McGintys' District. Also living in this district was Robert Jr., Washington, John, and several related Moores. Was this him, or one of his sons? More research is needed here.

He is shown in the 1813 Baldwin Co. tax list, living in Capt. Thomas' district. He is then shown in the 1818 Baldwin Co. tax list, living in Capt. Hightower's district with 145 acres of type two and 145 acres of type three lands. His land adjoined that of a Sanford on the waters of Rocky Creek. He also shows seven slaves. Apparently, he owned and operated a grist mill on Rocky Creek. The following was published in the *Georgia Journal*: "1818, December 1st. The subscriber, living in Baldwin County, Rocky Creek, 7 miles northeast of Milledgeville, wants to employ a man as a Miller, for ensuing year, who understands grinding and keeping a good geared mill (Signed) Robert

McGinty."

Robert and Deborah remained members of the Island Creek Church for twenty two years, departing by letter on November 17, 1821, when they moved on to Jones Co., GA, and he became pastor of the Bethel Baptist Church for a short time. He was then referred to as "Elder McGinty." The Ocmulgee Baptist Assn. minutes of 1822 show him as the messenger to the annual meeting from Bethel church in Jones Co. (Tarver Library, Mercer Univ., Macon, GA, reel # 1180).

Since it is known that Robert was very involved in association work from this point forward in his life, it is important to understand what changes were taking place in the Baptist church at this time in history. From the beginning, Baptist churches were not independent of each other. Whitney, in his *History of British Baptists*, covering the church history in the 1600's, shows that they always sought the fellowship between the different churches to carry on evangelistic work. This continued in America.

The first Baptist church that was established in GA was founded in 1772. It was the Kiokee Baptist Church in Columbia Co. near Augusta. Over the next two years several others were formed. In 1774 these churches formed an association called the Georgia because it was the only one in the State. It was constituted at Kiokee by the work of Elder Daniel Marshall, the pastor. Over the next ten years, the association flourished and by 1784 there were about fifty-five churches with over 5,000 members. Beginning in 1794 new associations were formed including the Hepzibah, the Serepta and the Savannah. About this time, the question of foreign missions began to be considered by GA Baptists. Cary, the great pioneer in modern missions, had already been to Hindustan for a number of years and by 1812 great interest was developing in GA. The first mission society is thought to have been in Savannah in 1813. This society sent out a stirring address on the subject of missions, which resulted in the formation of other societies.

By 1815 Jesse Mercer, one of the most influential Baptist of the day, started a society to "evangelize the poor heathen in idolatrous lands." In July 1815 the Ocmulgee Missionary Society was formed and proved to be strong and influential. Later, in 1819 Robert McGinty was elected president of this society.

At the same time a strong anti-mission spirit which condemned the whole movement was underway. This caused great division in the church with some becoming "Missionary Baptists" and others anti-missionary, or "Primitive Baptists." There was thought to be a need for a general organization where brethren from different views could meet and resolve their differences. The new organization was called the General Baptist Association of the State of Georgia. It was formed at Powelton, GA, June 27, 1822. Robert was the first moderator. He wrote the following letter following the session in September 1822: "The transactions of your first convention have been presented to our body, by our much esteemed brother, Jesse Mercer, and have been taken into consideration. We have now to state that your specified objects meet our unanimous approbation. We cannot close this poor token of love without expressing our hope that the General Baptist Association of Georgia will prove a lasting blessing to the cause of the Redeemer's kingdom. We further request your next convention be within our bounds. R. McGinty, Moderator." At the time there were eight separate associations in GA with about 16,000 members. The new association did not receive full support for many years. In 1828 the name was changed to the Baptist Convention of the State of Georgia (Georgia Baptist Convention). However, by 1846 it was representing only 38,000 members out of estimated 60,000 total in the association. There were bitter feelings and divisions within the church in the period 1830-1840 over the missionary issue.

The 1820 census of Baldwin Co., GA, shows Robert, over age forty-five (which is the highest age bracket on the census form) and his wife, also over forty-five, with son William living next door (pg. 36-37). In this census, Robert is shown with one male child, sixteen to twenty-six and three male and six female slaves. Robert and his sons, William and Josiah, are also shown in the Baldwin Co. land lottery draws of 1821, in Maj. Richard W. Ellis's Battalion. Robert is shown here as Robert, Sen. (senior).

In 1823 he moved from Jones Co., to Monroe Co. and around the age of seventy-six, became the pastor of the New Providence Baptist Church. *Monroe County, Georgia, a History*, pg. 275, says that this church was organized in 1820 and was located on Providence Hill near Tobosofkee Creek. This location is southwest of Smarr, GA. My brother and I have visited this area. He was pastor here until 1828. At this time he also became very involved in the Flint River Association and continued active there until 1830. According to the tax digest of

1828 located at the GA Archives in Atlanta, he owned lot 80 in the twelfth district that contained 202½ acres. This lot was adjacent to lot 91 and 92 that were owned by his son, Thomas. The original grantee of lot #80 was John Prescot. He sold the lot to Jos. Duckworth, January 26, 1822 (deed record vol. A, #253), for $200. Sometime after this, Robert came into possession of this lot, but the deeds transferring title to him have not yet been found. He then shows in the 1830 and 1840 census, living in Monroe Co. In the 1830 census, page 225, he is listed at age 70-80 with a female age 60-70 who I think was his wife, Deborah. She must have died in the early 1830's because she is not shown in the census of 1840.

The Flint River Association, tenth in the state, was formed October 16, 1824, at Rocky Creek meetinghouse in Monroe Co. It consisted of fourteen churches, five ministers and about 525 members. Robert McGinty was the moderator of this first session. In 1825 at the second session, Robert gave the introductory address. He was the moderator (chairman) of the association for the first five years, 1824-1828 (Flint River Assn. Minutes, Mercer University). This association was created out of the Ocmulgee and was a strong missionary group of churches. The association responded to the needs of people at home, such as the Indians and Negroes and abroad where they could. They heartily embraced the total world mission program. The minutes of 1824 show Robert, in the first circular letter had admonished the people of God, "In the name of Him in whose service you are engaged, go on." Robert chose the Missionary Baptist Church while some of his children, such as Washington and Thomas, remained in the Primitive Baptist Church. Robert remained active in the association until age and infirmity compelled him to decline service. In 1829 he notified the association that he wanted to be excused from the moderator position because of age and infirmity (Flint River minutes of 1829 item 3). However, in 1830 he accepted the position of "circular letter writer" for one more year. We think that after Deborah's death, he moved in with his son William near Montpelier Springs, south of Forsyth, GA, in Monroe Co. According to the *Christian Index*, William moved to this area in 1836. He shows as living in William's house in the 1840 census of Monroe Co., age 80-90 (pg. 158). We know that William was a member of the New Providence Primitive Baptist Church at this time. William was listed as "messenger" for this church to the Flint River Assn. in 1841. This means that he represented the church at association meetings. The exact church location and Robert's burial place have yet to be found. Various sources show the approximate location of the original church, and my brother and I visited the area in November 2004. Flint River Assn. records and other references show that it was originally located six miles south of Forsyth, GA and three miles southwest of Smarr, GA. Sometime after the railroad was completed in 1836 the church building was moved to its present location in Smarr, GA.

Court records in 1832 show Robert, "clergyman, residing in the county of Monroe" as a witness to a Revolutionary War pension application by a Mathew Durham.

In *Georgia Baptists: Historical and Biographical* by Jesse H. Campbell, published in 1847 he offers the following on Robert McGinty: "He was a man of general information, an excellent moderator, a person of easy and polite manners, and a sensible, sound preacher." In the book, *History of the Baptist Denomination in Georgia*, published in 1881 Robert is described as follows: "Rev. Robert McGinty was a man of high standing and good influence; polite and easy in his manners; pious in character; strongly missionary in spirit; an excellent moderator and a sound, sensible preacher. He was one of those who helped form the General Committee, at Powelton, in 1803 and was a member of the Committee. He was moderator of the Ocmulgee Association, president of the Ocmulgee Missionary Society, and for years the moderator of the Flint River Association. Raised (which is an error) in Wilkes Co., he was baptized at the same time and place as Jesse Mercer, in 1787 and was ordained before 1799."

He is also mentioned as one of the "most prominent actors among the historical characters of the Georgia Baptists who moved in the drama enacted in the first decade of the nineteenth century, and put in train events which molded the destinies of our denomination in the State." In this section his name is shown as R. E. McGinty, but it is thought that this middle initial was picked up from earlier research that was in error. There is no proof that he had a middle name.

Robert's last will and testament (Record of Wills, Book A, pg. 164, Forsyth, Monroe Co., GA) was probated February 10, 1841, in Monroe Co., GA. He gave his servant, Molly, her freedom. He gave all of his twelve children twenty-five dollars each with equal shares of everything else and appointed two of his sons, Thomas and William, executors for the balance of his estate.

In 1836, he his sons sold the following property on his behalf:

WILL be sold on the fifteenth day of December next, at the residence of Robert McGinty, Sen. in Monroe county, Ga. a part of the

Negroes,

belonging to said Robert; also 4 or 5 thousand weight of Pork, with stock hogs, corn, fodder, farming utensils, and various other things.

The above articles will be sold to the highest bidder for cash.   THOMAS McGINTY, } *Trustees.*
nov 1—4t   WILLIAM McGINTY, }

Prior to his death, this announcement then appeared in the *Macon Georgia Telegraph*, January 5, 1841, page 3. Here, he mentions granting the POA to his two sons for them to sell part of his property (above). His will was probably written around this same time because he mentions dividing the proceeds among his children.

GEORGIA, *Monroe County.*
      To all whom it may Concern.
BE it known, that I have this day revoked, and do make null and void a certain Power of Attorney, made by me to William McGinty and Thomas McGinty, my sons, in the year 1836, I think in the summer of that year, for them to sell and dispose of a part of my property, both real and personal at public sale, which was done, and the proceeds were equally divided between my children; and now be it known that I now set aside and revoke any and all other proceedings on the above described Power of Attorney. Witness my hand and seal, this 25th December, 1840.
      ROBERT McGINTY, Sen. (L. S.)
   In presence of
      JAMES WATSON.
Jan 5   14 1t

The newspaper announcement of the sale of his slaves shown below appeared in the *Southern Recorder*, published in Milledgeville,

April 6, 1841. It was also announced for several weeks in other publications.

WILL BE SOLD on the first Tuesday in June next, within legal hours, at the court house in the town of Forsyth, Monroe county, agreeably to the last will and testament of Robert McGinty, Sr., late of said county. deceased, four negroes, viz: Lucy, a woman 25 years old, and her three children—Henry, a boy 8 years old; Susan, a girl 5 years old; and Emeline, 1 year old. Sold for the benefit of the legatees.

THOMAS McGINTY, } Exec'rs.
WILLIAM McGINTY, }

April 6, 1841.   12 tds

On June 1, 1841, these four Negros, Lucy and her three children, Henry, Susan and Emeline were sold to James Bivens for $1,350. On June 2, all of his personal property was sold at the residence of son, William. This list of property is on file at the Monroe Co., GA courthouse, Court of Ordinary, Book E, pg. 322-324 and is very interesting. Several McGinty relatives purchased items including Robert C.C., William, James, Elijah, Thomas, Josiah, and Shadrach. The items included household furniture, kitchen utensils, toilet items, poultry, livestock, food items and his book collection. He was well-read and the books included law, history and religious titles. These purchases totaled $1,525. We have no record of Deborah's death. She shows in the 1830 census but is not shown in Robert's Will. It is thought that she died between 1830 and 1840.

The exact date of his death and burial site is still unknown. However, recent discoveries in the tax records show that at the time of Deborah's death, they lived on lot #80 in dist. 12. They should be buried nearby. His death was not reported in the minutes of the Ocmulgee Assn., probably because he had not been a member for some time. There is a notice in the *Christian Index*, December 3, 1841, with the minutes of the Flint River Association, October 16-19, 1841, which includes a report on the death of ministers. It reads as follows: "We notice with much reverence, and long won worth and merit, the departure of our honored and aged father and brother, Robert

McGinty, who we remember in useful life, and even when age had taken the vigor of youth and active usefulness, as one of the pillars: Yes, he has gone up to reap his reward!"

Robert McGinty had been a minister in the Baptist Church for more than fifty years. Many of his descendents were also noted ministers and his longevity is also found in several future generations of McGinty.

At the time of his death in 1840/1841 it is possible that all thirteen of his children were living because they are all mentioned by name in his will. The number of McGinty descendents from Robert and Deborah are so numerous that future researchers will have plenty of opportunities to sort out the branches of their family tree.

John McGinty

(unknown-ca. 1782)

John McGinty I, b. unknown but assumed to be between 1700 and 1720 in Ireland, d., ca. 1782 in Mecklenburg Co., NC. Land transactions in both PA and NC show that he was married to Rebecca (also spelled Rebeka), maiden name unknown. Her name is included with his on deeds in both states.

Children of John McGinty I and Rebecca:

Robert McGinty, b. ca. 1750-60 probably in PA, but possibly in Ireland, d. ca. 1840 in Monroe Co., GA. Married Deborah Jackson ca. 1770. Robert's life is covered in detail starting on page 163 of this book.

James McGinty, b. before 1755 probably in PA, because his father was living there by 1755, d. unknown, but thought to be before 1816 in Clairborne Co, MS, because his wife, Lydia, is listed in the 1816 census as head-of-house. He married Lydia Hood, daughter of Tunis Hood from Mecklenburg Co., NC, by 1783. Their known children were Reuben, Elizabeth, Mary, Lydia, Robert J., and possibly a Bertram G., John, Abner F. and others. He shows in Mecklenburg Co. court records in 1778 and 1779. During the Revolutionary War, James served as a private in Capt. Charles Polk's Company of NC militia foot soldiers, which was organized in Mecklenburg Co., NC. Records show that he received payment in July 1776 for twenty-five days service, and again on June 15, 1779 (Halifax), for twenty-six days service. His brother, John was the sergeant in this group of about forty men. They were involved in several campaigns including Cross Creek and Brunswick from 1776 until 1779. An article in the *Olde Mecklenburg Genealogical Society Quarterly, vol. 15, number 1, "Germans in Mecklenburg"*, published in 1997, shows that James was among 534 NC Militia captured at the Battle of Guilford Courthouse (Greensboro, NC), March 15, 1781, and after the British victory was paroled by Lord Cornwallis the British commander. This was one of the last battles in the Revolutionary War.

After the sale of his father's land in NC, he accompanied his brother, Robert and mother, Rebecka to Wilkes Co., GA. He show as James McGintee in the "remnant" tax list of 1785 in Capt. Karr's dist., Wilkes Co., with one poll. No land ownership is shown (*Early Records of Georgia*, vol. II, pg. 25, by Grace Gillam Davidson). He is shown in the substitute census of 1790 by Frank Parker Hudson, located in the GA Archives, as having land or a land grant in Wilkes Co., GA, in what is now Taliaferro Co., west of Crawfordville, GA. There is a footnote saying that he may not have actually been living there in 1790 but that he did pay taxes there in 1787. His brothers, Robert and John also show in this document. Sometime around this time, he relocated back to NC. In 1793 he received state land grant #1583 in Mecklenburg Co. for 100 acres on the waters of Stewart's Fork and Richardson's Creek. He actually purchased this grant on April 3, 1800. He shows in the 1790 census in the Salisbury District (#15), Mecklenburg Co. (since 1842 this is part of Union Co.) below Goose Creek. At this time his family consisted of wife Lydia with three males and three other females. This census also shows the Hood family (Tunis Sr., Tunis Jr. and Reuben) living in the same District #15. He shows as a witness to the deed of William Robinson, July 20, 1793. He is also seen as a purchaser of several bushels of corn and a wagon at the estate sale of Robert Walker that was held in Mecklenburg Co. in 1794. Capt. McGinty's company was already formed by 1794. In the minutes of the April 1796 session, *Mecklenburg Co. N.C. Court of Common Pleas and Quarters, Book 3*, Capt. McGinty's Company is shown as a political district. We can assume that James was Capt. McGinty since his other brothers were no longer in NC at this time.

The Phillips Mill Baptist Church conference record of July 8, 1797, shows that James, who had been excommunicated at an earlier date, was to be reinstated. The church minutes say "Bro. Robert McGinty from the Mount Pelia Church informed this conference that James McGinty who was formerly a member of this church and excommunicated for certain crimes committed among them, had of late given full satisfaction to the aggrieved members of said church, whereupon this church agreed to give up this matter to said church and their satisfaction should be ours. Dismissed by letter." James had already left Phillips Mill Church and was a member of a new church by 1797. He was living in NC by this date. James is shown as a juror from McGinty's Company in 1795. He is shown in the 1800 land valuations for taxes in Iredell Co., NC (formed from Rowan Co. in 1788) as owning one tract of 510 acres of land on 3rd Creek and another tract of 200 acres on 4th Creek along with a barn that measured twenty-six by fifty feet. He shows in the 1800 census of Iredell Co., NC (pg. 640), with a large family consisting of two males under 10; two males 10-16; one male 16-26; one male over forty-five (him), two females under ten, one female, 10-16; one female, 16-26; and one female, 26-45 (wife). His age bracket here is "Over 45," meaning that he was born before 1755. Beginning in 1798 he shows as a juror in Iredell Co. several times through 1804. On November 3, 1801, James purchased the 510 acres on the waters of 3rd Creek from Adam Kerrell *(Iredell Co. Deed Book D, p. 387)*. On February 3, 1802, he sold some of the land on 3rd Creek to William Astin. This was part of the same 510 acres *(Iredell Co. Deed Book E, p. 393)*. His daughter, Elizabeth, also witnessed this deed. On February 26, 1802, he sold another 335 acres on 3rd Creek to Butler Stonestreet for $750. This sale was witnessed by his son, Reuben McGinty *(Iredell Co. Deed Book E, pg.1)*.

James relocated to LA/MS before 1804. According to census records, one of his sons, Robert J. McGinty, is shown as being born in MS in 1804. Robert J. went on to become the first mayor of Vicksburg, MS in 1836. The Louisiana Purchase was in 1803 and the opening of the Mississippi River brought in many new settlers to the area. James and his family seem to have been part of this movement. However, his legacy lived on in NC and in 1810 there is a court document concerning the responsible party for road maintenance and Nathaniel Bagwell was appointed overseer of the road from "McGinty's to Concord Meeting House." In 1811 and 1813 we see this same road mentioned again. In 1814 Ross McLelland was appointed overseer of the road "from opposite William Stevenson's to McGinty's old place."

He shows in the Federal census of 1810 living in Concordia Parish, LA. At this time, Concordia Parish was quite large and took in what is now Tensas Parish. In 1810 the McGintys lived in LA, just across the Mississippi River from the mouth of Bayou Pierre, Clairborne Co., MS. Today, that area is in Tensas Parish. His family is shown as three males under ten, two males, 10-16; one male, 16-26; one male over forty-five (him), two females, 16-26; one female over forty-five (wife) and no slaves. He is listed in the 1816 tax roll for Clairborne Co., MS, but is then missing from a later 1816 federal census where his wife, Lydia is shown as the head of the household. This census shows Lydia with one male over twenty-one, two males under twenty-one, two females over twenty-one and one female under twenty-one. Based on this, James could have died in 1816. Lydia is not found in the 1820 census, so she could have died before then. A member of the Tunis Hood family, Dellmann Hood, wrote a book titled *The Tunis Hood Family: It's Lineage and Traditions*. It mistakenly shows that Lydia Hood married Alexander McGinty Jr., when in fact she married James McGinty.

John McGinty II, b. ca. 1760 probably in PA, d. unknown, but after 1830 in Pike Co., GA where three of his daughters lived. Name of wife unknown but based on having seven children by 1820, their marriage would have been before 1813. During the Revolutionary War, John was a member of Capt. Charles Polk's NC militia foot soldiers. He was the company's first sergeant. The unit was organized in Mecklenburg Co., NC, and consisted of about forty men. They fought in several campaigns including Cross Creek and Brunswick. Records show that he received payment for twenty-five days service (undated), fifty-three days service from March to May 1776 in Polk's "light horse" to Brunswick, and twenty-six days at Cross Creek, January 15, 1779 (Halifax).

Before leaving Mecklenburg Co., NC, we see his name in court minutes beginning in 1783 serving on juries. He was present at the 1785 estate sale of his father in NC, and purchased several items. Around 1785 John moved to Wilkes Co., GA. He shows as John McGintee in the 1785 "remnant" tax list of Wilkes Co., with one poll. No property ownership is shown (*Early Records of Georgia*, vol. II, pg. 25, by Grace Gillam Davidson). In the 1790 and 1791 tax lists of Wilkes Co., he is shown in what is now Taliaferro Co., in Capt. Callier's military district (172), just east of Sharon, GA. He shows as part of a Pugh 1811 sale of 240 acres, on the "waters of Reedy Creek." His wife's name is unknown. John was a member of the "petit jury" in 1791. He shows serving on this jury in several cases. He shows in the Wilkes Co., GA tax list for most of the years between 1785 and 1821. He shows as a witness to the will of Martha Stewart that was written in Wilkes Co., March 27, 1791, and probated September 20, 1793. The land mentioned in the will was on Harden's Creek. In 1805 he drew in the

Wilkes Co. land lottery.

We think, though have not yet confirmed that he had at least four sons, John A., James, William and Alexander. All but Alexander, fit into the 1820 Wilkes Co. census age brackets. A Nancy McGinty also shows in the Wilkes Co. marriages, Grace Davidson book (pg. 84), marrying John Rhodes, July 30, 1818. She could have been one of his daughters, but more research is needed on her. All of the sons show in the local tax records from 1819-1821. Alexander married Margaret Person, July 2, 1818, in Wilkes Co., GA (page 49) and then moved to AL and purchased land in Perry Co., as early as 1823. John II shows in the 1820 census of Wilkes Co., GA, pg. 254, with three male and four female children along with four slaves. His probable son, John A. also shows in this census, pg. 282/194. There is also a record in the Peugh (Pugh) family research that show John II with four daughters and this is confirmed by the 1820 census. Olive "Ollie," married Asa Peugh around 1824. The 1787 tax digest of Wilkes Co., Capt. Heard's district shows John II living next door to Elijah Pugh. John does not show owning any property here and might be actually living with Pugh. The 1830 census of Pike Co. shows Asa Peugh living near John II. His wife, Olive McGinty, is age 20-30. Martha, born ca. 1809 in GA, married Benjamin Borders in Pike Co., in 1832. They show in later census records in Carroll Co., GA. Catherine married his brother, Lewis Charles Borders in Pike Co., in 1828. They show in the 1830, 1850 and 1860 census of Pike Co. Mary married William D. Pender in Pike Co., 1844. John A. (b., ca. 1778) shows as living in the 34th Battalion, Warren Co., GA in 1845 and died in that county, April 16, 1853, at age seventy-five. His epitaph in the *Christian Index* reads, "John A. McGinty, having been a member of the Baptist church sixty odd years. He died in the triumph of faith. Blessed are the dead which die unto the Lord." His first wife was Nancy (maiden name unknown). She was the mother of all his children. His second wife was Jincy "Jane" Culverhouse, who died March 13, 1856, at about age sixty-five.

Note: Possible son, John A. was born ca. 1778. Some of the tax records and deeds, after he became of age in 1800 could be him and not John II. However, we do see several entries which are definitely him, because the A is shown in his name. Entries include 1815 Wilkes County, *No. 5, Captain John Hendrick's District*, John A. McGinty, 1 slave, 100 acres type #2 land, 242 acres type #3 land, 50 acres pine land,

Wilkes County, on Rocky Creek, adjoining J. Hendricks, originally granted to McCarty, plus one stud horse, Goliath, $6, with taxes $7.21. 1819 Wilkes County, *Captain Anderson Bates' District,* John A. McGinty - 1 slave, 200 acres type #2 land, 125 acres type #3 land, 50 acres pine land, Wilkes County, on Rocky Creek, adjoining J. Hendricks, originally granted to McCarty, taxes $1.31, and 1821 Wilkes County, *Captain Archibald Harry's District,* John A. McGinty - 250 acres type #3 land, 50 acres pine land, Wilkes County, on Rocky Creek, adjoining J. Hendricks, originally granted to McCarty, 490 acres pine land in Irwin County, 10th District, Lot # 279, One two wheel carriage. Total taxes $1.75. John A. lived in Wilkes Co. from 1785 until 1820 and then moved to Warren Co.

In 1799 we see a John II living in Wilkes Co., Capt. Patterson's District and listed as a "tax defaulter." In 1800 he purchased 220 acres of land on Steven's Creek. The 1801 tax digest shows him as having land in William Ogletree's District. He had one draw in the 1805 lottery (the first one in GA) where he is listed as "John Maginta." He had two draws in the 1806/07 land lottery, and was living in Capt. John Young's District, Wilkes County, GA (*Early Records of Georgia*, Grace C. Davidson, pg. 326). We see John in the 1809 tax list, still on Stephen's Creek. In 1813 he shows in Hiram William's district with three slaves. We find John selling his land on Stephen's Creek to Archibald Gresham. As noted above, in 1820 John II is shown in the Wilkes Co. census (pg. 254), living in John Bryant's district on Hardin's Creek. In this census, he has three male and four female children. His age is shown as "Over 45," meaning that he was born before 1775. He shows drawing in other land lotteries during this period. By 1827 he was living in Pike Co., GA, and had been there for at least three years because he was included in the 1827-28 "free land lottery" in Pike Co., and a three year residence in the county was required. He was eligible for this draw because of his Revolutionary War service. In 1832 he successfully drew two lots located in Cherokee Co., GA. He was living in Bustin's district, Pike Co., and is shown as a Revolutionary War veteran. He is still shown in the 1830 Pike Co. census, pg. 124. His age bracket is 60-70, showing a birth date of 1760-1770. He had to have been born in the early 1760's because he is shown serving in the Revolutionary War and then on juries by 1784. If his son, John A. was born in 1778 then John II would have been born closer to 1760. His wife is also shown in age bracket, 50-60. There is a marriage of a John McGinty to Anna Holmes, 2 May 1837 in Pike Co., GA. This is possibly him, because there are no other known John McGintys in Pike at this time. We do not know when he died. No will has yet been found. The last record we have of John are these land lottery draws in Cherokee Co. that he made while living in Pike Co., GA, one of which, lot 297, Dist., 8, Sect. 2, was granted to him May 7, 1838. He probably never lived on this land in Cherokee Co. Many draws in this north GA area were later sold.

The Life of John McGinty I

Recent discoveries from my research in PA have proven that John I and his family moved from PA to Mecklenburg Co., NC, in about 1766. Previous research, done up until the 1950's by Gertrude Harris Cook, who was the great-great-granddaughter of Robert McGinty, and research done by my grandfather, Wiley P. McGinty Sr., the son of William Pitts McGinty, had shown that John I moved his family to NC from VA. This was based on all of the research they had at the time. However, recent documentation has shown that the VA family was actually named McKinney (sometimes spelled McCinney) and not McGinty. It is interesting to note that the spelling of McGinty was the same on several documents we have from PA back in the 1700's as it is today. The current, official spelling has not changed in over 260 years. However, up until the time that I was a child, the "c" in Mc had two small lines or dots under it (= or ..). This is no longer done but it shows on some old gravestones and documents.

The earliest record of John McGinty I is from the book *History of that part of the Susquehanna and Juniata Valleys,* edited by F. Ellis and A.N. Hungerford, published in 1886. It recounts the history of Mifflinburg (also called Taylorstown) which was three quarters of a mile below today's Mifflintown, PA. We see that 278 acres of property near to where this town was located was warranted to Robert Campbell on September 8, 1755. It was described as being bounded on the west by the Juniata River, on the north by Alexander Lafferty's land and on the east by John McGinty's land. This area of PA had been purchased from the Indians on July 6, 1754, and he received a warrant in the new territory. In 1755 this area of PA was in Cumberland Co. and this property was in Fermanagh Township, east of the Juniata River. A few months later there is a warrant #112, for fifty acres of land that John received December 16, 1755.

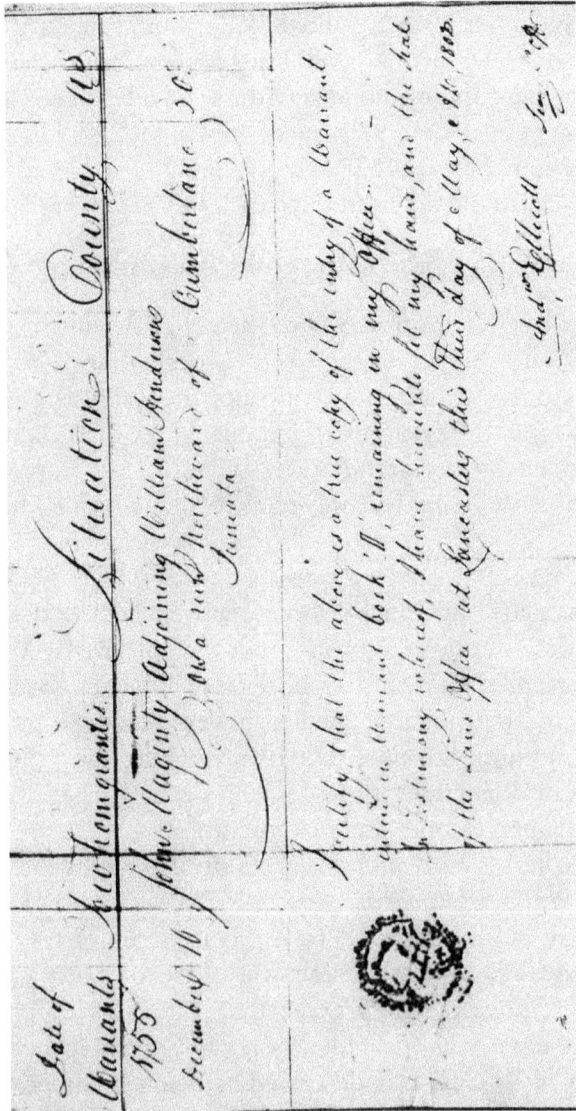

The Earliest Document Showing our McGinty Family in America. It reads: "Date of Warrants, December 16, 1755. To Whom Granted – John McGinty. Situation – Adjoining William Henderson on a Run Northward of Juniata. County Cumberland. Acres – 50"

This land was located adjoining William Henderson on a run northward of the Juniata (river) in Cumberland Co., PA. John also shows in a deed as having adjoining property in the sale of Alexander and Robert Campbell, dated 1757. This land was described as being on the north side of the Juniata River, in Cumberland Co. At this time, John actually lived in Donegal Township, Lancaster Co. The tax list of both 1758 and 1759 show John paying taxes in Donegal township (formed before 1741), which was in Lancaster Co. Donegal township was named for County Donegal, Ireland where the McGintys originated. It was formed in 1716-19. The part of Donegal where John lived became Mt. Joy Township in 1759. John shows here as a witness to a deed dated October 28, 1761 (Vanlear to Nisly, deed book M-444). A warrant #199, for 100 acres was issued to him on July 29, 1762, also on the north side of Juniata in Cumberland Co., and bounded by land of Campbell and Corran.

Later subdivisions of this land are shown in Mifflin Co., which was formed out of Cumberland Co. in 1789. Juniata Co. was then formed from Mifflin in 1831. This was well after John had relocated to NC, so the references are relating to the later county names rather than the original ones. Other records show this property, originally granted to John. It was subdivided several times in the 1800's and John's original warrant is always cited in these documents. On August 5, 1762, we see him selling 250 acres of land, located on the north side of Juniata in Cumberland Co., to John Wilkins for fifty pounds (Cumberland Co. deeds, 1-C-35). There is no warrant referenced in this deed, and I do not know how he obtained it. No deed has yet been located. His wife, Rebecka is shown with him in this deed. This deed shows John and Rebecka then living in Mt. Joy Township, Lancaster Co., PA. This deed confirms the name of his wife and she later shows with him on documents in NC. Sometime between 1762 and 1766 John and family relocated to this land in Cumberland Co. There were problems with the Indians in this area, and two of John's immediate neighbors, the White and Campbell families were massacred by them. This probably influenced John to move to NC, ca. 1767. John's land was also very close to the Lost Creek Cedar Springs Presbyterian Church meeting place that was founded in 1759 (per Penn. Hist. Soc.). He, no doubt, was also a Presbyterian, and continued to be one in NC.

The last document that has been located placing John I in PA is a deed dated September 29, 1766. In this deed, he is shown as being from Cumberland Co. He sold the 100 acres of 1762 warranted property on the north side of Juniata, mentioned above, to John Bayly of Donegal Township for £50 (Cumberland Co., I-D-270). This deed shows that the land included structures, improvements, etc.

Note: Research is currently underway to determine when John I arrived in PA. Many sources have already been examined by professional researchers in Lancaster, Cumberland and Chester Counties, PA, with only the results cited here. Quaker records in the area have also been examined because, as we have seen, John's son Robert married Deborah Jackson, a Quaker girl whose family was originally from PA. Nothing has been located to date showing the exact date that he arrived in PA from Ireland.

Around 1766-67 John I, Rebecka and their family relocated to NC, joining hundreds of Cumberland Co. families that had already trekked down the "Great Philadelphia Wagon Road," as it was called in the north, or "The Great Wagon Road from the Yadkin River through Virginia to Philadelphia distant 435 miles," as Joshua Fry and Peter Jefferson meticulously labeled it on their "Map of the most settled Parts of Virginia" in 1775. This heavily traveled road came through Cabarrus, Mecklenburg and Union counties in NC, close to where John acquired his initial property. Through the 1750's and 1760's the stream of Scotch-Irish immigrants into these areas grew larger. As PA's population steadily increased, both from immigration and a high birth rate, the demand for land drove prices to a point where a move to areas where land was still low cost and plentiful was appealing. John's possible brother, Alexander, had also traveled to this area in his trading business with the Catawba Indians. This Indian tribe's largest village was in SC. The violence of Indian disturbances in PA and VA were also reasons for the immigrations. Three NC governors had enthusiastically encouraged the immigration from the north of Scottish families. They were needed to expand the population and create economic development. Arthur Dobbs, governor of NC just prior to John's relocation (1754-1765) was born on Ireland and was himself an Ulsterman. John and Rebecka were among the later arrivals, along with the parents of President Andrew Jackson who settled in the Waxhaw community a few miles to the south in present day NC. Almost to a man, they were Presbyterians, but to date we have not obtained any actual church records from this period on John and his family.

The first evidence we have of John in NC is a deed dated January 4, 1767, showing John, the planter, purchasing 321 acres of land on Sugaw (Sugar) and McCalpin's Creek in Mecklenburg Co. It is very interesting to note in this deed that the land that John purchased was adjacent to land already owned by his possible brother, Alexander. We know that Alexander purchased land here as early as 1763. This land was near today's Pineville, N.C. Over time, these "bottom lands" along Sugaw Creek became known as some of the most productive in the country and no less an authority than President George Washington, who visited there in 1791 noted their "very rich look." John purchased this land from George Augustus Selwyn for thirty-two Pounds. Thomas Polk, who witnessed this deed, had arrived in this area in 1753 from Cumberland Co., PA, and was one of the Mecklenburg Signers, a document dated May 20, 1775, declaring independence from Great Britain, prior to the official Declaration of Independence in 1776.

George Augustus Selwyn, who sold this land to John I, had inherited the land from his father who was a British Lord who had been granted vast tracts of land in Mecklenburg by King George II in 1737. He was granted this land under the condition that he would settle 6,000 persons on the land and collect taxes from them. He was given until 1756 to fulfill this obligation. Because of the Cherokee uprisings, the time was extended until 1760 and when it became impossible for him to meet this date, a compromise was worked out whereby he could keep his land if he brought in one settler for every 200 acres. John I purchased one of these tracts. There were incentives offered to PA settlers like John, including a very attractive land cost. Prior to John's purchase, hundreds of Scotch-Irish settlers had already come to the area and settled on this land based on some promises from the colonial government in the Carolinas. Selwyn asked a young Henry McCulloh, whose name also appears on the deed of John I, to serve as his agent and to collect taxes that were due to him from the people who had settled on his property. McCulloh did not want to do this because he knew the reputation of the people with whom he would be dealing. He reluctantly consented. However, by 1762 there were over 150 families already settled on Selwyn's land, and they were not about to move or agree to pay taxes. In fact, they threatened to fire on any surveyor seen in the area. Thomas Polk who was the "head and chief" of these families finally agreed to a cease-fire if McCulloh would agree to make Polk's frame house the center of the new settlement. This was agreed and commissioners were appointed to build a new town. The date was around 1760. One of these commissioners was John Frohock, a very prominent citizen of the day, who also witnessed the deed of John I. Polk also wanted the new town to be the county seat and this sparked a seven-year political debate. Finally in 1767 the same year that John I purchased his land, Polk and other commissioners named the village Charlotte Town, in honor of King George III's new bride. In 1774 it became the county seat. It was in this area that John I settled. His property was actually a little south of Charlotte, near Pineville, N.C. Mecklenburg Co. was cut from Anson Co. in 1762. It was named for the German birthplace of the new queen of England.

If the land that John purchased had not been yet cleared and had a cabin, then his first priority after arriving was to build one, and then to plant a crop. Typically, families "camped out" in a sapling lean-to until a permanent log cabin could be erected. On these lots, settlers like John built log houses, usually one room, twenty feet square. Few houses had more than a single window, and only the most prosperous used brick for their chimneys. Both the hipped clapboard roofs and the wooden window shutters were fastened with iron spikes. As protection against fire and cooking odors, the kitchen was usually in a separate building near the cabin. As improvements were made, other out-buildings included the smokehouse, well and outhouse. Getting established also included the backbreaking work of clearing land in preparation for the first crop. It is said that in pre-Revolutionary Charlotte, only Thomas Polk's house was distinguished by a coat of white paint.

The indispensable equipment of every pioneer consisted of rifle, pouches, powder horn, axe and hoe. The cow was the most valuable domestic animal. Pigs were found on every farm, pork being the preferred meat on the frontier. The forests teemed with game, wild fruits, nuts, and berries, and the streams with fish. Even before the first harvest, families could survive off the land. The domestic economy depended on the women: cooking, baking, the making of clothes, washing, milking cows, making butter, spinning, weaving, pickling, and all the other duties of a housewife. Many were also mothers to large families of eight or ten children, which were nursed and cared for through illness without a doctor. If no school was available, their mother taught the children. Marriages were early, as no man who chose farming as his profession could survive without a good woman.

The next land transaction we see for John I was dated January 11, 1767. In this transaction, which is the same land we see him purchase on 4 January, he mortgaged the property to Henry E. McCulloh for 87.4 Pounds. There are no other land records of John I until April 10, 1779, when he purchased 230 acres of land on McCalpin's and Reedy Creek from Thomas and Susannah Polk (Deed Book 7, pg. 188).

By 1775 John was shown owning this land near the current Mint Hill, NC, which was sold after his death. In 1782 or 1784 (all records don't agree), we see that his wife, Rebecka and son James were asked by the governor of NC to present an inventory of his estate meaning that John I was deceased by then. This 1782 date, which appears on the original document, is also shown as October 1784 in other court records. The 1784 sounds more realistic because the estate sale of John I in 1784/85 is documented. We see purchases of items made by his possible brother, Alexander Sr. and his grandson, Alexander Jr. Also John's sons, James and John II, were there. Over the years, there were other friends and neighbors that show as witnesses on his deeds, etc., such as James Finney who married Alexander Sr.'s daughter and William Kenady, who purchased John's property in 1785. Kenady also married Mary Ann McGinty, one of Alexander Sr.'s granddaughters.

Studying the various items in his estate sale gives us a good picture of the environment where John I and his family were living in 1780's. As I mentioned earlier, the land that they settled was very fertile, and we know by the items sold that he was a farmer. There were many farm implements and several bushels of corn sold from his estate.

In 1785 John's son, Robert, who then lived in Wilkes Co., GA, sold his father's remaining 122 acres on McCalpin's Creek, (which had been purchased from the Polk's in 1779) to William Kenady for sixty Pounds. His mother, Rebecka, came to Wilkes Co. to live the rest of her life with his family. His brothers, James and John II accompanied him back to GA.

Note: The deeds cited here were collected over the years by me from many sources. In 2001 the recorded McGinty deeds in Mecklenburg Co. were published in the *Olde Mecklenburg Genealogical Society Quarterly, Vol. 19, Number 3, Pages 17-29*. This society is located at

P.O. Box 32453, Charlotte, NC 28232-2453.

John I had which is thought to be a brother, Alexander. Records show that they were together in PA and moved together to NC. John I is also thought to have possibly had another brother, James, who went to KY and settled in Harrodsburg.

Alexander McGinty

The life of John's possible brother **Alexander McGinty** is a very interesting story. I say "possible brother" because after John's death, his son Robert was the executor of his estate. If Alexander had been his son, with his status at the time, etc., he would surely have been named executor. The earliest record we see of him is in 1753. At this time, he was an Indian trader, associated with the Ohio Company. In 1748 several wealthy Virginians, including family members of George Washington, had established the Ohio Company. The investors secured lands west of the Appalachian Mountains from the British government. They would purchase the property from the King and then sell the land to settlers moving westward for a higher price than what the investors had originally paid. Many Indian traders and agents were involved in this venture. He was then living in PA and was captured by Indians on one of his journeys into KY.

A good account of this incident was published in the *History of Lancaster County, Pennsylvania* by Franklin Ellis and Samuel Evans in 1883. It reads as follows: "On the 26th day of January, 1753, when Daniel Hendricks, Jacob and Jabez Evans, William Powell (a half-breed), Thomas Hyde, Alexander McGinty and James Lowry were on their return from a trading journey among the Catawbas and were encamped on the south bank of the Kentucky River, about twenty miles from Blue Lick Town, with a large stock of goods, skins and furs, they were attacked by the French Caughnawaga Indians and were taken prisoners. The French government was unhappy about the way American traders were influencing the Indian tribes against France. A few men were wounded on both sides. While these prisoners were on their way to Detroit, Lowry made his escape and returned to his home in Donegal township, Lancaster Co. (Lowry was married to Susanna Patterson, sister of Capt. James Patterson who was a large land owner in what is now Mexico, PA in Juniata Co.).

The others were not so lucky. Jacob Evans and Thomas Hyde were sold to Monsieur Celeron, the French commander at Detroit (who sent them to Quebec); the others were taken to Montreal. Jacob Evans and Thomas Hyde were sent as prisoners to France. Jabez Evans, Powell, and McGinty were distributed among the Indians in the northern part of NY State. McGinty communicated these facts to the governor (of NY) and the Council of Pennsylvania who sent Conrad Weiser to Albany, NY to inquire about the matter, and if possible procure the release of the captive traders, all of whom belonged to Lancaster County. Weiser found that Jabez Evans was adopted by a squaw, and had some difficulty to get him away. All of these traders except Lowry were financially ruined by their misfortunes. McGinty (after being released and returning to Lancaster Co.), is said by one researcher, to have later became prominent in Cumberland Valley. I am not yet sure what "prominent" means. Research is ongoing.

An excerpt from *The Wilderness Trail* by Charles Hanna, published in 1911 reads as follows: "At a meeting of the Pennsylvania Council held August 7, 1753, there was read a letter from George Clinton, governor of NY, in which he stated that 'Some of our Indian traders were taken prisoners by a party of Cognawago, of Praying French Indians as they were trading with the Cuttawas, one hundred miles from the Lower Shawonese Town on Ohio, and stripped and plundered of their goods and skins, and carried prisoners to Montreal, from whence they sent a letter to Mr. Saunders, Mayor of Albany." Governor Clinton enclosed a copy of this letter from McGinty and the other captives, dated at Montreal, June 9, 1753, which read: "Loving and Unacquainted Friends. These come to let you know that there are six Englishmen of us here in this place that are taken prisoners by the French Indians. We were taken from off the south side of Allegheny River about one hundred miles, on the twenty-sixth of last January, and the Indians brought four of us along to this place, and two of us they sold to a French Captain on the road as we came; and when we came here to this place, the Indians thought to have sold us to the French General, but he would not buy us nor release us from the savages. So we live, us four, with the savages still; but we do not know how long, for our lives are in danger daily of being taken by them; and now the other two lads are sent down here, and them they have shut up in prison; so we are all in a very poor state, and to your hands, you will be so compassionate as to use the best endeavors you can to work our deliverance from them; for our lives seem bitter to us whilst with them...We are all of us from Lancaster County, Pennsylvania, and were all Indian Traders." The names of the six men captured, including Alexander McGinty are shown.

I recently discovered a book titled *The Life of Conrad Weiser, Iroquois Interpreter*, which was compiled by Rev. William M. Beauchamp in 1925. It is basically the diary that Weiser kept of his journeys.

Conrad Weiser (1696-1760) was the chief Indian interpreter for the Province of PA. He held this position for over twenty years. He had come to America from Germany in 1709. His parents lived for a time with the Mohawk Indians and he learned their language. Later in life, he became a valuable asset for the PA government, in their dealings with all of the Indian issues in those days.

After the capture of Alexander McGinty and the other Indian traders, Weiser was asked by Gov. Hamilton of PA to go to Albany, NY and meet with the mayor, a Mr. Sanders, and the commissioners of Indian affairs, and try to get them released. He arrived on August 7, 1753, and presented them a letter from Gov. Hamilton concerning the release of the prisoners. His diary entries are as follows: "August 7, 1753, at five o'clock arrived in Albany. The next day, in the morning, delivered Gov. Hamilton's letter to the mayor, Mr. Sanders, who thought it proper to call the commissioners of Indian affairs to meet at four o'clock in the afternoon, to concert measures to bring back the poor prisoners from Canada, belonging to Pennsylvania, taken in January last on the waters of the Ohio, the said prisoners having wrote several letters praying his assistance for their relief, which letters Mr. Sanders gave me to peruse.

"Accordingly, at four o'clock, the commissioners met me at the house of one Lottridge, and a French Indian squaw was sent for, who had one of the prisoners, to wit, Jabez Evans, in her family, given to her in place of Degerihogan, her son or relation, who died two years ago. The Indian woman's name was Susanna, wife of one Thanyuchta. She being a noted woman, and none of the Indians of that country being in Albany but young lads, she being asked how it came that these poor people were taken prisoner in time of peace, she made the answer that some of the Caghnawaga warriors went to fight the Oyadackuchraono, and happened to meet some of them at some distance from their country, accompanied by these white men, who when they saw the Caghnawagas would or had a mind to kill or take the Oyadackuchraono, they, the English, made resistance, and wounded one of their men with a musket ball in his arm, upon which they rushed to take the white people as well as the Indian, and brought them away to Canada, leaving their horses and things upon the spot; and when they came to Canada they presented their prisoners to the governor general and told him how things had happened, and that the governor made answer that he would have nothing to do with those prisoners, upon which the Indians took them away to their towns, and three of them were given to an Indian living in Caghnawaga, one to the Indians at Canassategy, and two were imprisoned at Quebec; for what reason she did not know.

"The commissioners told the woman that they had received several letters from these poor prisoners, praying for relief (this very woman had brought one from Jabez Evans) and as they were taken in time of peace they desired that they might be brought back again; that the commissioners would make reasonable satisfaction to those that had them in their houses and had used them kindly, if they would bring them over.

"The commissioners sent a belt of Wampum (which I did provide) to the chief man of Caghnawaga, called Anuchrakechty, to require his good office for the release of these prisoners, which the woman undertook faithfully to deliver; she being a very intelligible woman I desired Mr. Sanders to give her a Piece of Eight to buy some bread for her return, which she received very thankfully. I served the commissioner as interpreter, because it was thought fit that my name should not be mentioned, for fear that the expectation of the Indians would rise too high; but the woman asked me where I lived, because I could talk their language so well, she wondered that I was never heard of. I told her I had lived at Shohary and traveled up and down among the Indians.

"By way of discourse, she informed me that the conduct of the Indians that brought the English prisoners was not approved of at Caghnawaga, and the rest of the Indians were angry at those that took them, and in their drunkenness would call them old women and breakers of the peace, and that it was a shame to take people that had not offended and in time of peace, that it appeared plain to the Indians that those prisoners had done no harm."

There were more letters, and Alexander was finally released and returned to Philadelphia in early October 1753. He made a formal deposition on October 12, 1753, claiming that he had lost, "All that your petitioner had in the world, and was even stripped of his clothes;

and being now reduced to extreme poverty and want," and he also presented a petition for financial relief. He was granted a sum of six pounds to defray the expense of his return trip to PA.

In 1755 Louis Evans (the "Evans Maps") completed one of the first maps of KY. Alexander McGinty is credited with furnishing Evans much of the detail in those areas he had traveled as a trader. This map had been requested of Evans by the government in 1750.

Based on these events and his occupation as an Indian Trader before 1753, it is apparent that Alexander McGinty was in PA well before this date. The migrations from Ireland were well underway by 1725. Future McGinty researchers have the challenge of discovering more about the origin of the McGinty family in PA and Ireland.

The next record we have of Alexander is a land grant dated February 3, 1755, awarding him one hundred and fifty acres on the northwest side of Tuscorora Creek in what was then, Lack Township. Today, it is in Beale Township, Juniata Co., PA. This land was then resurveyed in 1770 and found to contain 312.3 acres. This area of land was purchased from the Indians in 1754. Alexander's parcel of land was later divided into several parcels and each was re-surveyed in the 1800's. There are several documents on record showing the subdivisions of this original land granted to Alexander.

In 1757 we see the first documentation showing that Alexander and John were together in PA. In a sale dated June 3, 1757, two hundred acres of land belonging to Alexander and a Robert Cambell were sold by the Sheriff in Cumberland Co. to satisfy a debt. The description of this property shows that it borders land owned by John McGinty.

We have no further documentation on Alexander until April 22, 1763 when he was granted (or purchased) three hundred acres of land in Mecklenburg Co., NC. This land was located on the east side of the Catawba River on Clement Davis Branch (Clement's Branch) including the "forks of the same." Old maps show that this property was south of Pineville, NC, where Four-Mile and McAlpin's Creeks pour into the Catawba River, and next to the line showing Indian lands. The next deed, showing his property transactions, is dated 1767 and there are several other deeds showing both purchases and sales up until 1799. One of the 1767 deeds for John shows that his land was bordered by that of Alexander. This is another documented tie between the two in NC. Alexander was shown as a planter and we know that the land in this area was very fertile farmland. He shows as a witness to the will of Thomas Neel dated November 28, 1766 (will book B, pg. 119). In 1770 a deed shows that he was still living on Clement's Branch.

Alexander was probably a Presbyterian, and on February 4, 1780, he witnessed a deed in Mecklenburg Co. that represented the sale of land by Samuel Montgomery, a farmer, to the trustees of the Rocky Spring Presbyterian Church. The name of this church was changed shortly after to the Philadelphia Presbyterian Church and it is still there today, in Mint Hill, NC. We also know that his son, Alexander II married Hannah McDowell and she was still a member of this church in 1837. She shows earlier in the 1810 census of Mecklenburg Co., NC, living in Capt. J. Wilson's company as a widow with three children and three slaves (pg. 486/69). (Alexander II became an attorney and was admitted to the bar in TN with Andrew Jackson). Also, Abner Alexander McGinty, Alexander's grandson, was a member here as evidenced by financial pledges he made to the church.

Alexander attended the estate sale of John in 1782. At this sale, he is listed as Alexander, Sr., and his son, Alexander, Jr., was also present at the sale. They both purchased several items. The next record we have of Alexander is in the first census of NC in 1790. His name is listed in the census index as McGintey (pg. 355). He is shown as head of the family in the Salisbury District of Mecklenburg Co. with one white male over sixteen (him), one white female over sixteen (his wife) and two slaves in his household. There are no children listed but since he was probably well into his sixties by then any children had probably all left his household.

Alexander's will was written April 2, 1802. At this time, he shows substantial acreage, makes generous cash awards to his grandchildren and refers to his home as a "plantation." He names his heirs as wife, Mary Ann, his grandsons Abner McGinty, Henry McDowell McGinty, Alexander Crawford, James Crawford and James Finney and granddaughters Sophia (Josephine) McGinty (she married Matthew Bain), Mary Ann McGinty, Mary Ann Johnson and Martha Crawford Miller. His children are not shown in his will. He appointed his wife, Mary Ann executor along with James Montgomery and John Gingles. He died in 1803, and his will was probated in July of that year. His wife Mary Ann's will was written in September 1803 and probated in April 1804. I have a copy of her estate settlement. It is felt that Alexander was born ca. 1725. Based on this, he would have died in his seventies after a very interesting life as a true American pioneer.

It is interesting to note that Alexander had a son, Alexander Jr. (ca. 1765-1798). Alexander Jr., grew up in Mecklenburg Co., NC, and became a lawyer. He married Hannah McDowell ca. 1787. Mecklenburg Co. records show that in October 1787 he along with Andrew Jackson (later president) took the oath of office to practice law in "the several county courts within this state." Greene Co., TN (part of the South West Territory then) court records dated August 1788 show that he, along with Andrew Jackson, were admitted to practice law there. That this Jackson is the one who later became president is confirmed because the Greene Co. court records show John McNairy being admitted to practice on the same date with McGinty and Jackson. Shortly after this, McNairy was appointed a judge and Jackson research shows that he and McNairy went to Nashville together later in 1788. Jackson was from Waxhaw, NC, close to where Alexander Jr., grew up. Records show that Alexander sold land in Burke Co., NC in 1791. He relocated to KY and shows as being admitted to practice law in the August 1794 (court records of Green Co., KY). Various documents show that he was living in Mercer Co., KY by 1794-95. He died at an early age, ca. 1798 cause unknown. There is speculation that he died or was killed by Indians in KY. We know that after his death, his wife Hannah was back in Mecklenburg Co., NC (1810 census and tax rolls) and according to the Philadelphia Presbyterian Church records in Mint Hill, NC, she died there in 1842.

We know that John and Alexander, the first McGinty family that we see in America, were originally in PA. If James is their brother, or otherwise related, then he also probably came through PA on the way to KY.

James McGinty

It is thought that a **James McGinty** in KY is somehow related to Alexander and John. He could have been their brother, but more research is needed to verify his relationship to them. All of the records that have been found on him are from KY. Remember that Alexander was an Indian trader and very familiar with early KY. James was an early pioneer in Mercer County, KY and there are several theories on how he arrived there. The first is that he was with the original thirty-one men from Pennsylvania under the command of Col. James Harrod in March of 1774. However, one source that lists these men does not include his name. Harrodsburg, KY is named for Col. Harrod. Another theory is that he arrived from southwest Virginia as a soldier under Gen. George Rogers Clark who was responsible for the protection of the KY settlers. James was one of the original landholders in Lexington, KY, when the city was first laid out into lots.

The earliest record available on him is a payroll roster for service in the Revolutionary War. He is shown on the payroll of Capt. Robert Patterson's Company of Militia, on duty in the late Shawnee Expedition and continuing in service for the defense of the County of KY from August 20 through November 1780. The DAR Patriot Index also confirms that his spouse was Ann (Kennedy), Wilson, Pogue, Lindsey, (Vol. III, *Index of Spouses of Soldiers & Patriots*, and shown in Vol. I, pg. 538). The next record, dated April 13, 1781, shows him listed as a laborer building the fort at Lexington under Patterson. There are several other accounts that included his name that were submitted by George Rogers Clark to the VA Assembly in hopes of getting paid for their services. In 1782 his name appears on a petition to establish the town of Lexington, and on December 26, 1782, he was awarded a town lot. In 1785 the town fathers took back this lot, probably because he had not yet built a home on it. He may have moved to Harrodsburg by then. He reportedly owned a "still house" near Gore's spring which was adjacent to the fort. He was a businessman and as old records show, he bought and sold lots and owned a considerable amount of property in the town and vicinity. He also was active in civic affairs, acting on various committees and as a trustee of the town.

On July 24, 1787, James asked the governor of VA to sanction his marriage to the noted Anne Kennedy Wilson Poague Lindsay. The purpose of this request was to make sure that the records were clear on her first marriages. Anne's maiden name was Kennedy and she was originally from Augusta Co., VA. James was her fourth husband and they were married July 24, 1787, (witnessed by David McFall). Her first husband, John Wilson died at an early age. She married her second husband, William Poague in VA (1762) and they moved with their five children to the KY area in 1775. He was killed by Indians in 1778.

Her third husband, Joseph Lindsey (m.1781), who was Commissary for George Rogers Clarke in several expeditions, was killed by Indians in the battle of Blue Licks in 1782. Two of her earlier husbands were killed by Indians. She was a true pioneer woman and her life was very interesting. Among other things, brought the first spinning wheel to KY and made cloth from buffalo hair and nettle lint. This cloth was called "Linsey-Woolsey." She learned to dye it from the original dull gray color using local items such as walnut hulls, oak bark, cedar berries, etc. She was extremely resourceful and was known as a "wonder among women." She taught the women how to weave and make brooms by shredding a hickory pole, grain by grain until there was a fluff at the lower end. She advised the women who had brought shoes from VA to save them for the winter and how to make moccasins for the summer.

She was the first to obtain a license to run a boarding house and restaurant or "Ordinary" as they were called (court order book 1, Mercer Co., KY court records, January 2, 1787). She became wealthy for her time with large parcels of land. Her third husband, Lindsay's will (will book A, pg. 6) shows that he left his entire estate, including Negroes and at least 2,500 acres to her. Records show that she owned additional property and a mill near the fort. She also served as the unofficial mayor of the town and was very active in various affairs, including the conduct of the people. She died November 14, 1815, and is buried in the pioneer cemetery at old Ft. Harrod. A bronze marker recognizing her service as a patriot was placed on her gravestone by the D.A.R. She is also listed in *DAR Patriot Index, Centennial Edition, Part III*, pg. 2328 for patriotic service, and is listed as being born ca. 1735 in VA and dying November 11, 1815, in KY.

The "Anne McGinty House," a reconstructed log cabin, is an attraction at the fort today. I visited the fort and cemetery as well as the

Harrodsburg Historical Society in November 2003.

A twelve section, one drawing room Pullman Sleeping Car that was assigned to the Chesapeake and Ohio Railroad was named *Ann McGinty* in her honor. This car was in service from 1933-1950 and was frequently part of their then famous *George Washington* train that traveled through Kentucky and Virginia. The C&O had begun calling itself "The Route to Historyland" in the 1920s, and emphasized its route through Colonial historical areas. Pullman cars were given famous Colonial names *(The Chesapeake and Ohio Historical Society, Clifton Forge, VA).*

This Anne McGinty poem was written by an anonymous author:

> She who had braved the red mans hate,
> With Harrod, Clark and Boone,
> First of her sex within the State,
> Before a way was hewn.
> Who heard the savage whoop and yell,
> With dead around her strewn,
> And helped the savage hoardes repel,
> To save the place from ruin.
> I scraped away the moss and mold,
> For on it at a glance --
> I saw characters perhaps which told,
> Of someone whose advance
> Into the western forest gave -
> The savage less expanse.
> And lo' I saw Ann McGinty's grave,
> Which I had found, by chance.

There was an article in the *Kentucky Gazette*, August 18, 1792, concerning James McGinty, Mercer Co., and an issue with a stray mare. I have not read the article but have seen the abstract in another publication.

James McGinty signed his will on December 17, 1804, and died in 1805. In this will, he divided his estate between two boys, C. Lewis, son of Thomas Lewis and Robert Palmer, son of Henry Palmer who could have been his nephews. Apparently, James had some sort of association with Palmer's family. His land was located on Elkhorn Creek. This area of KY is still the most coveted bluegrass land in the state. According to historians, this creek has watered many of the great KY horses. According to the will, his other property in Harrodsburg was to be rented or sold for the benefit of these boys and their education. He appointed the fathers of the boys as executors. The records show that his estate was inventoried on February 15, 1806, and settled on August 27, 1806. It is unknown as to why his wife was not mentioned in the will, but she is shown, along with her son-in-law, John Thomas, in the document dated August 27, 1806, as the administrator of his estate. There is some indication that Anne's former children did not approve of her marriage to James and also that he and Anne were not living together at the time of his death. Later, there was a long controversy and legal proceeding over the Elkhorn land and who was actually entitled to it.

We know that John and Alexander, the first McGinty family that we see in America, were originally in PA. If James is their brother, or otherwise related, then he also probably came through PA on the way to KY. The large Irish migrations to America began around 1725 so all three of them could have come over as young men or been born in America. We do not have their exact birth dates and based on the ages of their children and grandchildren, we can only estimate. Many immigrants from Ireland came into Philadelphia but others came in through MD, NY and even Canada. Many sources of information have been investigated including some in Ireland, and to date, there is no documented information showing when and where they arrived or their history in Ireland. This presents a challenge for McGinty researchers.

In May of 2002 a professional researcher in Ireland was commissioned to do a search for our McGinty family. No records were found. The Donegal Historical Society has informed me that they have no records that survived from the early 1700's.

The newspaper library at Belfast Central Library was included in this search. They have copies of the *Newsletter*, which is the oldest surviving newspaper in Northern Ireland and dates back to 1738. Locating a written account of Alexander McGinty's capture as an Indian Trader in 1753 was the objective. If it was written up in this publication, it might show where he was from in Ireland. Unfortunately, there is no index to the *Newsletter* and each daily copy would have to be searched manually. This type of extensive search was not done but might have merit in the future because his kidnapping was big news in PA. The *London Times* was also checked but their records go back only to 1795.

The Presbyterian Historical Society was contacted. No church records from Donegal survived before 1840. Derry was also checked and has no surviving records before the mid 1800's.

I visited the Donegal Ancestry center in Ramelton, County Donegal in August 2003. They have a large collection of records from all of the major genealogical sources including church records of baptisms, marriage and burials, civil records of deaths, births and marriages, census records, pre and post famine land records, gravestone inscriptions, school roll books and trade directories. I was told that it would be most unusual to locate any records as far back as the 1700's, except for one of two Church of Ireland parishes – and there are many gaps in earlier records. Civil registration did not commence in Ireland until 1864 (non-Roman Catholic-Catholic marriages were registered from 1845). The possibility of finding records that would positively identify our ancestors in the 1700's is very remote. The earliest recorded church registers start in 1691 for the Church of Ireland parish of Drumhome while the earliest Roman Catholic records for Donegal date from much later, generally around the mid 1850's. Some of the Presbyterian registers commence around the beginning of the 1800's. Despite this lack of very old data, it would be interesting to see what McGintys show up in the more recent data.

We should not be discouraged in the search for our McGintys prior to their arrival in America. There are many sources of information and new material on the family surfaces on a regular basis. It is a challenge, but one that future McGinty researchers should continue to pursue.

Dear Ancestor
Author Unknown

Your tombstone stands among the rest
Neglected and alone
The name and date are chiseled out
On polished marbled stone
It reaches out to all that care
It is too late to mourn
You did not know that I exist
You died and I was born
Yet each of us are cells of you
In flesh, in blood, in bone
Our blood contracts and beats a pulse
Entirely not our own
Dear Ancestor, the place you filled
So many years ago
Spreads out among the ones you left
Who would have loved you so
I wonder how you lived and loved
I wonder if you knew
That someday I would find this spot
And come to visit you.

Wiley P. McGinty Sr. Family Tree

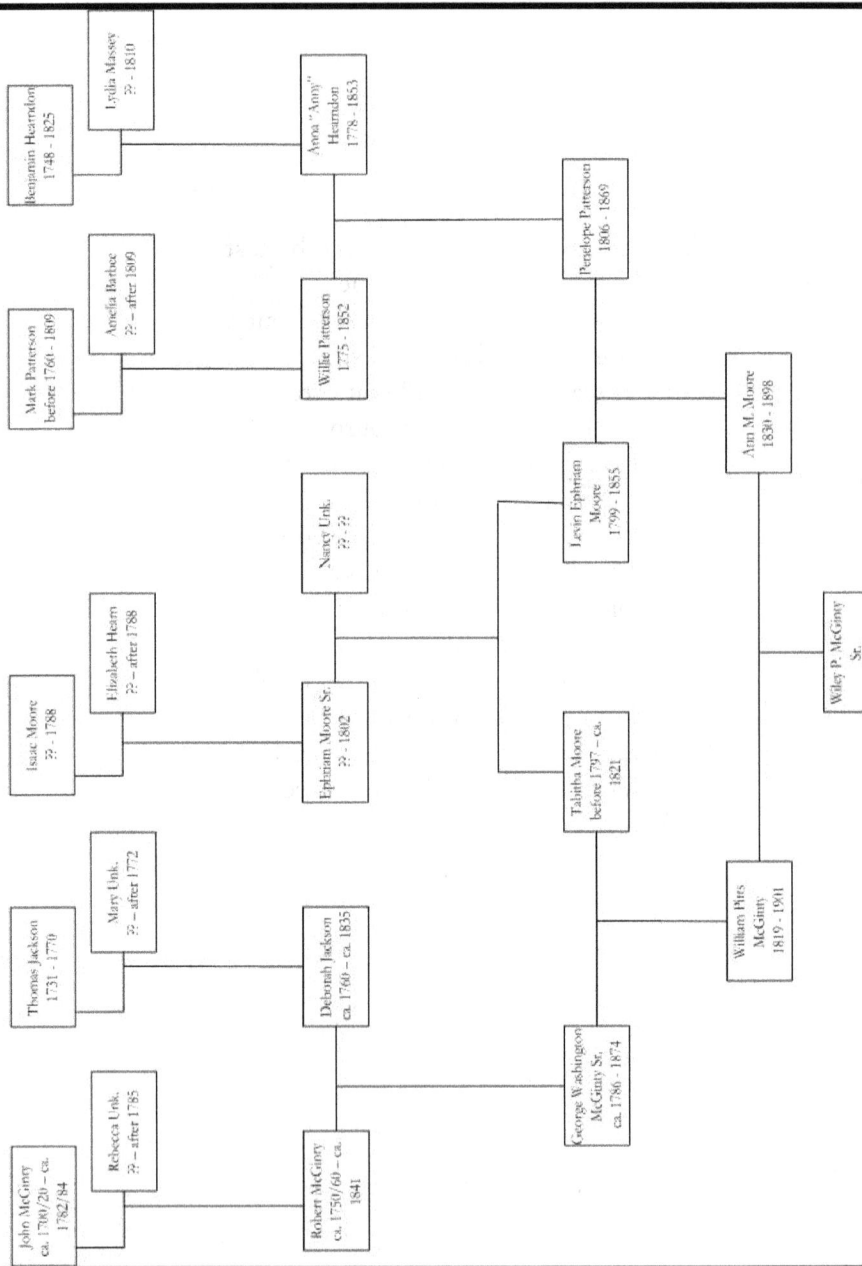

Benjamin Hearndon
1748 - 1825

Lydia Massey
?? - 1810

Anna "Anny"
Hearndon
1778 - 1853

Penelope Patterson
1806 - 1869

Mark Patterson
before 1761 - 1809

Amelia Barbee
?? – after 1809

Willie Patterson
1775 - 1852

Ann M. Moore
1830 - 1898

Isaac Moore
?? - 1788

Elizabeth Heam
?? – after 1788

Nancy Unk.
?? - ??

Ephraim Moore Sr.
?? - 1802

Levin Ephraim
Moore
1799 - 1855

Wiley P. McGinty
Sr.

Thomas Jackson
1731 - 1770

Mary Unk.
?? – after 1772

Deborah Jackson
ca. 1760 - ca. 1835

Tabitha Moore
before 1797 - ca.
1821

William Pitts
McGinty
1819 - 1901

John McGinty
ca. 1700/20 – ca.
1782/84

Rebecca Unk.
?? – after 1785

Robert McGinty
ca. 1750/60 – ca.
1841

George Washington
McGinty Sr.
ca. 1786 - 1874

APPENDIX

Macon McGinty Family Tree

INDEX

McGinty, Alexander Jr. (II), 238-239

McGinty, Andrea Laraine, 23

McGinty, Andrew Maurice, 173

McGinty, Andrew Jackson, 99-100

McGinty, Andrew Philip, 23

McGinty, Andrew Wilton, 99

McGinty, Anne Louisa, 188-190

McGinty, Ann, Wilson, Poague, Lindsey, 241-243

McGinty, Annie Margaret, 41

McGinty, Annie Sujette, 91

McGinty, Avery Inez, 11

McGinty, Basil Beasley (Rev.), 48, 60, 76-77, 91, 93-96, 102, 106, 161

McGinty, Benjamin F., 169

McGinty, Benjamin Franklin Sr., 129

McGinty, Benjamin Franklin Jr., 129

McGinty, Benjamin Franklin, 117, 160

McGinty, Benjamin R., 190

McGinty, Bertram G., 219

McGinty, Calvin Eudorus, 122

McGinty, Carey, 99

McGinty, Catherine

McGinty, Charles, 38

McGinty, Charles P., 51

McGinty, Christine, 40

McGinty, Clayton, 181

McGinty, Cornelius, 179, 181

McGinty, David, 190

McGinty, Donald Jordan, 24, 45

McGinty, Doriann D., 130-135, 160

McGinty, Douglas Clairfield, 69

McGinty, Elenora Narcissa (Carpenter), 129 -130

McGinty, Eli Hood, 164-165

McGinty, Elijah, 181

McGinty, Elisha, 181

McGinty, Elizabeth A., 124

McGinty, Elizabeth S., 128

McGinty, Elizabeth, 219

McGinty, Elizabeth, 221

McGinty, Elmo Leon, 93

McGinty, Emily Francis, 121, 171

McGinty, Emma C. "Cliffie", 87

McGinty, E.S.R., 168

McGinty, Fiona Lane, 24

McGinty, Francis, 181

McGinty, Frances, 186

McGinty, Frances "Fannie", 122

McGinty, Franklin Alexander, 88-90

McGinty, Garnie, 156

McGinty, Georganna "Lala", 96

McGinty, George, 190

McGinty, George Banks, 179

McGinty, George Carlton, 91-92

McGinty, George P., 122

McGinty, George Washington, 96

McGinty, George Washington, 188-189

McGinty, George Washington Sr., ii, 77, 81, 102, 117, 122,

INDEX

About the Author

Gerald "Jerry" McGinty has spent over 30 years researching McGinty family history. His searches have taken him to many county courthouses, the State Archives of Alabama and Georgia, and many cemeteries and churches. He has also visited and researched McGintys in County Donegal, Ireland. His research has been quoted in several publications, and some of his research articles have been published online. He has an extensive family tree on Ancestry.com. Jerry enjoys golfing and fishing. He lives in Tampa with his wife, Sylvia.

Notes